THE GOLDEN SUMMERS

An Antic History of Newport

THE GOLDEN SUMMERS

An Antic History of Newport

by

RICHARD O'CONNOR

G. P. Putnam's Sons
New York

The author is grateful for permission to quote from the following works:

The Glitter and the Gold by Consuelo Vanderbilt Balsan, published by Harper & Row, 1952.

The Last Resorts by Cleveland Amory, published by Harper & Row, 1952.

Who Tells Me True by Michael Strange, published by Charles Scribner's Sons, 1940.

Queen of the Golden Age by Cornelius Vanderbilt, Jr., published by McGraw-Hill, 1956.

King Lehr and the Gilded Age by Elizabeth Drexel Lehr, published by J. B. Lippincott, 1935.

The author also gratefully acknowledges the assistance of Mrs. Leonard Panaggio of the Newport Preservation Society and the Newport Historical Society's library staff.

SBN: 399-11324-X

Library of Congress Catalog
Card Number: 73-93738

CONTENTS

5

Part Four.   THE GLITTER OF DECAY

Illustrations appear after page 176

INTRODUCTION

THERE were few who disputed the claim of Newport, Rhode Island, that between 1890 and the First World War it held title as the queen of American resorts. The richest people in the country, the haughtiest of society's matriarchs, the most snobbish of their social advisers, the most gilded of visiting European nobility, made Newport their summer retreat. If there was some question about the social value of that privileged enclave—and there was—it was most pithily expressed by Finley Peter Dunne, whose perceptive Mr. Dooley quoted his priest as saying there had always been "some kind iv a Newport" in which the upper classes were enabled to "make monkeys iv thimsilves an' go back to the jungle. . . . I'm glad there is a Newport. It's th' exhaust pipe. Without it we might blow up. It's th' hole in th' top iv the kettle. I wish it was bigger."

Whether you viewed it as a sociological escape valve or as the most elegant of American watering places, there was no doubt whose creation it was. Men made the money for those marble "cottages," and male architects designed them, but it was the dream town of the American female. Its whole history was dominated by willful women, a pride of social lionesses, whose menfolk were pallid characters by comparison. Newport was the center of their struggles for social power, the scene of their matchmaking, the venue of their most extravagant activities.

Women had not yet been granted the vote, but their veto power in their own homes was notorious. Foreigners were appalled by the tyrannical manner of the American female: not only males like Rudyard Kipling, who found it impossible to meet some of the magnates of San Francisco because their wives and daughters monopolized his time and dismissed the heads of their households as unworthy of a great writer's time, but Mademoiselle Suzanne Beret, a well-born young Frenchwoman who taught French to the daughters of a wealthy Cleveland family. The rudeness of young women to men much older than they were was shocking to a properly raised French girl. "M. Eltinoit made Miss X a compliment on her costume at a dinner last week by saying she resembled Sarah Bernhardt. She responded: 'Shut up! How dare you compare me to such a woman!' They treat their sons and husbands as rudely before people as though they were bad servants. . . . They are much more loyal to each other than Frenchwomen would be."

It was the women of the middle and upper classes whom Thomas Beer in his masterly *Mauve Decade* defined as a new breed he called the Titanesses. Their ferocious pride dismayed him, as the pitch of their demanding voices deafened him. And it was they who conceived and constructed the Xanadu of the Gilded Age, Newport by the sea; their taste that dictated its extravagant follies.

Beer believed that the Titaness "existed rather as a symptom of America's increasing cheapness"—his viewpoint was self-consciously elitist—and that "her performance was listlessly sanctioned by men whose covert emotionalism she openly and more courageously expressed in an envy of all that was free, cool or unhaltered in life, art and affairs. She was an emblem, a grotesque shape in hot black silk, screaming threats at naked children in a clear river, with her companionable ministers and reformers at heel. . . . Everywhere the schoolteacher starved along on disgusting wages. But for the women of any means a terrific machine of flatteries had been patented. Her social importance had climbed higher and higher since the Civil War and in the following twenty years of rank commerce. There was no longer any talk of hosts in the great cities; social columns announced the acts of hostesses. The men were too busy to bother. . . . Women were listening to Oriental philosophers and reformers, sitting to expensive painters, running abroad to hunt down titled Europeans and making their menfolk 'damned miserable in all ways.' "

American males of the upper classes, through indifference, had lost control of their domestic lives and had become slightly less important than the second footman. In abdicating responsibility, they also surrendered their peace of mind unless they were unconventional enough to find consolation in an unofficial wife less shrill in her demands.

The neurologist S. Weir Mitchell (as quoted by Beer) scaldingly criticized one such husband, whose wife was his patient. The domestic tyranny of the Titaness was attributable to their husbands, according to Dr. Mitchell, who wrote the husband that he was responsible for his wife's neuroses because "you have accustomed her to spend money on herself and your daughters without stint and met all her demands in the way of entertainment. . . . The tendency of American men to leave the management of their homes and families to their wives without advice or supervision is growing malignant in its results. . . ."

So when you view one of the surviving marble cottages erected on the whim of one of those imperious ladies—a monument, you might think, to feminine caprice—you might also bear in mind the less visible culpability of the man lurking behind that awesome façade. He may have regarded his new summer home, with its corps of servants, its sweeping lawns, its gazebos, teahouses, equipages and stables, as a lot of female foolishness. But he had his own reasons for tolerating the extravagance, the social rivalry it reflected. As a Titan he had more important things to do than curb the follies of his Titaness.

The result was the creation of a seaside fun house without mirrors in which the lords and ladies of the Eastern seaboard reveled in display rather than enjoyment, pursued pleasure in what seems to have been a desperately joyless fashion and set standards of extravagance in manner and customs which can never be equaled again.

Part One

FUN HOUSE WITHOUT MIRRORS

1.

THE HAPPY FEW

NEWPORT was "discovered" many times before the immensely wealthy decided it was the ideal place for the world of fashion to spend its summers. It is an island whose location is strategic enough to have attracted the attention of the colonial maritime trade and the United States Navy, beautiful enough to have caught the eye of Boston intellectuals and artists of the Hudson River School, long before high society converged on its beaches, cliffs and groves.

The loveliness of its seascapes, the eye-filling sweep of its beaches, the natural stateliness of its every aspect brought, on a January day in 1729, possibly its most distinguished resident. He was Dean George Berkeley, not only a celebrated churchman but the poet and philosopher who concocted the line every schoolboy once had to learn and every statesman feeling the twinge of Manifest Destiny felt compelled to quote: "Westward the course of destiny takes its way." Which, eventually, it did.

Born in County Kilkenny, Ireland, forty-five years before, he had quickly risen to be Dean of Derry (Church of Ireland, a branch of the Church of England), and had come to the new world with an imposing mission. With the promise of a king's Charter and the pledge of 20,000 pounds sterling in Crown funds, he was supposed to establish in Bermuda a university ordained for "the Better Supplying of Church in our Foreign Plantations, and for converting the Savage Americans to Christianity." While he awaited the charter and the funds, he decided to settle down just outside Newport, where he built Whitehall in the fashion of the Anglo-Irish great houses. And waited for three years. During that time he exerted a considerable influence on the colonial scholars who flocked around him. He was as impressed by colonial Newport as it was by him, and wrote a friend that though Newport was divided religiously by four sorts of Anabaptists, Presbyterians, Quakers and Independents, there were "fewer quarrels about religion than elsewhere, the people living peaceably with their neighbors of whatever persuasion. They all agree on one point, that the Church of England is the second best. The island is pleasantly laid out in hills and vales and rising ground; hath plenty of excellent springs, and fine rivulets, and many delightful landscapes of rocks, promontories, and adjacent lands . . . very pretty and pleasantly situated. . . ."

After three years in Newport, waiting for the charter that never came, Dean Berkeley learned that he had been betrayed by the King's ministers, who felt they had better uses for Crown funds than the establishment of Bermuda University. Berkeley sailed back to Ireland to become the Bishop of Cloyne and continue his brilliant career. He left a number of legacies, one of which was the gift of Whitehall to Yale University, another was Peter Harrison, the architect, who had come over to America with Berkeley to design his university but stayed behind in Newport to design some of its lovelier colonial buildings.

Ninety prosperous years of history had unreeled before Berkeley sojourned in Newport.

It was founded in 1639 by William Coddington, a disciple of Anne Hutchinson, and several other citizens who with a small group of others had been forced to leave Massachusetts because of their religious beliefs. They had been headed for Delaware but were intercepted at Providence by Roger Williams, who persuaded them they could find religious freedom and political democracy in the astringent atmosphere of Rhode Island. Williams himself guided the party down the bay and acted as their interpreter in negotiating with the local Indians. The founders of Newport soon made a clearing and laid out their first thoroughfare, Thames Street, which ran along the waterfront. And the town thrived surpassingly; it became an entry port for rum and molasses from the West Indies and—alas for the liberal principles of its founders—African slaves. This was known as the Triangular Trade: molasses from Jamaica was converted into rum in Newport's twenty-two distilleries, the rum was transported to Africa to be traded for slaves, the slaves were shipped to Jamaica in exchange for more molasses.

The money that flowed into Newport from this sinister traffic provided its cosmopolitan air and brought an influx of aristocratic Southerners as well as Sephardic Jews, astute merchants to a man, who were encouraged to go there by the colony's professions of religious tolerance. The Jewish community made a great success of itself, and on Touro Street built the first synagogue on American soil. The temple was designed by Peter Harrison and dedicated in 1763. Most of the Sephardic Jews so valued Newport that they elected to be buried there rather than in their native Spain or Portugal. A long time later Longfellow wrote of the Hebrew burying ground:

> How strange it seems! These Hebrews in their graves,
> Close by the street in this fair seaport town;
> Silent beside the never silent waves,
> At rest in all this moving up and down!

Thus the paradox: Newport was a place founded on the principle of inclusion, but it would become famous for being the site of social exclusion, systematized and dogmatized snobbery.

At any rate the town grew to a population of 12,000 less than a century after it was founded—an amazing rate of growth in colonial America—and its prosperity increased year by year until the Revolutionary War.

Its most eminent citizens then were not men like Dean Berkeley and his little circle of American and British devotees, but the traders. Foremost among them was Godfrey Malbone, merchant prince and slave trader, who had migrated there from Virginia. He built the first of the Newport showplaces in 1744 at a cost of $100,000, the equivalent of which today is incalculable by any reliable standards but must be more than a million dollars. Certainly it would be difficult now for a million to build a stately mansion surrounded by a terraced garden of ten acres, not to mention a tunnel from the mansion's cellars to the beach. It was suspected, certainly not without cause, that much of Malbone's success was derived from smuggling; that the tunnel allowed his privateers to bring cargo offloaded on the beach past the custom's agents prowling overhead.

Slaver and smuggler he may have been, but Malbone did possess a style to match his effrontery. His returning ship captains were not only entertained royally but at the conclusion of the feast were permitted to break all the china and glassware on the table. Such privileges apparently did not extend to young George Washington, a fellow Virginian who celebrated his twenty-fourth birthday as a guest of Colonel and Mrs. Malbone. At the height of the conviviality our future Founding Father dropped a punchbowl. Young Washington was required to pay for the bowl on the spot. In his records, preserved at the Library of Congress, there is the notation, "By cash to Mr. Malbone's servants, four pounds. To a Bowle broke, four pounds."

In 1766, ten years after he entertained George Washington, Malbone gave a dinner party for every Newport personage he considered important enough to grace his table. Just as the first course was being served, a fire broke out in one of the upper stories. Guests and servants pitched in to fight the flames, but their efforts were unavailing. "By God," Malbone roared, "if I have to lose my house, I shall not lose my dinner!" He then ordered the servants to place the tables out on the lawn. Grimy from their firefighting efforts, the elite of prerevolutionary Newport dined by the light of Malbone's burning mansion. Malbone rebuilt his mansion and was more convinced than ever that money was the root of all good. "What will not money buy?" he once rhetorically asked. The next day an anonymous poet supplied an answer. His verse was posted at the Town Hall: "All the money in the place/won't buy old Malbone a handsome face."

Old Malbone would be the last of the high-handed gentry to be seen around Newport for more than a century, and Newport-

ers had to make the best of his boisterous legend during the long
somnolent decades.

Newport's prosperity ended abruptly with the Revolutionary
War. Her hour as one of the great colonial ports was struck on
December 7, 1776, when a British convoy of eleven warships and
seventy transports sailed up the West Passage and anchored in
Newport Harbor. Commerce, of course, came to a halt as the
years of British occupation began; the wealthy merchants were
driven to Providence after their homes were requisitioned, and
Hessian mercenaries looted and burned their way through the
surrounding country. Newport was simply a British garrison
town and supply base until a French fleet finally drove out the
invaders.

It would never regain its importance as an entry port. Its
slowly returning prosperity had to come from other sources,
mainly the loveliness of its vistas and the glory of its summer
weather. As late as 1788 a visitor to Newport reported that it
"seems to me a tomb where living skeletons quarrelled over a few
herbs."

Slowly, during the ensuing four decades, Newport became
known as a quiet, unostentatious place to spend a summer by the
sea. Visitors from the hinterland began appearing. They were, of
course, moneyed folk, because in those days no artisan or farm
laborer could entertain the notion of taking a summer vacation
unless, of course, he was a fugitive from justice. The harbingers of
a modicum of prosperity again came from the South, which
seemed to appreciate Newport to a marked degree. As early as
1784 a group of Charleston planters, brought up the coast aboard
the sailing packet *Governor Gerard*, began summering in Newport.
Other families from South Carolina and Virginia followed them.
It became their custom to spend every summer from then on in
Newport's boarding houses or in rented farmhouses.

By 1830 the summer people were a dependable part of the
local economy. A number of hotels sprang up to accommodate
them, most notably the Ocean House, which a New York
journalist termed a "huge yellow pagoda factory" and which
became nationally celebrated as a pleasure dome of those

comparatively few Americans who could stop working in the summertime.

From being an important seaport the town had sunk to the few available pursuits of a decaying gentlewoman. In addition to taking in boarders of the more respectable sort, she could also properly concern herself with education of the private and genteel variety. Thus, a number of academies preparing boys for Yale or Harvard, girls for a suitable marriage, were established in Newport.

To one of those girls' academies, in 1806, came a Scarlett O'Hara prototype, one of those Southern women with voices like nightingales and psyches hammered out of the most durable metal, the sort who would keep the Civil War going long after their cavaliers had wearied of the struggle. She was a young woman named Ann Cary Randolph, always called Nancy. Though somewhat threadbare, she was employed as a teacher, with all the transferable manners and airs of one of the Randolphs of Virginia, of kinship-by-marriage with Thomas Jefferson.

Nancy Randolph came to Newport at the age of thirty-two as the central figure of a scandal which, after fifteen years, was still the talk of the Virginia taverns. During her brief life Nancy had been accused of infanticide, of ruining the lives of three brothers and her own sister, and worst of all, refusing to hang her head in shame.

Her tale, in fact, antedates writers of the Southern Gothic school by more than a century. It began in 1791 when her sister Judith married Richard Randolph of the plantation Bizarre near Roanoke (her family, which came from Richmond, was not directly connected with the Randolphs of Roanoke). Her own family was poor while her brother-in-law's was a part of the plantation aristocracy. Nancy was brought along as an afterthought. Pretty, prideful and ambitious, she was determined to marry one of Richard's two brothers, Theo, who had tuberculosis, or John, who was only nineteen but already on the verge of a notable career in reactionary statesmanship.

A year later, when Richard Randolph, his wife and sister-in-law Nancy were visiting a neighboring plantation, came the thunderclap Nancy and most Virginians would hear the rest of their lives. The body of a newly born infant was found on the woodpile. Indictments followed: Richard was charged with having fathered Nancy's child and then killing it to avoid scandal. He was tried before sixteen magistrates, with Patrick Henry and John Marshall appearing for the defense. John Randolph saved the situation by testifying that Nancy had been engaged to his brother Theo, who had died 229 days before the child was born. Richard was acquitted. With a truly Southen talent for closing family ranks, the household at Bizarre was reconstituted, Nancy returning there with possibly guilty Richard, her outraged sister, her suspicious brother-in-law John. Several years later Richard died and John became the master of Bizarre plantation. He tolerated Nancy's presence, despite the seething hatred and suspicion between them, until a stormy winter night in 1805 when, after conferring with her sister Judith, he charged her with "intimacy with one of the slaves" and threw her out.

Nancy made her way to Richmond and sank rapidly to the squalid level of living in a room at Prior's Public Garden, where her vengeful brother-in-law John alleged she "declined into a very drab."

Just as her uncle, Thomas Jefferson, was being inaugurated for his second term as President, Nancy found employment in the Newport academy. Later in 1806 she fell ill, was dismissed from her post and was destitute in Newport. But that place was the luckiest of all her stopping places. Just then Gouverneur Morris, an old friend of her father's, happened to visit Newport and heard of her distress. He was not the man to scorn anyone solely on the grounds of morality. He had not only been a member of the Continental Congress, the inventor of the federal currency system and U.S. Minister to Paris, but was the survivor of a number of hectic love affairs, not least the one with Countess Adelaide Flauhaut, the former mistress of Talleyrand—and certainly not the man, at fifty-five, to be overly concerned with past indiscretions.

Morris swept Nancy off to his estate at Morrisania, in New York state, and several years later, over the protests of two nephews who had hoped to inherit his fortune, married her. She made her position impregnable by producing a son when she was forty and Morris was sixty-one. An incredible melodrama came to a quiet closing.*

Newport could claim credit for providing the backdrop for the happiest chapter in Nancy Randolph's spirited career.

Some years later, in 1844, it would witness the coming of William Beach Lawrence, a man whose self-importance greatly exceeded that of the more accomplished Gouverneur Morris, and learn that confronting the imperious manners of its summer visitors would often be exacting.

Lawrence was Newport's first millionaire, the son-in-law of Archibald Gracie, the New York merchant, and himself a prosperous authority on international law, the author of a book on *The Law of Charitable Uses*, which would serve as a guide for philanthropists. Maud Howe Elliott, whose mother was Julia Ward Howe ("The Battle Hymn of the Republic"), was invited to tea by the Lawrences and described her host as "a tall, gaunt man with a blanched face and faded blue eyes."

There was nothing pallid about his character, however, as Newport soon learned. In 1844 Lawrence bought almost the whole of Ochre Point for $14,000 and made the farm there his summer residence. Some years later he sold one acre of his property to a friend named Pendleton for the same amount, but soon regretted that strikingly profitable transaction. His privacy, he decided, was worth more than $14,000. So he built a stone wall between his and Pendleton's properties. The wall, of course, cut across Cliff Walk, which had long been a favorite strolling route for Newporters.

* But not without a final set-to between Nancy and her implacable enemy, John Randolph, now one of the paladins of the U.S. Senate. In a letter to Morris, Randolph charged Nancy with having poisoned his brother Richard, among a whole catalogue of crimes. Nancy replied with a 4,000-word letter, copies of which were broadcast far and wide, denying if not completely refuting his charges, and outdoing him at vituperation. She died many years later as the much-venerated matriarch of the Morris clan, unassailably respectable.

Unawed by their first millionaire outsider, Newporters turned out en masse to tear the wall down. Lawrence responded by building a thicker wall and studding it with broken glass, and by stationing a large unfriendly bull in a pasture nearby. The citizenry once again tore down the wall, and this time heaved its fragments into the sea. Legal action was Lawrence's only feasible recourse, and the issue was fought through the courts for several years. Litigous as he was by disposition, Lawrence was confronted by a native uprising, by a conflict with local tradition, which a more temperate man would have avoided. There was an old statute on the books that gave fishermen access rights to the shore. On that basis, the United States Supreme Court decided in favor of the natives. It was a famous victory. Ever since, the public has enjoyed the right to stroll along Cliff Walk between the shore and the lawns of the great estates, right down to Bailey's Beach, gawking as much as they please at the remaining quality folk.

Experiences like that with William Beach Lawrence undoubtedly made many Newporters wary of yielding to what was probably inevitable, the establishment of Newport as a resort, dependent on the patronage of outsiders. No community willingly succumbs to becoming part of the tourist or summer-vacation industry; there is something subtly degrading about the process, in which communal pride and dignity are submerged by the necessity of catering to summer guests. The seasonal nature of the business, flush with prosperity three or four months of the year at most, not only unbalances the local economy but afflicts the spirit of those involved. The temptation, as anyone who has lived the year round in a resort area knows, is to take the tourists and summer people for everything you can and thus tide yourself over for the winter months. All this contributes to a sort of defensive syndrome, an exercise in self-justification, by which the natives bolster their self-esteem through regarding outsiders as interlopers legitimately to be shorn. Certainly it encourages a warped viewpoint and a servant mentality.

Newport struggled briefly against its fate and did not gladly consign the descendants of Godfrey Malbone's smugglers and

privateers to the humbler occupation of serving summer residents
as coachmen, grooms, footmen, parlor maids and gardeners. It
had little choice if it hoped to prosper. By 1850 it was apparent
that the port would never regain its colonial standing in
maritime commerce, that no sizable industry would prefer it to
Providence or Woonsocket, that its principal assets were its
setting, its summer climate and its gemlike specimens of colonial
architecture.

And yet the editor of the Newport *Mercury* could only view the
summer influx with a jaundiced eye. "While we throw no
obstacles in the way of summer business," he explained in an
editorial, "and are quite willing for all who can to reap the fullest
benefit from the summer visitors, still we are firm in our belief
that the greatest calamity which has ever befallen Newport is
making it a fashionable resort in the summer."

The family of Robert Dunn, one branch of which descended
from Godfrey Malbone, had long been established in a stately
residence on Kay Street. The Dunns watched the coming of the
wealthy sojourners with equal skepticism and could only frown
on the Vanderbilts taking over a pew in the old Trinity Church
and cushioning the hard pews with maroon brocade. "Original
Newport settlers might have felt toward those ancestral Mal-
bones, Waltons and Hunters as Mama and Aunty felt toward the
new rich now," Dunn wrote. His aunt delighted in sitting on her
porch, waving the scandalous weekly *Town Topics*, which the
newcomers detested, and loudly proclaiming, "This is my Bible.
Can't anyone find *me* a lover?" The permanent residents were
distressed by the slack morality exhibited by the flashy people
from New York. "At lawn parties on Bellevue Avenue, boys in
sailor suits and girls in starched white piqué took the latest
scandal in stride. One father of pretty daughters went to the
asylum for shooting a Frenchman caught in bed with his wife.
. . . A foursome traded wives. . . . We heard, too, about the
Broadway showgirls, and the dinners on gold plate, and the
rivalries between rich washerwomen's daughters and hotelkeep-
er's wives. One day two victorias passed the Casino; from one the
dowager called 'Sitting Bull' [Mrs. James Kernochan] glared

without speaking as, from the other, another leader of 'society' burst into loud coughs and sneezes to disparage a fortune made in snuff."

In the coming decades there would be a continual guerrilla warfare between the townspeople and the summer residents. The territorial imperative asserted itself in only slightly more dignified terms than the conflict between street gangs over their turf.

To the summer people from Fifth Avenue, the natives were merely a quaint discordant chorus of bumpkins forming the background to their revelry, tolerable only so long as they stayed in their place. They were generically classified as "townies," a pejorative term. To the townspeople, the summer residents were interlopers at best; overdressed, overbearing, overfed, and often of dubious morality by New England standards. As one longtime summer resident would write:

"The townspeople despised the 'cottagers,' the summer colony of millionaires, and boasted of their ability to make them toe the mark. What harm was there in charging the idly rich prohibitive prices for two months and then living in comfort for the rest of the year on the proceeds? . . . The cottagers on their side were only concerned in excluding the townspeople from any of the pastures they considered their own. They themselves might wander at will in the lovely old town with its quaint old-fashioned streets nestling down by the waterfront. But the inhabitants must not dream of returning the compliment. Not for them the sacred purlieus of Bellevue Avenue and Ocean Drive, where they might catch a glimpse of the forbidden splendors of villas which were only occupied for six or seven weeks in the year. Even their humble mode of transport, the streetcar, was not permitted to invade the privacy of the Avenue for after one or two tentative attempts the offending lines were always uprooted at the instigation of W. K. Vanderbilt, Jack Astor or other autocrats."

Thus, it would seem to the natives that they had, somehow, been swindled. Neither party would ever be comfortable in the relationship.

The Civil War ended the patronage of the Southern planters, but they were replaced by what Newport historians called "nice millionaires"—that is, unobtrusive ones—and by a stately, somewhat self-infatuated circle of New England intellectuals. When the driveway along the beaches and cliffs was opened in 1869, Newport entered its period of high culture, elevated thought and genteel rumination.

Every summer there was an ingathering of the happy few, intellectually as exclusive and snobbish as their successors would be in the social and economic sense—the time of Dr. Oliver Wendell Holmes, Henry Wadsworth Longfellow, Julia Ward Howe, Henry James, George Bancroft, Helen Choate Bell, Thomas Gold Appleton, John Singer Sargent, Clarence King, and for one summer, in a flush and sober period, Edgar Allan Poe. The time of which Henry James wrote, "Where in the world, the hard American world, they *could* have hibernated, how they could even, in the season, have bowed their economic heads and lurked, if it hadn't been for Newport," Mr. James was unable to say. It was the refuge, he added, of "slightly disenchanted cosmopolites." It was an ingathering whose modern parallel is the intellectually fashionable and commercially successful colonies which now establish themselves on Nantucket and Martha's Vineyard.

In addition to Sargent, the Newport scenery had long been attractive to artists, beginning with Gilbert Stuart, whose patron had been Godfrey Malbone, and later including John LaFarge and William Hunt, whose brother Richard would design many of Newport's more extravagant villas.

Besides the Boston-based intellectuals, academics and artists who made Newport their summer headquarters, there were occasional drop-in visitors attracted by Newport's growing fame as the watering place of literary celebrity. Robert Louis Stevenson sojourned there one summer in hopes that the sea air would restore his health. Maud Howe Elliott, the daughter of Julia Ward Howe and Dr. Samuel Gridley Howe, would remember him as "Very ill during this visit, and rarely visible—spending his days lying full length on a couch, wrapped in a scarlet dressing gown, smoking endless cigarettes, and at times pouring forth a stream of talk that left his listeners tingling with the thrill of his rare and exquisite personality."

Another ambassador from the world outside that closely linked circle of New England intellectuals was Bret Harte. In 1871 young Mr. Harte and his wife journeyed from California, where he had won fame for his picaresque tales of the frontier, to receive the plaudits of the Eastern literary establishment. One of the honors bestowed on him was delivering the annual Phi Beta Kappa poem at the Harvard commencement exercises, an occasion somewhat enlivened by Harte's insistence on wearing green gloves. That summer the Hartes sojourned in Newport, where Harte was a star performer at dinner parties given by the Brahmins. Any man who would wear green gloves at a Harvard commencement obviously was the sort who could let a little fresh air into the close atmosphere of such a circle. His wit, his uninhibited storytelling charmed the Boston intellectuals. At one gathering, whose hostess was a rich lady, the stately Julia Ward Howe was also a guest. Inadvertently Harte propelled his hostess into making a sizable gaffe. As another guest recorded it, "Mrs. Julia Ward Howe was asked by Mr. Harte if she would not give him the privilege of hearing from her lips 'The Battle Hymn of the Republic.' Mrs. Howe had a beautiful and highly trained voice. . . . After 'The Battle Hymn' Mrs. Howe sang an Italian song and ended up with an English ballad, full of pathos. At the finish Mrs. Howe rose slowly from the piano, and the eloquent silence was broken by her hostess' voice at the extreme end of the room saying, 'Oh, Mrs. Howe, do now sing something comic!' "

Harte had arrived in Newport with ten thousand dollars' worth of magazine contracts to fulfill, but was so enchanted by the Newport atmosphere that he turned out only one short story during a summer largely devoted to lazing on beaches and verandas. He also produced a poem titled "A Newport Romance," which, for many residents of the summer colony before the super-rich invaded in full force, condensed much of Newport's historic charm. It was built around a house on the Point that had been the setting of an ill-starred romance between a

young French officer and a Quaker girl; the house was said to be
haunted by the ghost of the girl nightly searching for her
vanished lover. Harte ended his sentimental verse with the
stanzas:

> And ever since then, when the clock strikes two,
> She walks unbidden from room to room,
> And the air is filled that she passes through
> With a subtle, sad perfume.
>
> The delicate odor of mignonette
> The ghost of a dead and gone bouquet,
> Is all that tells her story; yet
> Could she think of a sweeter way?

Other literary celebrities would pass through the Newport
summers, some leaving no stronger trace than the ghostly scent of
mignonette in Bret Harte's poem. One of the more famous was
Edith Wharton, a member of an old Newport family, whom Mrs.
Elliott would remember as "Pussie Jones of Pen Craig Cottage,"
not quite so impressive a byline as the one that graced her many
novels. "Our acquaintance was slight," Mrs. Elliott recalled,
"she belonged to the ultra-fashionable crowd, and I in quite
another group. Though the intellectuals and the fashionables
sometimes met, they never quite fused. She was slender, graceful,
and icy cold, with an exceedingly aristocratic bearing. We were
all amazed when Pussie Jones brought out a book of verses in her
early twenties."

Social fusion between the Boston intellectuals and the first
wave of wealthy summer people that arrived during the postwar
years was out of the question. Each group regarded the other
with suspicion bordering on contempt. To the Brahmins and
bluestockings there was something insufferable about the display
of wealth and possessions, the obsession with "position" based on
acquired or inherited money. They prized a person for his wit
and perception, and passed the long golden summers trading
epigrams, coining phrases and exchanging philosophies. Some of
those sub-Athenian discourses were nicely touched with asperity.

Professor Wolcott Gibbs, who loved nature with an unbridled passion, observed during one of those long afternoons on the veranda: "Who loves his fellow man plants trees."

"Go kick a tree," snapped Mrs. Helen Choate Bell, "for me."

The happy-fewness of Newport's days before the Gilded Age millionaires decided it was the only feasible place to spend the summer would soon come to an end. Its distinction as the place where Longfellow and Holmes held forth, rather than the watering place of William Beach Lawrence and a few other nabobs, ironically was what attracted the attention of the wealthy people down the coast. Rich people, sadly enough, are bored by each other; they value nothing more highly than "amusing" persons of talent or intellect who can distract them, provided they are housebroken and can be trusted not to make off with the silver. One could weary quickly of listening to old Commodore Vanderbilt tell how he made his first fortune out of leaky ferryboats. But the Boston Brahmins were not inclined to stay around and act as court jesters or resident philosophers for the moneyed newcomers. The new Newporters were thrown on their own resources, to the extent that Edith Wharton explained her avoidance of Newport in later life by saying, "I did not care for watering-place mundanities." Gossip and tittle-tattle replaced civilized discourse; not a Bret Harte or Robert Louis Stevenson but a Russian archduke would be the star attraction of a Newport summer, and the display of wealth in every conceivable fashion became the dominant pastime. By the 1880's Newport was the mundanest place in the United States.

2.

THE COMING
OF THE WHITE ELEPHANTS

THE EXACT date on which Newport was transformed from a summer colony of New England intellectuals and a few unostentatious wealthy people cannot be exactly determined. Yet it all seemed to happen overnight, a stampede to the Rhode Island seaside that swept away the modest hotels, boarding houses and farmhouses in which summer people had indulged in their quiet pleasures and replaced them with castles and chateaux of the most depressing magnificence. The "marble cottage" type of architecture overwhelmed its setting, and soon Ocean Drive from Bellevue Avenue out past Ochre Point to Bailey's Beach was dominated by structures that seemed to combine the more grandiose features of Florence and Versailles with those of the nineteenth-century American railroad station. They were white elephants, Henry James said, "all cry and no wool."

James returned to the States from long expatriation to produce his observations on *The American Scene* in 1907. He could only deplore what three decades and too much money had done to the perfection of Newport as he had known it in the lovely past. "What an idea, originally, to have seen this miniature spot of earth, where the sea-nymphs on the carved sands, at the worst, might have chanted back to the shepherds, as a mere breeding-ground for white elephants! They look queer and conscious and lumpish—some of them, as with an air of the brandished proboscis, really grotesque—while their averted owners, roused from a witless dream, wonder what in the world is to be done with them. The answer to which, I think, can only be that there is absolutely nothing to be done; nothing but to let them stand

29

there always, vast and blank, for reminder to those concerned
with the prohibited degrees of witlessness, and of the peculiarly
awkward vengeances of affronted proportion and discretion."
Henry James' malediction on the great houses that towered over
Ocean Drive and overwhelmed the natural grace of their setting
has been carried out. They still stand as a monument to the
hubris of the Gilded Age.

Yet it was a humble native of Newport who seized upon and
profited from the coming of the white elephants. Plain Alfred
Smith he was, a tailor catering to the local merchants, not
fashionable enough for summer people who had their suits made
by Poole's of London. For many years he had been content to
follow his trade. Then, rather suddenly, his imagination was fired
by the sight of all those New York millionaires staying at the
Ocean House. Soon, he believed, they would be building their
own houses in Newport instead of putting up at a hotel. A frugal
man, he had saved up $20,000 from his tailoring business, which
he used to go into real estate promotion. With another solid
citizen named Joseph Bailey, he bought 140 acres of farmland on
the southern edge of town and bullied the town council into
extending Bellevue Avenue from the Ocean House through his
fields of scrub growth and rocky outcroppings right down to
Bailey's Beach. By 1880 it became evident that his plunge from
the safety of the tailoring trade to the risks of trafficking in real
estate was justified when he sold a parcel, for which he paid
$2,000, to an outsider for $16,000. And that was only the
beginning of the tidal influx of real estate profits. Seventy-five big
Victorian cottages were built on Bellevue Avenue. Soon a few
acres of hitherto worthless land on Ochre Point would be selling
for a million dollars.

The money rolled in for Smith, who would die in 1886 leaving
an estate of several millions, but he was a shrewd, hardheaded,
plain-living Yankee who didn't propose to have his style altered
by riches. A style diametrically opposed to that of those who
bought his land and who believed wealth was an excuse for
flaunting, not concealing, one's good fortune. Instead of lolling
on the back seat of a carriage, he drove a horse and buggy

around town. When he built a larger house, it was located on Mount Vernon Street, several unfashionable blocks above Bellevue and its lordly establishments. His wife was equally invulnerable to the attractions of high life among the summer cottagers, and busied herself with the pieties and good works of a New Englander. For both, a church supper was a brilliant enough social event. To townspeople like the Smiths, no matter how their financial position improved, the world of fashion down on Bellevue Avenue was as remote as the court of Kubla Khan.

Perhaps the real villain from Henry James' viewpoint was not a local promoter like Smith but the Civil War itself, which made so many people suddenly rich without making them suddenly capable of acquiring the aristocratic graces. While that war was reddening the sky over the sundered nation, some of our oldest and mightiest fortunes were being built on a foundation of immense profits made on supplying the Union armies, speculating in gold and smuggled Confederate cotton, gambling on the stock-market reaction to various victories and defeats.

So much wealth flowed into New York that Mayor Fernando Wood, whose devotion to the Union was minimal, proposed that New York City secede from the Union and stop sending its money to the U.S. Treasury. Gold speculation reached such heights that the speculators in that commodity were called "General Lee's left wing," endangering as they did the integrity of the greenback. Congressional investigations revealed that the country's leading financiers made tens of millions out of selling the government unseaworthy ships, outmoded and defective rifles acquired from European armories, shoddy uniforms, cardboard-soled boots and rotting foodstuffs.

The Vanderbilts would strive to keep the Goulds out of the circle of socially elect by claiming their wealth was "tainted" by Jay Gould's hectic speculations in the railroads, yet old Commodore Cornelius Vanderbilt made a large fortune out of one venture alone—equipping General Nathaniel Banks' ill-fated expedition to New Orleans in 1862. The ships Vanderbilt supplied for that thrust against New Orleans, an Iowa senator remarked after listening to testimony before his investigating committee, weren't capable of making a safe voyage around New York Harbor. "In perfectly smooth weather the planks were ripped out of her," he reported regarding one of the hulks, "and exhibited to the gaze of the indignant soldiers on board, showing that her timbers were rotten. The committee have in their committee room a large sample of one of the beams of this vessel to show that it had not the slightest capacity to hold a nail." If it had encountered one of the frequent storms off Cape Hatteras, the whole fleet would have been sunk. The government estimated it had been swindled out of twenty-five million dollars by contractors dealing in ships alone.

J. Pierpont Morgan, another stately name in finance and society, made his first big killing on an arms deal so crooked that even his fellow entrepreneurs were shocked by its audacity. His agents bought 5,000 obsolete Hall's carbines, condemned five years earlier by army inspectors as more dangerous to their possessors than any enemy framed in their sights, for $3.50 apiece. He then sold them to the western army headquarters at St. Louis for $22.00. The whole shipment of Morgan's carbines had to be junked when soldiers firing them had their thumbs blown off. And that is only a quick sampling of how America's New Class enriched itself.

All that new money, producing a crop of new millionaires, meant more people battering at the gates of New York society. There were so many new aspirants that it was no longer possible to know all the claimants or sort out their claims. The survivors of the old Knickerbocker group were overwhelmed; few of them had battened on war profits, and they found themselves displaced by the thrusters, elbowed aside at the opera, confronted by vulgarians, ablaze with diamonds, whenever they ventured on the social scene. The term "social climber" was frequently heard, in hostile accents, and it was apparent that so-called high society would lose its meaning, its reason for being, if somebody didn't assume the role of arbiter and decide who was worthy of inclusion and who must be told to wait in line.

Restless, avid for associations that would certify their claim to "belonging," the swollen membership of New York's grandee class began looking for new places in which to exhibit itself. A summer retreat, to match the Fifth Avenue town house in splendor, was regarded as a necessity. Saratoga, with its racing and gambling, its unbuttoned style, did not offer the cachet required for consolidating one's social position. The New Jersey beach resorts were also a trifle common, though favored by President Grant and his friends. So the social vector swung waveringly, then firmly toward the beaches and vistas of Newport, which possessed that aristocratic quiet, that cultivated manner, that lingering touch of colonial gentility seemingly transferable to anyone who could afford to establish himself there in an expensive style.

Already it was the summer seat of such enviable hostesses as Mrs. Nicholas Beach, Mrs. Paran Stevens and Mrs. Sydney Brooks, who had introduced such genteel entertainment as musicales and salons. Certainly it would be elevating, and socially ennobling, to listen to string quartets and participate in witty discourse instead of pigging it on a Jersey beach or bringing the winners home on the Saratoga track.

And there was an even more lustrous attraction: the glamorous Belmonts gilded with all that Rothschild money. There was no image more suggestive of high-class living than Caroline Belmont, the daughter of Commodore Matthew Perry, tooling down the avenue in her *demi-daumont,* a carriage imported from Paris, drawn by four horses and driven by two postillions outfitted as jockeys.

The coming of the senior August Belmonts and the construction of their villa By-the-Sea in Newport—their lavish style and what it portended—was not wholly welcomed by the old guard. The latter was offended not only by the magnificence of By-the-Sea but the corps of servants required to keep it functioning. As Mrs. Belmont's daughter-in-law, the former actress Eleanor Robson, would recall in her memoir, there were "sixteen servants for indoor housekeeping and four men in the garage, three in the stable and several gardeners."

A lady of waspish temper, Mrs. John Francis was disturbed by the florid style of the Belmonts, especially when her only servant, a maid, who had been employed by the Belmonts the previous summer, kept comparing Mrs. Francis' austerity with By-the-Sea's splendor. One day the maid would inform Mrs. Francis, with the air of one who has come down in the world, that "Mr. Belmont keeps twenty servants," the next that "Mr. Belmont keeps ten horses."

After listening to her maid's "Mr. Belmont keeps" litany one day, Mrs. Francis snapped, "Mr. Belmont keeps . . . everything but the Ten Commandments."

August Belmont, Sr., may have broken one or two commandments in his time, but his social and financial position was impregnable by the time he built By-the-Sea in his wife's hometown. He was not only the Rothschilds' representative in the United States, but for many years had been chairman of the Democratic National Committee, a director of the Metropolitan Opera, a founding member of the sportive New York clique that included the Jeromes (one of whom was the grandfather of Winston Churchill), William Travers, James Gordon Bennett, Jr., and other high-flying clubmen. His Jewish ancestry, it appeared, was only the slightest of handicaps, one he shed at the earliest opportunity. Thus, he did not suffer from the virulent anti-Semitism of the Civil War years, when it was charged in the press that the Jews were speculating in gold, thereby destroying the national credit, and smuggling supplies to the Confederacy in exchange for contraband cotton.

The suave and worldly Belmont was born in the Rhine Palatinate in 1816, more South German in appearance than anything else, and at the age of thirteen served as an unpaid apprentice in the Rothschilds' Frankfurt bank. Still in his teens, he was sent to serve the Rothschild interests in Naples and Havana until, in 1837, he migrated to the United States. With Rothschild backing he soon became one of the three principal bankers in the country. He was converted to the Episcopal faith, he married a beautiful Christian girl, Caroline Slidell Perry, of the seagoing Perrys, and from then on the Belmonts were totally Christian, to the extent that his son raised pigs and fed them on Jerusalem artichokes to improve the flavor of the bacon they provided for his breakfast table. "Since the first August Belmont set foot in America," as Dixon Wecter remarked, "no member of that Family has ever married a Jewess, but invariably a Gentile of social standing. In this way, plus an exchange of the synagogue for Episcopal communion, a constant association with non-Jews, and the adaptability of Nature which has given Belmonts scarcely any Semitic cast of feature except in their patriarchal age, a complete break with their Old World background has been successfully effected. In social acceptance no later Jewish Family can compare with them."

Thus, the Belmonts would spearhead the socialite invasion of Newport and abstain from joining the wealthy New York German-Jewish families in their summer migration to what later was called, variously, the "Jewish Newport" and a "gilded ghetto." The Jewish version of Newport was centered on Elburon on the New Jersey shore and spread to surrounding resorts at Long Branch, Sea Bright, Deal Beach and Allenhurst. It was a close approximation in style of Christian Newport which, in contravention of its historic hospitality toward people of the Jewish faith, became a severely restricted area (and not only for Jews). At Elburon and surrounding Jewish colonies, Emanie Sachs would recall, the atmosphere was quite as stuffy as at Newport; the residents, she wrote, were "padded with red damask, built of a pattern in a piece, dancing round and round in a golden trap, getting nowhere."

Thoroughly Americanized and Christianized, August Belmont surged ahead, an outstanding example of upward mobility to inspire the flood of immigrants soon to follow, and eschewed all morbid reflections on living in a "golden trap." It was more like a golden three-ring circus.

His marriage was happy and fruitful; his sons carried on along the path he marked out for them, and he became an American version of his patrons the Rothschilds. There was no landed gentry or titled aristocracy to which he could attach himself, as the Rothschilds did in England, France and Austria, but he found a more than adequate substitute. This was the hedonistic element he found among his peers in Wall Street, a sort of jet-set

prototype that soon became known as the "Belmont Clique."
Witty, amoral, cosmopolitan, they included Leonard, Lawrence
and Addison Jerome; Henry Clews, the English-born broker,
who chronicled their antics in his candid memoir *Fifty Years in
Wall Street*; William Travers and Addison Cammack, all of them
risk-taking operators on Wall Street; and subsequently young
James Gordon Bennett, the madcap son of the publisher of the
New York *Herald*. With Leonard Jerome and several others, he
organized the American Jockey Club and built a racetrack
called Jerome Park. He built up a racing stable and established
the Nursery Stud at Lexington, Kentucky. An association with
horseflesh, he had shrewdly noted, was necessary to creating an
aristocratic impression; knights rode while varlets walked.

Bolstered by his friendships, protected by his claim to being as
Christian as the next parishioner, he rode out the anti-Semitism
that afflicted the North (much more than the South) during the
Civil War. The fact that he headed the Democratic National
Committee subjected him to charges that he was a Copperhead
and a traitor to the Union. The more rabid Abolitionist
newspapers and streetcorner demagogues assailed him and "the
whole tribe of Jews," as Rufus Learsi (*The Jews in America*) noted.
But August Belmont was adept at counterpropaganda and
quelled suspicion by raising and equipping a Union regiment
and exerting his (and the Rothschilds') considerable influence in
European financial centers on behalf of the Union cause.

Thus, Belmont, his elegant wife and their sons established New
York society's bridgehead on the Newport shorefront. If the old
guard had any objections to Belmont's flashy reputation, it could
not withhold acceptance from his wife. Her family had provided
in her father and uncle two of the local heroes. Caroline herself
displayed the coolly aristocratic manner imparted by a French
education and wore the most expensively tasteful imported frocks
and jewelry.

The old guard might have objected strenuously, despite the
impeccable Caroline, if it had realized that the Belmonts were
not only introducing ten-course dinners attended by liveried
footmen in the midst of its revered simplicities, but would shortly

serve as bellwether for a whole flock of New Yorkers in their summer migrations. After the Belmonts came a task force composed of various Kips, Tiffanys, Rhinelanders, Van Rensselaers, Lorillards, Kernochans, Livingstons, Schermerhorns, and Stuyvesants, followed by the Astor and Vanderbilt clans. And then the floodgates were open.

For Newport by now had received the imprimatur of Ward McAllister. Even more than the example of the Belmonts, his seal of approval encouraged the presence of any New Yorkers who aspired to social position. After all, he had concocted the Four Hundred—or whatever the precise number, it varied from time to time—the list of the elect in the social world of the metropolis. McAllister made a career out of social arbitration, of acting as adviser to the dowager queens, of serving as grand vizier over their courts and cotillions. Indubitably he was a throwback to older courts on another continent, courts equally obsessed with relieving the boredom of having too much of everything.

Samuel Ward McAllister could claim deep roots in Newport and Rhode Island, though he was a member of the Southern branch of the Ward family. Thus, to the staider New England members of the clan, including his cousin Julia Ward Howe, he might appear to be a traitor to family tradition in encouraging the migration of New Yorkers to Newport. Certainly when Cousin Ward's friends and followers appeared in force, much that was valuable about Newport to the old-guard intellectuals was destroyed.

Like the New England Wards, he was a descendant of Richard Ward, the Royal Governor of Rhode Island, and Samuel Ward, the Revolutionary Governor. He was the son of Judge Matthew Hall McAllister of Savannah, Georgia, where he was born in 1827. Certainly he was not educated or reared to be the dancing-master type, the prop of old ladies' social pretensions— that vocation came to him naturally—but started out in life as a lawyer. With his father and brother he migrated to California during the Gold Rush. The gold dust showering almost everyone inspired him to join his father and brother in practicing law, always a lucrative profession where sudden wealth, quick tempers and disputed property claims are combined. "Gloom settled upon me," he recorded after learning that eggs cost $2.00 apiece in booming San Francisco, "until my noble parent requested me to bring back to the office our first retainer (for I was a member of my father and brother's law firm). It was $4,000 in gold ounces. I put it in a bag and lugged it to the office, and as I laid them ounce by ounce on my father's desk, he danced a pirouette, for he was as jolly an old fellow as ever lived. I went to work at once in earnest; it struck me that in that country it was 'root, pig, or die.' "

After three prosperous years McAllister left San Francisco and its frontier barbarities to immerse himself in a politer society. Trying to wangle an appointment as secretary of the American legation in London, he appeared in Washington in 1853, failed to obtain his appointment but did find an eminently suitable wife, Sarah Gibbons, who was not only an heiress but becomingly self-effacing. She was so shy, in fact, that few people during his grandest period could recall having met Mrs. McAllister. Had she been much less content with remaining in the background, of course, it would have been impossible for him to pursue his career as New York society's guardian of the gates.

McAllister spent some years sojourning abroad and learning continental etiquette, wine snobbery, various national cuisines and other things necessary to the career of a gentleman-in-waiting. When he returned to New York, he was determined to carve out a sizable niche for himself in post-Civil War society. Aside from his European schooling in gentlemanly conduct, and a decent income, he did not have a great deal to offer. His appearance, except for a Vandyke and a Napoleon III mustache, was undistinguished. He was not amusing, was devoid of humor, and took the trivia of social intercourse far too seriously; pompous was probably the word for him, if not pretentious.

Returning to his native Savannah on a visit, he exhibited his innocent pride in being a real swell, a certified toff, by recalling in his memoir that "I naturally prided myself, on appearing in my native city, in putting my best foot foremost, and entertaining as well as I knew how, or, rather, in giving to my Southern friends, the benefit of my European education in the way of dinner giving. I found this, at first, instead of gratifying my father's friends rather piqued them; they said—'Heyday! here is a young fellow coming out here to show us how to live. Why, his father did not pretend to do this. Let us let him severely alone,' which for a time they did." When the sons of the Duke of Devonshire and the Earl of Shaftesbury appeared in America, McAllister appointed himself their host in Savannah. It was his first top-drawer social triumph: "My *filets de boeuf aux truffes et champignons,* and the scions of noble English houses, placed me in the front social rank in that little, aristocratic town, and brought forth from one of its oldest inhabitants the exclamation, 'My dear boy, your aunts could give breakfasts, but you, you can give dinners!' "

His contemporaries undoubtedly found McAllister an oddity. Most men with his training and position would have plunged into a real man's work, gambling on the stock exchange, dreaming up new railroad lines to the Pacific, thimblerigging, stock-jobbing and all the other occupations of the upper-class male of his time. Instead McAllister—soon to be referred to as Make-a-Lister—wallowed happily in a woman's realm and concerned himself with social precedence, guest lists and directing the arch little niceties of a cotillion.

He soon assumed the burden of molding New York society on the English and continental patterns. By 1872 he was drawing up the first of his celebrated lists—a committee he called the "Patriarchs," which would "have the right of inviting to each ball four ladies and five gentlemen, including himself and family." This was one way of excluding the unworthy, a problem that greatly exercised his talent for sniffing out the "right" people. It was obvious from his list of Patriarchs that he relied heavily on pedigree, rather than native wit or charm, in singling out the members of his new order of chivalry. They included John Jacob Astor, William Astor, Delancey Kane, George Henry Warren, Eugene A. Livingston, William Butler Duncan, E. Templeton Snelling, Lewis Colford Jones, Benjamin S. Welles,

Frederick Sheldon, William R. Travers, Royal Phelps, Edwin A. Post, Archibald Gracie King, Lewis M. Ruthurfurd, Robert C. Remsen, William C. Schermerhorn, Francis R. Rives, Maturin Livingston, Alexander Van Rensselaer, Walter Langdon, F. G. D'Hauteville, C. C. Goodhue—and, of course, Ward McAllister.

No one, fortunately, demanded to know just why Ward McAllister should decide who was who in New York society. There was a vacuum, caused by the pressure of outsiders trying to get into the dress circle, and McAllister filled it. Until he assumed the role of social arbiter, such matters were generally referred to an even odder specimen, Isaac Hull Brown, the 300-pound sexton of Grace Church. For many years Brown had swayed like a captive balloon over the social scene. He had started out in life as a carpenter. Having no social ambitions for himself, but having a keen interest in the pecking order, he served as a sort of unofficial social secretary, confidential adviser and public-relations man for the Fifth Avenue hostesses. His early vocation saved the day, or night, in 1860 when a ball was held in honor of the visiting Prince of Wales at the Academy of Music. A section of the floor collapsed when a horde of people converged on the Prince and clamored to be presented all at once. With his great bulk and immense authority, Brown cleared that section of the ballroom, hauled people who had fallen through the splintered boards to safety, then led a crew of volunteers to the basement and did a quick repair job that allowed the ball to proceed.

Brown presided at weddings and funerals as well as other social occasions, stationing himself at the door and reaching a hamlike fist for any gate-crashers. McAllister, naturally, observed him with the interest any man takes in his predecessor. "His memory was something remarkable," McAllister recalled. "He knew all and everything about everybody, knew always everyone's residence, was good nature itself, and cracked his jokes and had a word for everyone who passed into the ballroom. You would hear him *sotto voce* remarking upon men as they passed: 'Old family, good old stock,' or 'He's a new man; he had better mind his p's and q's, or I will trip him up. Ah, here's a fellow who intends to dance his way into society. . . . Here comes a handsome boy, the women are crazy about him,' etc." One of his services to society was to organize what was called "Brown's Brigade," a carefully selected list of about a hundred presentable bachelors who could be recruited as "extra men." Brown's recruits were required to have "commanding figures," as he said, be fashionably tailored and have "an ample supply of small talk at their tongue's end."

Self-tutored as he may have been in the mores and manners of the rich, he understood and sympathized with the great affliction of their lives: ennui. It was his job to minister to that pervading malaise of the brownstone mansions, the fanciful chateaux going up on Fifth Avenue. One of his dictums was, "The Lenten Season is a horridly dull season, but we manage to make our funerals as entertaining as possible."

His own funeral in 1880 was held in Grace Church and done in a style of which, it was felt, he would have been proud. A parishioner wrote a poem that would serve as his eulogy:

> Oh, glorious Brown, thou medley strange
> Of churchyard, ballroom, saint and sinner;
> Flying by morn through fashion's range,
> And burying mortals after dinner!
> Walking one day with invitations—
> Passing the next at consecrations;
> Tossing the sod at eve on coffins;
> With one hand drying tears of orphans,
> And one unclasping ballroom carriage,
> Or cutting up plumcake for marriage . . .

By then Ward McAllister had already elbowed him aside as the chief arbiter of social ranking. He saw that the momentous decisions of who was to be invited to tippytoe through the next cotillion, who would be presented to the next visiting royalty, who would be seated below the salt, could not be left to the intuitive efforts of a mere sexton, no matter how trustworthy and dedicated, but must be entrusted to a man of breeding. And the

process must be conducted with all the scientific system of a
first-rate stud farm. There were too many aspirants now to be
sorted out, rejected or accepted in the pecking order. All those
Civil War fortunes had to be weighed and social or financial
taints detected. People like the Goulds would have to wait a
generation before their money was sanctified.

He divided New York society into two groups, the Nobs (the
older aristocracy) and the Swells (new money). "Beauty before
brains," he decreed, "mind before money." He was ready with
advice on how the newcomers could upgrade themselves: "If you
want to be fashionable, be always in the company of fashionable
people. As an old beau suggested to me, if you see a fossil of a
man, shabbily dressed, relying solely on his pedigree, dating back
to time immemorial, who has the aspirations of a duke and the
fortunes of a footman, do not cut him; it is better to cross the
street and avoid meeting him. It is well to be in with the Nobs
who are born to their positions, but the support of the Swells is
more advantageous, for Society is sustained and carried on by the
Swells, the Nobs looking quietly on and accepting the position,
feeling they are there by divine right; but they do not make
fashionable Society, or carry it on. A Nob can be a Swell if he
chooses, i.e., if he will spend the money; but for his social position
this is unnecessary. A Nob is like a poet—not so a Swell—he
creates himself."

What was needed, he thought, was "organized social power,"
which would be "capable of giving a passport to society to all
worthy of it. We thought it would not have been wise to allow a
handful of men having royal fortunes to have a sovereign's
prerogatives, i.e., to say whom society shall receive. . . . We
thought it better to try and place such power in the hands of
representative men. . . ." Foremost among the representative
men, of course, was himself.

Aside from presiding over the selection process, McAllister was
at his lordliest organizing cotillions for various hostesses and
mincing through the stately patterns of the quadrilles. He was
the organizer, the veritable field marshal, of the Banner Ball,
which celebrated the 1876 centennial. His account of the ball is

drenched in self-satisfaction at the commanding figure he presented. "I led the way to the ballroom with the 'fairest of the fair,' the daughter of one of the most distinguished men in this country (who had not only been Governor of this State, but Secretary of State of the United States). We were surrounded by a noble throng of old New Yorkers, all eager to view the opening quadrille. The ladies were in Colonial costumes, representing Lady Washington and the ladies of her court." At another ball, celebrating the centennial of the battle of Yorktown, French and German officers whose antecedents had participated in that climactic victory were the guests of honor. But it was McAllister, in his view, who dominated the proceedings, "flitting from one group to another, instructing each of them what they were to do. The position was indeed droll. I stood behind the Governor, who was to all outward appearances conversing with General Boulanger, but was literally squeezing my hand and asking me what he was to do. One distinguished German general promptly said, 'I go it blind! I will simply do what the others do.' These were the forces I had to marshal and put through a quadrille."

No one, obviously, could do a better job of satirizing Ward McAllister—willing to make a career out of "flitting" around ballrooms—than McAllister himself. He busied himself with conceiving the quadrilles and designing the costumes proper for each, as engrossed in providing an hour or two of distraction for Fifth Avenue as any chamberlain of a European court. At the ball given for Lady Mandeville, as he described it, the staging was worthy of a David Belasco. They consisted, he wrote, of " 'The Hobby Horse Quadrille,' the men who danced in it being dressed in pink and the ladies wearing red hunting-coats and white satin skirts, all of the period of Louis XIV. In the 'Mother Goose Quadrille' were 'Jack and Jill,' 'Little Red Riding Hood,' 'Bo-Peep,' 'Goody Two-Shoes,' 'Mary, Mary, Quite Contrary' and 'My Pretty Maid.' The 'Opera Bouffe Quadrille' was most successful; but of all of them, 'The Star Quadrille,' containing the youth and beauty of the city, was the most brilliant. The ladies in it were arrayed as twin stars, in four different colors, yellow, blue, mauve and white. Above the forehead of each lady, in her hair, was worn an electric light, giving a fairy and elf-like appearance to each of them." The host of the Lady Mandeville ball appeared as the Duc de Guise, his brother as Louis XVI (it was not explained how Louis XVI turned up at Louis XIV's court), and his wife as "The Electric Light, in white satin, trimmed with diamonds, and her head one blaze of diamonds." Thus, in McAllister's fancy, the world of Louis XIV melded gracefully with the age of Edison's mazda bulb.

He was not at all dismayed that New York society was being transformed by floods of new money and its possessors. Formerly a man with one million would be ranked as a Nob or Swell, depending on how long the money had been in his or his family's possession, but now it took a man with fifty to a hundred million to make a really sizable splash in the social swim. Small dinner parties were passé. "Fashion demanded that you be received in the hall of the house in which you were to dine, by from five to six servants who, with the butler, were to serve the repast. . . . Soft strains of music were introduced between the courses, and in some houses gold replaced silver in the way of plate, and everything that skill and art could suggest was added to make the dinners not a vulgar display, but a great gastronomic effort, evidencing the possession by the host of both money and taste."

As he passed into middle age, McAllister found the New York scene a bit exhausting, with all those demands on his social sense and his impeccable taste, and he began spending much of the year in Newport, where he had bought the Bayside Farm. "The crème de la crème," as he put it, would surely follow him to Newport in the summer months. He wintered in the West Indies, but was still available for top-drawer organizing for New York's more expensive hostesses.

His description of his Newport activities was no less fatuous or self-infatuated than those of his New York period. His picnics— or fêtes champêtres, as he insisted on calling them in deference to the contemporary belief that a French phrase was incomparably more elegant than English—soon began advertising Newport and its well-curried pastoral life as the only fashionable place to be seen in the summertime. A McAllister picnic was regarded as socially more elevating than a dinner at the Belmonts. An arbiter and cotillion leader in New York, he became a social force in his own right in Newport. And he left no doubt that he was impressed by his newly enhanced position, the following bit of his memoir conveying precisely his self-satisfaction:

"Riding on the Avenue on a lovely summer's day, I would be stopped by a beautiful woman, in gorgeous array, looking so fascinating that if she were to ask you to attempt the impossible, you would at least make the effort. She would open on me as follows: 'My dear friend, we are all dying for a picnic. Can't you get one up for us?' 'Why, my dear lady,' I would answer, 'you have dinners every day, and charming dinners, too; what more do you want?' 'Oh, they're not picnics. Any one can give dinners. Now, my dear friend, do get one up.'

"This was enough to fire me, and set me going. So I reply: 'I will do your bidding. Fix on the day at once, and tell me what is the best dish your cook makes.' Out comes my memorandum book, and I write: 'Monday, 1 P.M., meet at Narragansett Avenue, bring *filet de boeuf pique*,' and with a bow am off in my little wagon, and dash on, to waylay the next cottager, stop every carriage known to contain friends, and ask them, one and all, to join our country party, and assign to each of them the providing of a certain dish and a bottle of champagne.

"Meeting young men I charge them to take a bottle of champagne, and a pound of grapes, or order from the confectioner's a quart of ice cream to be sent to me. My pony is put on its mettle; I keep going the entire day getting recruits; I engage my music and servants, and a carpenter to put down a dancing platform, and the florist to adorn it, and that evening I go over in detail the whole affair, map it out as a general would a battle, omitting nothing, not even a salt spoon; see to it that I have men on the road to direct my party to the farm, and bid the farmer put himself and family, and the whole farm, in holiday attire."

Aside from ordering his farmhands into their finery, he often rented a flock of Southdown sheep, along with a few yokes of

cattle, to give the Bayside Farm an "animated look." Then, like
Marie Antoinette and her milkmaids, the whole party could
enjoy the illusion of going back to nature.

Ranging over the farmlands outside Newport, McAllister and
his frolicsome friends even invaded farmhouses and made
themselves at home in peasant dining rooms. The farmers, he
affirmed, just loved it. "They threw open their houses to us, and
never heeded the invasion, on a bright sunshiny day, of a party of
fifty people, who took possession of their dining room, in fact of
their whole house, and frolicked in it to their heart's content."
He did not claim that the local yeomanry tugged their forelocks,
but it is rather difficult to imagine Rhode Islanders, with their
tradition of stubborn independence, actually beaming with
pleasure when a clatter of socialites descended upon them and
exclaimed over their quaint, poky ways.

At least one McAllister-led expedition came to grief, as he
admitted in his memoir. A procession of carriages and coaches
journeyed from Newport to a country hotel at Bristol Ferry,
where McAllister and his friends feasted on Spanish mackerel,
softshell crabs, woodcock and partridges, with lashings of champagne. On the way back to Newport, his coach toppled off the
road and spilled the socialites into a ditch, with several of them
slightly injured. A young man in the party, who had just started
his career in the diplomatic corps, was sent to a nearby
farmhouse, the lights of which could be seen from the road, to ask
for a glass of water for one of the bruised passengers.

The young diplomat banged on the farmhouse door and
bawled, in Ivy League accents, "House, house, won't you hear,
won't you hear?"

An old man poked his head out of the window and roared
back, "Why, man, the house can't talk! What do you want here
at this time of night? I know who you are, you're some of
McAllister's picnickers. I suppose you want milk, but you won't
get a drop here."

Aside from that misadventure on the road from Bristol Ferry,
his primacy as an arranger of rustic gambols, he maintained, was
unchallenged. An outing without McAllister in charge of food

and entertainment was all but unthinkable. Once, he admitted, some young bloods from New York decided to hold a country dinner and dance at a country teahouse six miles from Newport without consulting McAllister. Instead they engaged Delmonico's to cater the affair. All afternoon there was dancing on the porches and lawns of the establishment. When the guests went inside to fall on the collation Delmonico's staff had arranged for them, they beheld a disaster of proportions that could have been duplicated only in a Mack Sennett comedy.

The servants, without a watchful eye kept on them, had turned the interior of the teahouse into a shambles. "All the coachmen and grooms had made a foray on the abundant supplies, tumbled Delmonico's French waiters into the cellar and locked them up; then, taking possession of the dining room, held high carnival. Every mouthful of solid food was eaten up and all the champagne drunk . . . every coachman and groom was intoxicated. . . ."

The party broke up at once, with drunken coachmen "swaying like pendulums" on their boxes, the postillions riding the *demi-daumonts* hanging on by the manes of their horses. One peppery old gentleman suggested that the varlets be rounded up and given a sound thrashing on the spot, but "prudence dictated that at that work man was as good as master, that the result might be doubtful." So the guests rode home behind their tipsy stablemen. "My man is beastly intoxicated," one old beldame declared, "but I shall appear not to notice it." The only satisfaction one employer got from his Irish coachman was the reply, "I own up, sir, but indeed I'm a weak creature."

That occasion on which McAllister's controlling hand was brushed aside, with the result that the lower orders went berserk, would always be remembered with a shudder by Newport's quality folk, to whom it had seemed like a preview of a second American revolution.

One of the highlights of McAllister's Newport career was the visit of President Chester A. Arthur. The President was viewed with mixed feelings in Newport; he was a Republican, but his earlier career had been tainted by the corruption of the machine

politics of New York City. It was felt that raffish Saratoga was
more his style. But that wasn't Ward McAllister's view, he was
more concerned with celebrity than social qualifications. Over
the objections of the Governor of Rhode Island, who wanted to
keep the President to himself, McAllister insisted on inviting
Arthur to one of his country picnics. He bustled into the parlor of
the governor's mansion with a bottle of Madeira in each hand,
which he presented to the President. Knowing that Arthur had
as sharp an eye for beautiful women as he had an appreciative
palate for wine, he promised the President that he would have "a
bouquet of such exotics as are grown only in a Newport
hothouse" as fellow guests at the picnic.

McAllister's outing took place at the Paradise and Purgatory
Rocks on the shore, with "one of the most beautiful women in
America" chosen as his dining companions. The wine was
plentiful and sparkling, and "we had a merry dance on the
green." McAllister was overjoyed when the President told him,
on leaving Newport, that "you did indeed redeem your promise."

Even with McAllister's imprimatur, however, President Arthur's visit was not a resounding success. Regarded as an old
boodle hound, though his administration in Washington was free
of the corruption that had attended his career as Collector of
Customs in New York, he was snubbed by many of Newport's
hostesses. Even the servants, aping their masters, treated him
without the respect due his office. When he left the Newport
Casino one afternoon, the club servants ostentatiously ignored
him. The President of the United States was reduced to going out
in the roadway and whistling up his own carriage.

3.

NEWPORT'S FIRST QUEEN

THE ATMOSPHERE surrounding the first of Newport's successive "queens" was usually described, with pardonable hyperbole, as something approaching the regal, the monarchial. Certainly no dowager empress was accorded more deference.

On formal occasions, to further the illusion, she invariably wore a diamond tiara and was surrounded by a "court" of ladies whose social qualifications came close to matching her own. Her hauteur, her sense of self-importance, certainly was no less than that of Queen Victoria.

Mrs. William Backhouse Astor, Jr., who insisted on being referred to as The Mrs. Astor, was the first of the majestic ladies to ascend the Newport throne. She came to Newport and established herself at Beechwood on the advice of Ward McAllister, her chief of staff and longtime collaborator in shaping the stateliest of all American social careers, that Newport was the only decent place to be on display in the summertime. Beechwood was her summer palace, long a local showplace with its piazzas extending around three sides, to which she added a ballroom.

After Mrs. Astor established herself on Bellevue Avenue and encouraged a wholesale migration from Fifth Avenue and its tributaries all over the nation, the Newport of the old quiet days vanished forever and was replaced by the super-rich and their possessions. It would be mourned with feeling, with a nostalgia more bitter than sweet, by people like Senator Henry Cabot Lodge of Massachusetts, the crusty descendant of one of Boston's first families, one of the victims of the law that holds that wealth

49

will always displace lineage in a democracy. In his memoir
published in 1913, Lodge left no doubt about his loathing for the
Newport that sprang up when Mrs. Astor and Mr. MacAllister
took over:

"I often look back to those quiet days of Newport with positive
regret. Then it was a place where one went to meet friends, not to
make them; culture and charm were the passports into Society,
but now wealth seems to be the Golden Key which unlocks most
doors in this place of rich men's houses. Bellevue Avenue, with its
melee of expensive cars and expensive owners, is as artificial as
the unnatural-looking clumps of hydrangea which is Newport's
favorite flower. What a contrast to the dignified Avenue as I
remember it! But it is an age of change, and Newport has shared
the universal fate. . . ."

There was no doubt, however, that The Mrs. Astor was
well-qualified for her essay in social imperialism.

Her pedigree and her marriage, linking the old Dutch
aristocracy with the more potent force of the Astor millions,
entitled her to believe that if leadership was required, she was the
person to supply it. If there was little queenliness about her
appearance—she was as dumpy as a Dutch housewife and could
have played Hans Brinker's mother if it were a matter of
typecasting—she made up for it with a breathtaking display of
jewelry. Only at night, of course; one of her homilies for
debutantes was that "Jewels are not worn in the daytime; glaring
colors and striking contrasts are to be avoided." But at night, on
any public occasion, she glittered with diamonds like a sultana,
and only Diamond Jim Brady himself could outflash her. In
jewelry, at least, it was an age of excess. A diamond tiara was *de
rigueur,* and below that she was literally encrusted. She wore a
diamond necklace containing 204 stones then valued at $60,000
(diamonds, like everything else, were only a fraction of today's
cost); a twelve-row fall of diamonds over her bosom, and a
stomacher which, belying its name, was a diamond-studded
brooch, also on her bosom. Her fingers were beringed with
diamonds and other precious stones. On a topflight occasion she
would also wear diamond stars in her hair, which was jet black in

her youth and the same color, thanks to hair dye, in her old age. All that fretwork of jewelry had the effect of providing her with a commanding posture. Her gowns, usually white satin, were so stiff with embroidery of pearls and silver, reinforced by all those diamond gewgaws, that she *had* to sit up straight.

Aside from all those visible signs of her wealth and her awesome dignity, her force of character, Mrs. Astor impressed herself on her peers, and laid claim to sovereign rights over her class, through possession of a judicious mind. Or so Ward McAllister claimed: "She had a just appreciation of the rights of others and, coming from an old colonial family, a good appreciation of the value of ancestry; always keeping it near her, and bringing it in, in all social matters, but also understanding the importance and power of the new element; recognizing it, and fairly and generously awarding it a prominent place."

But it was her driving ambition rather than any judicial quality ascribed to her by the adoring McAllister that was responsible for her ascendancy. Caroline Webster Schermerhorn was the descendant of a satisfactorily remote ship chandler who rose to wealth and prominence in the Knickerbocker period. Her own father reportedly was worth half a million, a fortune perhaps but not an overpowering one any longer. It would take the Astor wealth, growing out of the malodorous Western fur trade and multiplying on New York real estate (including acres of Manhattan tenements), to propel her upward at a dizzying pace. In 1853 she married William Backhouse Astor, Jr., grandson of the original John Jacob and brother of John III.

Her first wifely imposition was to persuade her husband to drop his middle name, so redolent of outdoor plumbing in the humbler sections of national life.

William did not share her ambitions to rule society. A rather dour character, he took after his grandfather, who insisted on eating peas and ice cream with his knife and once disturbed a genteel dinner party by wiping his fingers on the sleeve of the young lady next to him, though his manners were better and his appearance less uncouth. Few could understand why he married Caroline Schermerhorn with her large nose, heavy jaw and

dumplinglike figure. Eventually they produced the shy and plain
Carrie and several other children, but their union otherwise was
largely a formality. Astor devoted himself, not to playing Prince
Albert to her Queen Victoria, but various other pursuits. At
Columbia he had been accounted a brilliant student and on
graduation he had undertaken the Grand Tour to further his
studies of the art and literature of Greece and the Middle East.
Then he had married Caroline Schermerhorn as a means of
asserting himself in the Astor family and proving himself, at
twenty-three, as worthy of sharing in the management of the
Astor estate. The Astors, however, were strict followers of the rule
of primogeniture, and the managerial role was reserved for his
older brother John Jacob III.

Caroline's husband was too intelligent to be satisfied with
helping her attain the top rung on the social ladder. Playing the
society gentleman does not come naturally to an American, who
traditionally leaves the social game to his wife and daughters.
Even the wealthy labor under the compulsion of doing something—grow wealthier if nothing else. William Astor turned to
various pleasures that had little or nothing to do with his wife.
He spent much of his time aboard his sailing yacht *Ambassadress*,
on which pretty girls often outnumbered the crew, and at his
horse-breeding farm in Dutchess County. On land or sea he
drank heavily.

Just as her husband felt himself overshadowed by his older
brother, Caroline Astor initially was outranked by her sister-in-
law Augusta, Mrs. John Jacob Astor III, who was a woman of
great charm, kindliness and popularity. Augusta spent much of
her time in good works; even Jacob Riis in his condemnation of
Manhattan's tenement owners (*How the Other Half Lives*) praised
her "noble and useful life." Her parties were regarded as the
epitome of good taste and even had that rare quality of restraint.

Fortunately for her ambitious sister-in-law, Augusta Astor
lacked any aspirations to dominate the Astor family or the wider
society. She even went along with Caroline in the latter's
insistence that the old Astor enclave on Lafayette Place was no
longer suitable, so many pushy newcomers having moved into

the neighborhood, and joined in a concerted move uptown. The Astor brothers and their wives built mansions side by side at Thirty-fourth Street and Fifth Avenue.

Caroline launched herself as the sultana of New York society early in the 1870's when she formed an alliance with Ward McAllister. They agreed that postwar society was in disarray, that balls and other social functions were becoming a hurlyburly of climbers, muckers, vulgarians and other undesirable types. It was largely on her behalf that McAllister formed the Patriarchs Committee to cull out the wrong people and guarantee the integrity of her guest lists.

For the next ten years Mrs. Astor and her "prime minister," as some of the newspapers called him, labored to perfect a caste system largely based on McAllister's borrowed dictum that it took three generations to make a gentleman (a tactful limitation since Caroline's husband happened to be a member of the American Astors' third generation). By this standard the upstart Vanderbilts were rejected. As the Vanderbilt's most recent biographer has observed, "Mrs. Astor hardened the lines, raised the fiscal requirements, and set out to create a caste in which snobbery and money would make up for lineal shortages. The second and third generation Vanderbilts were still in trade, still actually *working* the railroad lines. So when the Vanderbilts married and moved into houses on Fifth Avenue, they found the doors of high society closed to them. They were a generation too soon for Mrs. Astor."

It was most discomfiting for Mrs. Astor when the new Metropolitan Opera House was opened for the 1883–84 season, and not only were the Goulds to be found basking in a box in the Diamond Horseshoe but the Vanderbilts had captured Box Six right next to the Astors' Box Seven. So many newcomers to society had edged their way into the Diamond Horseshoe, which Mrs. Astor always insisted was named in honor of her collection of jewelry, that one newspaper remarked on the "odor of crisp greenbacks" noticeable that opening night.

During those years it was generally acknowledged that Mrs. Astor was the leader of New York society, that she (in collaboration with McAllister) decided who was in and who was out. Not only people "in trade," not only people whose money was tainted by too recent possession, but other types were ruled distinctly unworthy of recognition.

Jews, of course, were out. The Irish and most Catholics of any origin would have to prove themselves and were usually found wanting. Germans were acceptable; the Astors had come from rooms over a butcher shop in Germany.

Mrs. Astor was human enough to let the bars down, once in a while, out of friendship. A girl long accepted in the Astor family circle, Ellin Prince, confessed in tremulous tones to Mrs. Astor that she had fallen in love with a Jew, James Speyer, the member of a family long prominent in Wall Street, but she was hesitating to marry him because she feared it would banish her from the upper echelons of society. Would Mrs. Astor receive a Jew and his wife? "I don't think we have any alternative," Mrs. Astor sighed, "for we are all so fond of you. Marry him, my dear, if you want to. I for one will invite you both to my parties and I think everyone else will do the same."

But she made few such exceptions, and it was generally agreed that she would have been highly disturbed if she could have foreseen that her Fifth Avenue mansion one day would be replaced by a synagogue. In that massive establishment at 350 Fifth Avenue, she held court, surveyed the expensive glitter of her little world, entertained, separated the social sheep from the unacceptable goats. Her footmen wore blue livery copied exactly from that of Windsor Castle. The dinner parties at which she presided were, on the advice and counsel of Ward McAllister, the height of contemporary elegance, and if there was a little too much of everything—if her dining room seemed to be overburdened with heavy gold plate, with hundreds of Gloire de Paris roses, with candelabra and crystal—that was just the style of the times. Her guests stayed at table for three or four hours. It took that long for them to work their way through nine courses of a menu usually selected by McAllister: *Tortue claire, mousse aux jambons,* salmon in the spring, terrapin in the winter, *filet de boeuf, riz de veau à la Toulouse,* maraschino-flavored sherbet, Nesselrode pudding, Camembert with biscuits. Champagne was served until the beef course, when it was replaced by vintage red and white wines. Often she had more than a hundred guests.

But it was her magnificent ballroom that served as the center of her social triumphs. Her major ball in January was the premier event of the season in New York; if you weren't invited to that, you might as well resign yourself to social inferiority, to taking up philanthropy or spending your money on racehorses and yachts. The anxiety of ambitious mothers on Fifth Avenue waiting for Mrs. Astor's invitations to be delivered by her coachman may be imagined. On the judgment of that one woman—who would have looked like a grocer's wife without her dyed pompadour and her filigree of diamonds, and her social adviser, the fatuous McAllister with his alternately arrogant and obsequious manner—depended so much hope and despair.

For the elect, however, Mrs. Astor's January ball was a splendiferous occasion. It was carefully stage-managed by McAllister to show Mrs. Astor at her most imposing. She and her daughters posed themselves beneath her portrait, painted by Caroline Duran, an idealization that Mrs. Astor in the flesh could never quite attain. Their guests were then shepherded into the immense ballroom with its gilt cornices and crystal chandeliers, with its walls almost completely covered by the paintings of Millet and other exemplars of the Barbizon school. On the balcony was John Lander's orchestra, the Meyer Davis of his time, ready to start playing Viennese waltzes. Not until 1:30 A.M. would the cotillion begin under the direction of McAllister and his chosen quadrille leaders.

It wasn't the waltzing or even the quadrille that was uppermost on her guests' minds, but the evidence, soon to be provided, of who her seasonal favorites were. It was good to be invited to her January ball, it was even better to be singled out for her personal attention.

Just before the music and dancing began, with a hush falling over the ballroom, Mrs. Astor in her shower of diamonds would proceed to the raised platform at the far end. On it was what facetiously, but with some symbolic accuracy, was called The

Throne. It was a long divan—but not long enough to accommodate all who yearned to sit there, in which case it would have to
extend approximately to Central Park South—with a scattering
of red silk cushions. Mrs. Astor carefully placed herself in the
middle, wary of bending too much in any direction for fear her
bodice with its encrusted pearls, beads and sequins would crack
like an armadillo's carapace. From time to time her courtiers
would be dispatched into the throng to pick out someone
honored with an invitation to join Mrs. Astor on The Throne.
Their progress to the platform was followed by hundreds of eyes
bitter with envy or misted with wistfulness. Those granted a
personal audience knew their careers were made, at least until
they made the wrong marriage or stumbled into scandal or
misconduct. Some of those who were not invited to the dais were
simply crushed. One lady from Philadelphia's Main Line (a
Drexel) broke down when the summons to Mrs. Astor's divan did
not come, openly sobbed, walked the length of the ballroom as
everyone stared, and left in disarray.

Yet Mrs. Astor, despite all the evidence of her supremacy, felt
herself threatened from a northerly direction on Fifth Avenue. At
660 Fifth Avenue was the social powerhouse of the Vanderbilts, a
replica of the Chateau de Blois, of which Mrs. William K.
Vanderbilt was the chatelaine. Her dinner parties and parties
were as extravagant as Mrs. Astor's. Her husband was the
grandson of the uncouth old Commodore, and therefore by
McAllister's definition a gentleman. Alva Vanderbilt, too, was as
ambitious and imperious as Mrs. Astor. Her claims to superior
ranking were recognized by McAllister, who was beginning to
dance attendance on her as he had Mrs. Astor.

But in 1883 Mrs. Astor indubitably was Number One, and she
had so far refused to extend diplomatic recognition to 660 Fifth
Avenue. Alva Vanderbilt could not be said to exist socially until
she was acknowledged by Mrs. Astor. She plotted to win that
recognition, possibly with the advice of Ward McAllister, who
saw that the Astors and Vanderbilts, as possessors of the two
mightiest fortunes, must learn the virtues of coexistence. Early in
1883 Mrs. Vanderbilt let it be known that she was planning a

magnificent ball for the night of March 26, 1883. When details of
the preparations leaked out, there was a stir of anticipation up
and down Fifth Avenue, consultations with costumers, much
rehearsal of the various quadrilles.

Mrs. Astor's daughter Carrie, just out of finishing school and
an entry in the matrimonial sweepstakes, was a member of the
Star Quadrille with seven other debutantes, and they drilled
almost as fervently as a ballet company under the eye of
dancing-master McAllister. Both Mrs. Astor and her daughter,
though the former had not acknowledged Alva Vanderbilt's
existence, were confident they would receive an invitation. As the
great night approached, however, none came. Carrie was
despondent, the only girl in her set who had not received an
invitation.

Now, briefly, Mrs. Astor knew the pangs of exclusion, which
only grew sharper when she made discreet inquiries as to
whether Mrs. Vanderbilt intended to invite her and her daughter and the reply was negative. Mrs. A., it seemed, would have to
make her obeisance. Until then, she was a nonperson. Being a
fond mother, she decided to make the required gesture. A few
days before Alva Vanderbilt's ball, she summoned her carriage,
drove up Fifth Avenue to Number 660, and sent her footman in
with her calling card. That oblong of engraved pasteboard,
which said simply "Mrs. Astor," solved everything. Alva Vanderbilt considered herself a member of the top echelon, now that
Mrs. Astor had formally called (though she had stayed in her
carriage at the curb), and Mrs. Astor and her daughter received
their invitations forthwith.

One thing that neither a Vanderbilt nor any other rival would
ever snatch from her was her title as the reigning sultana of the
Four Hundred. For that she could thank Ward McAllister, who
by 1888 had come to the conclusion that there were just 400
persons in the top drawer of New York society. It did not escape
notice that that was just about the number of people who could
be crowded into Mrs. Astor's ballroom.

"There are only about four hundred people in fashionable
New York society," he told a newspaper reporter in 1888. "If you

go outside that number, you strike people who are either not at ease in a ballroom or else make other people not at ease."

He may have flirted dangerously with the Vanderbilts but he left no doubt that he owed complete fealty to Mrs. Astor, whom he generally referred to as his "Mystic Rose," a poetic flight that puzzled most people who knew her. For four years he coyly refused to name those he considered worthy of inclusion in his Four Hundred, while society fretted and the newspapers badgered him for details. And he swelled in self-importance as the publicity made his name better known than most politicians, or even actors. Mr. Ward McAllister, in fact, had made himself more famous than most of the people, aside from Astors and Vanderbilts, whose names might be on his sacred list.

He held out until the eve of Mrs. Astor's ball on February 1, 1892, and though he had had four years to mull it over could come up with only a few more than three hundred actual members of his Four Hundred. In addition to himself, the list included the big men on Wall Street and their families, railroad and banking magnates. It was short, strikingly so, on anyone who might have been considered talented and amusing or artistic. At least one socialite, unimpressed by his list, though she was included, remarked that "The Four Hundred would have fled in a body from a poet, a painter, a musician or a clever Frenchman."

Mrs. Astor evidently accepted McAllister's designation of those worthy to tread on her ballroom floor; perhaps it was simply a culling of her guest lists.

She allowed herself to be persuaded in the late 1880's to join the summer migration to Newport. Her "cottage," Beechwood, like her New York townhouse, was the seat of social authority, with McAllister always at hand to sort out problems of precedence.

One problem he couldn't solve concerned her right to the title of The Mrs. Astor, which was vigorously contested for a time in Newport. Mrs. William Waldorf Astor, the daughter-in-law of the John Jacob Astor III's and therefore Caroline's niece by marriage, moved into the nearby and equally palatial Beaulieu.

There was no love lost between Mrs. Astor and her nephew, who insisted that henceforth all letters addressed to "Mrs. Astor, Newport" must be delivered to his wife, the former Mary Paul. She was a rather shy and retiring young woman and wanted no part of the family feud, but there was a long wrangle, involving the U.S. postal service and the opposing cliques of Astor friends, over whether Caroline was entitled to be addressed as the one and only Mrs. Astor.

With McAllister's help, Mrs. Astor won the dispute on the grounds of seniority, and the William Waldorf Astors fled to England. Her reign from then on was undisputed, even when Mrs. William K. Vanderbilt deployed her millions on the Newport scene and built The Breakers, the most overpowering of all the Newport cottages. "The Vanderbilts," it was whispered, no doubt to Mrs. Astor's satisfaction, "only went to Newport because the Astors were there."

Her Newport balls were as elaborate, the guest lists as carefully composed, as those she gave in New York. One couldn't be too careful, there were so many climbers and pretenders scheming to gain acceptance through tripping the measures at her cotillions. It was thus recorded that "would-be socialites schemed and bribed her friends and servants to procure for them invitations to her balls. A rumor was current then that fifteen-thousand dollars paid into the right hands would get one into Mrs. Astor's annual ball." But that didn't really solve the gate-crasher's problem; gaining acceptance was a lengthy process. Even with money and polished manners, according to McAllister, it took at least four seasons for a family to be accepted by Newport's most fashionable. "If you were not of the inner circle," he wrote, "and were a new-comer, it took the combined efforts of all your friends backing and pushing to procure an invitation for you. For years whole families sat upon the stool of probation, awaiting trial and acceptance, and many were rejected."

Mrs. Astor herself became a little more flexible after being maneuvered into acknowledging the Vanderbilts, but "Mystic Rose" was still adamantly opposed to admitting those besmirched by present or too recent contact with the marketplace, never mind that the founding father of her own clan had been a ship chandler. The phrase "in trade" was a killing frost when issued from Mrs. Astor's mouth. Alexander T. Stewart, the department store magnate, lived across Fifth Avenue from the Astor mansion but he was socially a nonperson. When she was asked to receive the wife of a worthy, long-established carpet manufacturer, she replied, "I buy my carpets from them, but is that any reason why I should invite them to walk on them?"

Mrs. Astor needed all the assurance such pronouncements indicated, all the regality she displayed in welcoming guests to her balls, all the composure she had acquired in four decades of queening it, when she was confronted by gossip and scandal concerning members of her family.

William, with his maritime girlfriends, his obvious determination to keep a continent or an ocean between him and his wife, was a recurrent problem. It must have been difficult to face down all the talk of a loveless marriage. William spent most of his time living aboard the *Ambassadress* and later the *Nourmahal*, the largest steam yacht then afloat. Usually it was anchored off Florida, where he was much prized and appointed a member of the governor's military staff. He could not be coaxed to take his rightful place in New York society, or even to assume the responsibilities of fatherhood. Sometimes he did anchor off Newport but reports, relayed promptly by the members of her court, would reach Mrs. Astor's ears of parties aboard his yacht to which she was never invited.

On receiving such unwanted intelligence, Mrs. Astor would smile bravely and remark that sailing was so good for her husband's health, and what a shame it was she couldn't join him because she was such a poor sailor. "I have never even set foot on his yacht," she would add. "Dreadful confession for a wife, isn't it?"

Queen Caroline held her head even higher when scandal touched her family. There had been some difficulty over the marriage of their daughter Emily to James J. Van Alen, the son of a Civil War cavalryman and railroad investor. The senior Van Alen's reputation as a playboy was almost as colorful as William

Astor's, but the latter objected to Emily's marriage on the grounds that the former wasn't worthy of being the grandfather of an Astor descendant. The elder Van Alen challenged Astor to a duel—the code duello was still accepted by high-class gentlemen as an ultimate means of settling their differences—but the pistols-at-dawn meeting was averted when Astor was persuaded to send Van Alen a letter of apology.*

It was another daughter, Mrs. Charlotte Astor Drayton, who became involved in the most lurid scandal in the Astor family history. She had married James Coleman Drayton of Philadelphia and after producing four children was accounted happily married. Then she fell in love with a caddish fellow named Hallett Alsop Borrowe, a New York clubman. The affair became public knowledge when Borrowe sold her letters to a scandal-mongering newspaper, though as a vice-president of Equitable Life he should not have been forced to such lengths for walkaround money. Drayton challenged Borrowe to a duel, and the latter accepted. The two men couldn't seem to get together on just where and when they would meet over pistols. Too many other pressing engagements, perhaps. More challenges were hurled and promptly accepted but the duel never came off. Charlotte received a divorce on the curious grounds that she had been deserted under "cruel suspicion of marital infidelity." Eventually, after touring Europe with Borrowe in spite of his unconventional methods of financing his escapades, she married still another man, George Haig, a wealthy Scotsman.

Despite his own extramatrimonial ventures, William Astor was outraged by his daughter's misconduct and cut her out of his will shortly before he died.

Mrs. Astor, however, was staunchly loyal to her daughter. No one dared to criticize Charlotte in her presence. During the trial

* Their daughter Carrie married Orme Wilson in a wedding notable for its extravagance. Ex-President Grant got drunk and burned himself by putting the lighted end of his cigar in his mouth. Their son John Jacob Astor IV married Ava Willing, a Philadelphia society beauty, but later fell in love with and married the eighteen-year-old Madeleine Force. Returning from a trip to Europe in the spring of 1912, they sailed on the first and last voyage of the *Titanic*; Astor stoically went down with the ship but his bride was among those rescued.

of Charlotte's divorce suit, she received her guests at a large reception at her Newport cottage, Beechwood, and insisted that Charlotte stand beside her. Anyone who fancied there was a scarlet letter "A" embroidered on the bodice of Charlotte's gown had the choice of accepting it or facing Mrs. Astor's wrath.

By that time Ward McAllister was slipping badly both in Mrs. Astor's esteem and as a social arbiter over Newport's summer colony. In 1890 he had published his famously foolish memoir, *Society As I Found It*, the pomposity of which made him a laughingstock. The snickering became a roar of laughter when he witlessly involved himself in a dispute over the quality of Chicago's civilization.

McAllister's attention was drawn to Chicago when its mayor, beating the drum for the World's Columbian Exposition of 1893, jovially told the world that his city's hospitality was a little rough around the edges but hearty and genuine, and added that he had bought 200 barrels of whiskey for official entertaining. McAllister was perturbed that genteel New Yorkers might be subjected to such crude western embraces. He readily granted an interview to the New York *World* for the purpose of instructing Chicagoans on how to properly entertain the tender blooms of New York society. "It is not quantity but quality that society people here want. Hospitality which includes the whole human race is not desirable," he told the *World* reporter.

He went on to instruct Chicago hosts in various recondite matters, taking it for granted that they knew more about forty-rod whiskey than fine wines. "I would suggest that Chicago society import a number of fine French chefs. I should also advise that they do not frappé their wine too much. Let them put the bottle in the tub and be careful to keep the neck free from ice. For, the quantity of wine in the neck of the bottle being small, it will be acted upon by the ice first. In twenty-five minutes from the time of being placed in the tub it will be in perfect condition to be served immediately. What I mean by a perfect condition is that when the wine is poured from the bottle it should contain little flakes of ice. That is a real frappé."

Insecure as it was on its foundation of hog-butchering fortunes,

Chicago society and its journalistic defenders were outraged by McAllister's gratuitous advice. Sharp exchanges between New York and Chicago, then bitter commercial and financial rivals, followed. It soon became apparent that though Chicago may not frappé wine properly, its journalists were well schooled in invective. The Chicago press addressed McAllister variously as "A Mouse Colored Ass," "A Popinjay," "Head Flunky," "The Premier of Cadsville," "Head Butler" and "A Delightful Duffer." The Chicago *Journal*, reporting preparations for a banquet the mayor was giving for foreign naval officers, assured him that "the mayor will not frappé his wine too much. He will frappé it just enough so the guests can blow the foam off the tops of the glasses without a vulgar exhibition of lung and lip power. His ham sandwiches, sinkers and Irish quail, better known in the Bridgeport vernacular as pigs' feet, will be triumphs of the gastronomic art."

The New York newspapers, except for the *World*, were only too eager to reprint the remarks of their Chicago colleagues, having begun to take a sardonic view of McAllister's homilies on correct social behavior. Their readers, for the most part, were equally delighted by his comeuppance. To which he only added by granting more interviews with the *World*. "I never intended to convey the impression that any New Yorker as a man is necessarily superior to a native of Chicago," he stated, but then added, "We in New York are familiar with the sharp character of Chicago magnates and many of us have learned to our cost that the Almighty Dollar is the trail they are following. I do not think these Chicagoans should pretend to rival the East and Old World in matters of refinement. Their growth has been too rapid to allow them to acquire both wealth and culture. Their leaders of society are the successful Stock Yards magnates, cottolene manufacturers, soapmakers, Chicago gas trust speculators and dry goods princes." He was distressed by reports that wealthy Chicagoans had bowling alleys instead of art galleries installed in their mansions. They should be willing to learn from a man who had spent most of his life studying how to live graciously. "In these modern days, society cannot get along without French chefs. The man who has been accustomed to delicate fillets of beef, terrapin, pâté de foie gras, truffled turkey and things of that sort would not care to sit down to a boiled leg of mutton dinner with turnips."

McAllister's well-intentioned defense of Eastern social standards, his anxiety over whether high-toned New Yorkers would be properly cosseted in Chicago if they visited the exposition, were ill rewarded. Only the *World* chose to point out that McAllister was sincerely hopeful that "the society of the West elevate itself by observing the society of the East."

That summer of 1893 McAllister was a figure of covert ridicule, and neither Mrs. Astor nor any of the other dowagers of the resort would call him into consultation again. He was not quite an outcast, but his pedantry on the subjects of wine and food, his quibbling over social qualifications, his sheer stuffiness, made him seem an outdated bore. Society by then was opening up in all directions; it was almost as important to be amusing as to have a grandfather with a pre-Civil War fortune.

Even so, society's ingratitude for all he had done by way of preserving its pretensions was strikingly brutal. An executive committee that presided over balls in Newport and New York, and included Stuyvesant Fish, Elbridge Gerry and Colonel William Jay dropped him as its functionary. "McAllister," Fish announced, "is a discharged servant. That is all."

The doyen of the French chateaux and Italian Renaissance palaces that had sprung up in Newport largely through his promotional talent died shortly thereafter in 1895. The lackluster style of his funeral should have aroused morbid reflections in any philosophers who might have been present. His passing was hardly noticed by the society he had so assiduously served as master of ceremonies; only five of the old Patriarchs and about a score of those he had nominated for the Four Hundred found time to attend. To the lower orders he had always scorned, however, he was still a celebrity; the most remarkable of his postmortem tributes was the crowd of nonentities who clamored for seats in the church. If he had hoped remembrance of his endeavors, self-appointed as they were, he might have done better to stay in San Francisco, which named McAllister Street after his brother.

Mrs. Astor had not found time to attend McAllister's funeral, but apparently it made her realize that her own primacy's days were numbered and the standards she had set, with McAllister's advice, might soon be questioned. "Many women will rise up to fill my place," she reflected, "but I hope my influence will be felt in one thing, and that is in discountenancing the undignified methods employed by certain women to attract a following."

One of the women to whom Mrs. Astor was referring was Mrs. Stuyvesant Fish, who would be one of her successors. On hearing of Mrs. Astor's remarks, she commented with a sort of poisonous kindliness, "Mrs. Astor is an elderly woman."

Elderly, true enough, but determined to stay propped on her thronelike divan, the tiara on her black pompadour still glittering like a lighthouse over the assemblage. Her position seemed secure as long as she wanted to hold it. When an Episcopal clergyman named Rev. Dr. Charles W. Nichols, possibly in emulation of Sexton Brown, published his supposedly magisterial *The Ultra-Fashionable Peerage of America* in 1904, an incredible compost of fake genealogy and uninhibited snobbery, he described Mrs. Astor as "one of the most far-descended ladies in the United States," an invitation to whose dinner parties placed one not only among McAllister's Four Hundred but the "ultra smart 150." She may have felt aggrieved, however, that he could not number her along with J. P. Morgan, Ogden Mills, the Vanderbilts and several others who "descend gracefully from Kings."

In her middle seventies, failing mentally and physically, she began to consider the matter of her abdication. Society was becoming hoydenish, too informal and inclusive by her standards. Too many hostesses were presiding over "entertainments that belong under a circus tent rather than in a gentleman's house." That was the last tart reproof known to have issued from Queen Caroline. The last dinner party she gave was for Prince Louis of Battenberg, the British sea lord and a member of the royal family. Only seventy-nine persons were regarded as worthy

of meeting Prince Louis, though her usual dinner parties ran to
twice that many. Among those significantly missing from that
last fling were the Vanderbilts; it was her final back-of-the-hand
to that upstart clan.

The staid and traditional sector of society waited with
accustomed anxiety for invitations to her annual January ball in
1906, but none came. Mrs. Astor had gone permanently into
seclusion. Then in her seventy-fifth year, with two more years to
live, she was either unable or unwilling to continue the career
which had obsessed most of her adult life. The only persons who
saw her were her personal physician, two nurses, the butler and
three maids. But she was still a legendary figure and a matter of
curiosity to the world from which she had retired.

Nothing regarding her condition was allowed to leak from her
seclusion at Beechwood, her Newport cottage, but "innumerable
rumors passed through society in New York, Newport, and the
rest of the nation," according to a recent Astor family historian.
"Her mind, and this at least is true, was affected, possibly by a
stroke, or senility, or by the accumulated pressures of her tragic
personal life. . . . People said she wandered about the house . . .
talking to the ghosts of her past. . . ."

After she died in 1908, the most striking image she left
imprinted on the minds of those who had contested for her favor
was that of an addled majesty. In a house empty except for
nurses and servants, she would dress in a Worth gown and
festoon herself with her chains of diamonds, station herself in the
foyer as she had on so many momentous evenings in the past,
"greeting imaginary guests long dead," as one social historian
recorded, "exchanging pleasantries with ghosts of the utmost
social distinction."

4.

THE COTTAGE INDUSTRY

THE WEALTHIER people sojourning in Newport would display the best taste that money could buy.

Their cultural advisers supplied them with classic models, interior designs and exterior settings; Mediterranean *palazzos* on the austere coast of New England, Japanese teahouses and Ottoman kiosks in rustic groves, extravagant fancies in marble set against sand and pine landscapes better suited to the simplicity of the Yankee carpenters whom the fashionable architects displaced.

They would rear the most palatial structures in which to spend two months each summer, but nothing could dispel the cold sterility that clung to them like invisible shrouds. There was no accommodation made for family life, for simple domestic pleasures, for plain enjoyment. No architect or decorator, no amount of tapestry or application of the fine arts, could remove their museumlike chill or moderate their studied ostentation.

The concept behind those "white elephants" was the establishment of one's credentials among those just above or on an equal footing in the order of social precedence; certainly it wasn't to overawe the masses or encourage thoughts of revolutionary action. One had to flourish something more substantial than a Dun & Bradstreet rating or a genealogy dating back to the Dutch burghers who settled Manhattan; even the older New York families, including the Van Alens and Goelets, felt a compulsion in joining the Newport cottage-building competition. "Social competition was acute among the rich," Russell Lynes has observed, "and standing was determined, to some extent, not

only by the lavishness with which one entertained but by the size
and magnificence of one's house and by the richness of its
collections of paintings and tapestries and tiger rugs and
chandeliers and by the number of such houses one owned and
where they were situated."

In Newport one "marble blockbuster" (as Cleveland Amory
described them) after another was erected side by side in a
relatively small area. Like thirsty behemoths, they crowded
toward the water. The serenity and majesty of the view, one of
the factors that made Newport a summer resort in the first place,
was obliterated by walls, roofs, turrets, Queen Anne fretwork,
and magnificence shading into monstrosity. Even the names
given those rearing, forbidding mansions that dominated the
shore and disrupted the harmony of sea, sky and sand were
ludicrous misnomers. As Amory has pointed out, "Chateau Sur
Mer is not on the ocean, Champ Soleil is in the shade, Land Fall
is the home of an admiral, Quatrel means the home of four 'L's,'
or Lorillards, and such a name as Bel'Napoli was apparently
never meant to mean anything except that it was once owned by
a family named Belknap."

This was no Xanadu transported to the nineteenth century,
but a show-ring, a social adjunct of the marketplace. It almost
seemed that its builders had decided that the display of wealth
was a worthy substitute for happiness. Newport was an arena of
social competition, an unflagging continuation of the rigadoon of
upmanship into which the participants flung themselves the
other ten months of the year down in New York. If you were
young, you came to Newport to be bred to someone of equal or
superior rank; if you were middle-aged, you were concerned with
maintaining your position; and if you were older, you imposed
your presence on the scene to arbitrate the claims of newcomers,
flatter your ego by adopting protégés and see to it that the old
forms were observed.

It was a straitjacketed existence, any deviation from which was
swiftly punished. If you submitted to it in the first place, you
would abide by it and live under the threat of ostracism. The
pattern of behavior was as inflexible as the etiquette of a

Hapsburg court. "Mrs. Astor and her fellow matrons and their daughters," as one writer observed, "wore a different dress for each occasion all summer, requiring a wardrobe of at least ninety gowns. Parasols were matched to each daytime dress, as were the feathers of the great-brimmed hats that topped coiffeurs made bouffant by 'rats,' chignons, switches or wigs. The summer's heat was considered no reason to abandon the white, elbow-length kid gloves in daytime or evening, and a popular lady might run through three or four fresh pairs a day. . . . A resplendent parade of ladies in carriages driven by liveried coachmen set off down Bellevue Avenue at three o'clock every day when the weather was fine. . . . Protocol was followed as rigidly as at a state dinner. No one would dare to overtake the carriage of a lady of superior rank."

To outlanders who did not aspire to acceptability, or foreigners who could survey the scene with an amused objectivity, it seemed that the more toplofty Newporters were stifling themselves in conventions that had little to do with normal human conduct, were suffering as much from a surfeit of materialism as any Strasburg goose whose liver was being distended by forced feeding to make the pâté, which in turn contributed to the stuffing of wealthy Newporters. The excess was almost dizzying to the outsider.

One of the few Newporters not blinded to the follies of her contemporaries, Mrs. Philip Lydig, recalled the impressions of a French writer who came to stay with her during Tennis Week. "He was a comic figure against an American background, because he dressed always in white—a white suit, white shoes, white socks, even a white cravat—and he wore an immense Panama hat with an elastic under his chin to keep it on, and he had a heavy black beard, and the elastic caught it up and held it protruding ridiculously. . . ."

The Frenchman studied the Newport scene with the scientific curiosity of an anthropologist noting the characteristics of an exotic tribe, a role disguised by his comic appearance. "Everyone laughed at him. He was very small, alert in his mind and quick in his movements, bright-eyed with curiosity and as unself-con-

scious as some sort of precociously bearded small boy. The
general laughter did not embarrass him. He had the air of an
explorer in Africa who sees that his appearance amuses the
natives, and his private comments on us all were deliciously
cold-blooded and detached.

"I took him driving, one afternoon, to show him the sights, and
whenever we passed a conspicuously luxurious home, he would
ask eagerly: 'What is really going on inside there? Are they
happy? What do they make of life?' He asked it as one might ask
what sort of social relations existed in an Eskimo igloo, and in
trying to give him a truthful answer, I found myself, to my
surprise, invariably relating the most shocking histories of grief
and scandal.

"He became as excited as a street gamin in the chamber of
horrors of a musée of wax-works. 'What misery!' he would cry.
'What drama! What a plot of Dostoievsky! Do they write these
tales, your American authors? How I wish I knew this American
scene! We have nothing so colorful in France.' "

The Frenchman's slant on Newport as the setting for the
grimmest of tragedies imbedded in a style of life envied by most
Americans caused Mrs. Lydig to see her summer home in a new
and more lurid light. It should not have been news to Mrs. Lydig
that wealth and misery could go hand in hand. Yet the more she
thought about it, the more it seemed that there was something
grand, operatic rather than cheaply melodramatic, something
that couldn't be captured entirely on the society pages of the
New York *Herald*, about the domestic tragedies that occurred so
frequently on Bellevue Avenue and on Ochre Point. She came to
realize that "The tragedies of our lives had seemed tedious and
commonplace, dragged out over years of dullness and happening
so imperceptibly that they went unregarded. Now, gathered
together in this way, briefly, I saw them as he saw them—as
dramatic as the two hours of concentrated incidents that make a
stage play. They came home to me, for the first time. I was
almost as surprised as he. The display and the luxury, the
appearance of success and the envy of the world, had blinded me
to the real miseries of our existences. I began to look around me

with astonishment. I began to ask myself: 'Where is there a happy home amongst us? Is it possible that there is none?' " She came to the conclusion that there was a deep flaw in the fashionable life and wondered "what went wrong with us, with our ideals and our ambitions, that we nearly all seemed to get ourselves in miseries so destructive."

The memoir Mrs. Lydig wrote, aptly titled *Tragic Mansions*, searched for answers to the dilemma of the very rich—something sensibly short of Lord Buddha's example of giving all his possessions to the poor and wandering the world as a mendicant-saint, of turning Newport's mansions into poorhouses and orphan asylums. A later generation would settle for "social conscience," a still later one for a smarmy sort of liberalism that left its fortunes and privileges intact while diminishing those of the middle class. Mrs. Lydig did not pretend to find any easy answers, only the conclusion that she and her class had been misled by false ideals. "They are not truly American," she added. "They are largely an importation from abroad, and they are much more pernicious here than they are in the social systems that originated them."

For all the determined gaiety of its summers, Newport was haunted by disquieting suggestions that too many had sacrificed too much to attain their place, by "a quality to shudder about," as Blanche Oelrichs (who, as Michael Strange, would write poetry and marry John Barrymore) defined it. She would never forget a middle-aged couple who arrived in Newport, the man prematurely aged by his struggle for wealth and success, his wife still young and vibrant. "Then it happened that after only a few years' enjoyment of their wealth and social prominence Mr. X had a stroke and became paralyzed when, one night, his wife, coming into her husband's sickroom, glitteringly fresh on her way to a dinner party, had gotten some of the mush that he was attempting to lift to his mouth spilt on her frock. 'She had to go back and change,' said my mother, 'and imagine, she was so angry with the poor man that she never even went back to wish him good night.' "

In the several memoirs of Newport society figures, all of them

women and all of them unusually perceptive despite their
frivolous backgrounds, it is evident that a terrible price was paid,
in many instances, for those overbearing and overfurnished
summer palaces. From one point of view, however, they were
simply professional tasks to be performed with due deference to
the tastes and ambitions of those who paid for their construction.
To the builders and decorators, the members of Newport's
cottage industry, they were not "tragic mansions" but challenges
to their ability to spend their customers' money in large and
awe-inspiring amounts.

The leader of that industry was Richard Morris Hunt, the
master of that mélange of architectural styles that produced the
Newport "cottage." A summertime Newporter himself, his
esthetic eye would not be affronted by the creations demanded
by his clients. "The first thing you've got to remember," he once
instructed his son, "is that it's your client's money you're
spending. Your business is to get the best results you can
following their wishes. If they want you to build a house upside
down standing on its chimney, it's up to you to do it, and still get
the best possible results."

A practical and comfortable philosophy, but one that would
not endear him to aesthetes unburdened by a businessman's
principles. Architectural critics of later generations would regard
Hunt as a man who created monstrosities, who cast aside his
classical education in favor of catering to the marketplace.
"Though he may have been a more expert designer and a man of
more refined tastes and greater knowledge than most of his
contemporaries," one authority on the nineteenth-century tastemakers has written, "his influence on American building is
looked upon darkly. It is not that his own buildings are
considered any more ridiculous than those of his fellow architects, but the style that he played so large a part in setting has, in
many expert opinions, been a disastrous backwater in the
progress of our architecture. Actually Hunt was in no sense an
innovator; he was a sail that caught the ambitious breeze that
blew off the great fortunes of the seventies and eighties and drove
the ship of taste into luxurious and splendid harbors."

It was not that he lacked artistic principles or personal taste somewhat more conservative than the "formalized barbarianism" charged against him when he built one of the Vanderbilt mansions on Fifth Avenue. His own summer home in Newport was built for comfort and openhanded hospitality; it had none of the daunting magnificence of the mansions he built for his clients, though he could have afforded it; the house and outbuildings, usually overflowing with guests, resembled a hotel during the high season.

One landmark of his long and distinguished career was the American Institute of Architects, of which he was a founder and first secretary. Until it was established, as one of his first pupils, Henry Van Brunt, recalled, the architectural profession was in disarray bordering on anarchy. "The hand of each was turned with jealousy and suspicion against his brother. His processes of design and his business methods were personal secrets. Each concealed his drawings from the rest, as if they were pages of a personal diary. Even books and prints were carefully secluded from inspection by a rival. Pupils were apprentices and as in my own case, often looked with eager and unsatisfied eyes through the glass of their master's locked bookcases. There were no ethics of practice, no common ground of mutual protection, no national literature of architecture. The current professional periodicals of England and Germany furnished the sole inspiration of nearly every architectural office in the land."

Newport's master builder was a Vermonter born in 1827. His widowed mother took him and his brother, William Morris Hunt, who was to become a distinguished painter, to Europe when Richard was sixteen. She was a painter herself and determined to provide her sons with the best possible grounding in their respective fields. While William studied painting in Munich, Richard enrolled at the École des Beaux Arts in Paris and became the first American architect to study there. Soon every American architect would aspire to a Beaux Arts background. He spent almost a dozen years in France, first in school, then as assistant to a French architect designing additions to the Louvre ordained by Napoleon III.

By the time he was twenty-seven and outwardly a "Frenchified Yankee" and a tolerable imitation of the Second Empire dandies, he decided that America was ready for something grander than the Cooper Union. He wrote his mother, "There is no place in the world where they are more needed, or where they should be more encouraged. Why, there are more luxurious houses put up in New York than in Paris! At any rate the desire is evinced and the money spent and if the object is not attained, it is the fault of the architects. . . . There are no greater fools in America than in any other part of the world; the only thing is that the professional man has got to make his own standing."

His first job on repatriating himself was assisting the architect in charge of placing a dome on the Capitol in Washington. Setting up his own studio a short time later, he quickly learned that he was correct in assuming that what his profession needed most in those pre-Civil War years was respect, standing in the community, equal footing with other professional men. His first solo flight was designing a house for a wealthy dentist. The house was built at a cost of fifty to sixty thousand dollars and Hunt presented his bill for five percent of that amount. The dentist had paid him $450 on account and refused to pay the additional amount Hunt demanded. Hunt, realizing that his profession would never amount to much until it had a legal basis for obtaining fees, took his case to the New York Supreme Court. The court awarded him only two and a half percent as his fee, but a precedent had been established and an architect's remuneration was as sacred a matter as a lawyer's or doctor's.

After joining in the establishment of the American Institute of Architects, Hunt flung himself into the "battle of styles" then—aside from their fees—the main obsession of his colleagues. One school was that of the Gothic revival, the other that of proponents of the "classic"—though bastardized—style in which Hunt had been indoctrinated. Hunt became his school's most eloquent and diligent advocate, the standard-bearer of what was eupeptically styled the American Renaissance.

The handsome, genial and persuasive Hunt found the necessary patrons to indulge his expensive fancies. He became the architect-of-record for the Vanderbilts, the Astors, the Goelets and Belmonts. He designed George Washington Vanderbilt II's incredibly massive limestone chateau Biltmore, with its library of 20,000 morocco-bound volumes under a ceiling painted by Tiepelo, on his 130,000-acre domain in the North Carolina woodlands; William K. Vanderbilt's lordly French chateau at Fifty-second Street and Fifth Avenue, and the Vanderbilt mausoleum on Staten Island, a $300,000 replica of a Romanesque chapel at Arles, in which the founder of the line was entombed under round-the-clock guard by watchmen charged with protecting the old Commodore's corpse from body snatchers.

He was the preeminent figure in his profession by the time wealthy New Yorkers fell to the task of what staid Bostonians called the vulgarization of Newport. With his clients' millions at his disposal, with all those French chateaux and Italian palaces to adapt, with all those Beaux Arts visions from his youth to sustain him, Hunt proceeded to convert Newport into a sea-girt enclave of fantasy and extravagance. The American plutocracy took its manners and tastes from what it regarded as impeccable European models—particularly the French—and did not concern itself about any possible taint of decadence, as Mrs. Philip Lydig and other commentators would point out. Naturally it was more than willing that its premier architect design their summer retreats along the lines suggested by largely defunct royalty and nobility; anything European was certified to have stood the test of time, to have the imprimatur of the elegant past—never mind whether it was compatible with its natural setting or adaptable to the human needs of people not inherently the residents of palaces or ducal chateaux.

They were mainly concerned with housing themselves in a manner that would not attract the sneers of any possible cultural superior—a bankrupt Ruritanian nobleman, say, on the hunt for an American heiress. "Where the arts were concerned," Russell Lynes has observed, "the vulgarizers of Newport were a timid, unadventurous lot. They were willing, indeed eager, to spend vast sums from their fortunes on palaces and on all manner of arts, firm and applied, to furnish them; but where taste was concerned they wanted to be absolutely safe. Paul Bourget, the French novelist and critic, spoke of 'the sincerity, almost the pathos, of this love of Americans for surrounding themselves with things around which there is an idea of time and stability.' And he added, 'It is almost a physical satisfaction of the eyes to meet here the faded colors of an ancient painting, the blurred stamp of an antique coin, the softened shades of a medieval tapestry. In this country, where everything is of yesterday, they hunger and thirst for the long ago." But Bourget, though he may have satisfied himself with this explanation of the houses he visited, only half-glimpsed the truth, and the half he saw was sentimental. The fact was that the rich were rich enough and lived enough apart from the world to be conservative; they could look only to the models of wealth and station that they could find that were comparable with their own—the great houses of Europe and the palaces of Renaissance princes, who had also made their money as traders and financiers."

Richard Morris Hunt sensed the anxieties of his patrons. Like the somewhat younger Stanford White, who would build the Newport Casino and many of the statelier cottages, he was something of a psychologist and knew the rich suffered from their own insecurities. One thing no Victorian of wealth and standing could bear to be accused of was petty economizing, he wanted everything showy and did not flinch at the grandiose; nor could he understand the value of subtlety and understatement. Thus, as Mr. Lynes analyzed Hunt's style, "Entrance halls were two or three stories high, layer upon rich layer of balconies and balustrades, of carving and wrought iron, of chandeliers and sculptured nymphs and graces, of tremendous allegorical ceiling paintings and friezes. With a lavish hand he used white marble and pink marble and green marble and gold and still more gold. Hunt gave his clients Moorish rooms and Palm Courts and Jacobean suites; bowls of orchids ornamented the marble-topped tables he helped his clients to select, exotic birds sang in Oriental cages he had suggested for their solariums, and the grand staircases would have been fit setting for a princess in train and coronet to descend to meet her courtiers. No wonder Hunt was the trusted darling of the New York rich. He was their taste and their sense of fitness."

By 1890, when Newport's golden age began, Hunt was at the summit of his profession, not only the architectural caterer to the super-rich but the man who designed the base of the Statue of Liberty, the new façade of the Metropolitan Museum and the Astor Library on Fifth Avenue. Hunt was in his sixties and his energy was flagging, but when the Vanderbilts called, he responded. Mrs. William K. Vanderbilt simply had to have the most impressive of all the Newport cottages. On Hunt's drawing boards appeared the plans for Marble House, the most expensive summer home ever built for a commoner. Eleven million was the total cost. Its façade was that of a Greek temple fashioned from pure white marble with a two-story portico of Corinthian columns and pilasters and capitals modeled on those of the Temple of the Sun at Baalbek. The driveway was no mere graveled road but a marble ramp that swept up from the Bellevue Avenue gates to the formal entrance of the Marble House. Mrs. Vanderbilt carried on from there. She fancied an authentic Chinese teahouse on the grounds and imported a corps of Chinese artisans to satisfy her whim. It was a splendid creation in red and gold lacquer overlooking the Cliff Walk and the sea, but it had this one little drawback. There were no facilities for making tea. Mrs. Vanderbilt solved that problem by having a miniature railway built from the pantry of the Marble House to the teahouse. When she gave a tea party, her corps of impassive footmen, each holding a silver tray over his head, rode out squatting on the miniature cars. It must have been for other reasons, however, that she became the first woman to be elected to the American Institute of Architects.

The classical elegance of the Marble House, though modeled on the Grand Trianon in the park at Versailles, was a discomfiting memory to Mrs. Vanderbilt's daughter Consuelo. "Unlike Louis XIV's creation," she wrote, "it stood on restricted grounds, and, like a prison, was surrounded by high walls. Even the gates were lined with sheet iron." Like so many children of the overprivileged, she felt a mortuarial chill rather than domestic warmth in such showplaces. "The hall and staircases were built of yellow marble, and there were fine tapestries flanking the entrance depicting the Death of Coligny and the Massacre of St. Bartholomew's Eve, which always gave me a momentary chill. . . . Upstairs my own room was austere. It was paneled in a dark Renaissance boiserie. There were six windows but at best one could only glimpse the sky through their high and narrow casements. An unadorned stone mantel opposite my bed greeted my waking eyes. To the right on an antique table were aligned a mirror and various silver brushes and combs. On another table writing utensils were disposed in such perfect order that I never ventured to use them. For my mother had chosen every piece of furniture and had placed every ornament according to her taste, and had forbidden the intrusion of my personal possessions. . . ." One may come to understand that there was pathos as well as irony in the phrase "poor little rich girl."

The final ornate masterpiece from the studio of Richard Morris Hunt was the three-million-dollar remodeling job he did on the Cornelius Vanderbilts' great square Italian *palazzo*, The Breakers. By no coincidence whatsoever, the mistress of that house, "Alice of the Breakers" as she was somewhat snidely known, was renovating it at the same time Alva Vanderbilt was building the Marble House. Alva and Alice, sisters-in-law, had long been deadly rivals in the family circle. Thus, the Marble House and The Breakers were an architectural confrontation.

Though he died in 1895, just before the reconstruction of The Breakers was completed, Hunt performed as nobly on Alice's behalf as on Alva's. Not one board-foot of lumber was used on its five floors and seventy rooms, thirty-three of which were servants' quarters. It was designed to be absolutely fireproof, and if almost eighty uncharred years are any proof, it apparently is. (Since 1948 it has been entrusted to the Newport Preservation Society and is open to the public.) The central hall rises forty-five feet, and its majesty, its numbing magnificence, seems to have been designed more to overawe than to welcome the visitor. The Breakers seems no more likely a place for human habitation than the interior of the Great Pyramid. Even in its relatively cozy billiards room, its walls faced with pale-green Cippolino marble, there is scant evidence that anyone was supposed to relax and enjoy himself.

The forbidding aspect, in fact, begins well outside the establishment. More than a hint of fortification surrounds the place; it was built during the panic and depression of '93, after all, and wasn't there a whiff of revolution about the march of Coxey's Army on Washington? The wrought-iron fence around the property could have helped repel a mob of Rhode Island sans-culottes. The entrance is guarded by a double set of doors. One set alone weighed seventy tons and, according to local legend, took four footmen to swing open.

The chilling effect of all that grandeur on a small boy was recaptured by a Vanderbilt grandson who wrote, "The bathtubs were carved of solid marble and were so icy cold that young Reggie Vanderbilt reportedly refused his evening bath until his tub had been sufficiently warmed with hot water. . . . Downstairs, the kitchen was the size of a small house, with five immense wood-burning ranges, each with eight or ten burners. The butler's pantry was two decks high, and lined to the ceiling with fine glassware and china, all chosen from samples brought to Mrs. Vanderbilt's house, for it was said she had never entered a shop. At The Breakers she could give a dinner party for two hundred, it was rumored, without calling in extra help. And each morning, Mrs. Vanderbilt, wearing immaculate white gloves, inspected her household, running a gloved finger over table tops and picture frames and stair railings. And when she was through, the gloves had better be white!"

No one can say that Richard Morris Hunt didn't leave durable monuments to the taste he conferred on the generation that made Newport the American capital of conspicuous consumption.

It was frosting on the wedding-cake architecture of Newport, which Hunt created almost singlehandedly, that its marble castles were surrounded by masses of hydrangea, a blue flowering shrub, which blended with the white marble houses, the mani-

cured lawns and the summer sky as though Luther Burbank or
some other botanical genius had developed it especially for
Newport.

The hydrangea somehow exuded a quality of expensive chic,
as though the landscape gardeners had touched up its intense
blueness with shadings of mauve and pink. (A Paris fashion
house with a branch in the Newport Casino recognized this
quality by bringing out a princess frock with white chiffon
imprinted with hydrangea in full bloom.) The blossoms of the
shrub somehow looked artificial; they were just too perfect, and
thus it seemed fitting that they were the floral epitome of the
Newport that sprang from the studios of fashionable architects.

Part Two

CONSORTS AND BILL PAYERS

5.

THE MASCULINE GENDER

IN THE recorded history of Newport, most of the masculine sector of that society seems shadowy and inconsequential. Newport was a centrifuge in which their womenfolk's whims and ambitions rose to the roiling surface. The men, seemingly, were drones whose only function was to provide a proper setting for their queen bees. Many were, of course, haggard fellows who had worked themselves half to death to provide passage to Newport for their wives; or had spent most of their lives guarding their inheritances from thrusters coming up from the under classes. Michael Strange would always remember her glimpses of Ogden Goelet tottering on the arm of a nurse behind the immense iron gates of his summer home. Goelet, she was told, could digest nothing but hothouse grapes, and her father told her that "Goelet has worked himself to death." That phrase would never be used to describe any of their ladies.

The menfolk, however, were necessary figures on the scene, and not only as paymasters. Every society queen needed her Prince Albert as a consort on official occasions. In addition, she required more or less unattached gentlemen to flirt with and flatter her. "The Newport ladies of those days," as Michael Strange recalled, "were trying hard to emulate their sisters in cosmopolitan Europe, and it would have been thought extremely 'bourgeois' for attractive matrons not to have gentlemen about them who were 'attentive.' "

The men who paid the bills—as distinguished from the male butterflies, the extra men, the courtiers, who adorned the ladies' drawing rooms and listened with apparent fascination to their

83

prattle—had their own existence in a resort dominated by feminine attitudes. Many lived on their yachts out on the bay and stayed away from the palatial cottages they had built unless and until their presence was commanded by Madame for an occasion at which a husband was required. If their wives had courtiers for purposes more social than sexual, the men often entertained young women from the Broadway chorus lines and elsewhere on their yachts, or repaired on shore to an exceedingly well-appointed whorehouse.

There was a male underground, none of whose members, unfortunately, turned out those frank and revealing memoirs produced by some of the females, which sardonically distanced itself from the high-handed activities of the resort's senior lionesses. It did not participate in the jungle war of social dominance, or give a continental damn which of the ladies had scrambled to the top and taken charge of the exclusion/inclusion process.

Their headquarters was a fusty old building, merely a frame house with a large piazza, at the corner of Bellevue Avenue and Church Street, in the center of the oldest part of Newport and a few hundred feet from the Touro Cemetery. It was—and still is—the Reading Room. A splendidly innocuous name for what was not only one of the most exclusive men's clubs in the United States, but the place where old bucks could get quietly drunk, exchange salacious memories, and be well out of earshot of Madame's recriminations. There were brass cuspidors every few feet in the club's corridors, not because there were many members who chewed plug tobacco, presumably, but as a symbol of masculine defiance. This was their territory, their sanctuary, their safe house, their retreat from feminine concerns. No woman could have approached the first step of the piazza without being confronted by a phalanx of choleric, purple-faced clubmen prepared to defend their turf against intrusion.

Needless to say, there was precious little literary discourse, or of leafing through morocco-bound volumes, in the Reading Room. This was a refuge for full-blooded men, old rips whose arteries may have been brittle but whose memories were as raucously libidinous as a midnight conclave of tomcats, and younger men still fully capable of hot pursuit. The talk was redolent of clandestine suppers in red-plush private dining rooms in the Broadway lobster palaces, of the girls who displayed their limbs in *The Black Crook* and the young things who twirled their parasols as members of the Floradora Sextette. And when it didn't center on the satiny contours to be found in the demimonde, it dealt with thoroughbred horseflesh. Wives were unmentionable. Domestic affairs were never discussed; this was a refuge from that sort of clamor.

The summer afternoons wheeled by on the wide cool piazza of the Reading Room in an amiable fog of mint juleps and cigar smoke. The urbanity of its members was often remarked on. They would stroll into the flossiest of the local parlor houses, Blanche's, quite as unhurriedly as they walked into Merker's barbershop for a shave. Blanche's eventually went out of business. The house was sawed into four parts and moved to other parts of town. One section was hauled, as if in final nostalgic review, past the Reading Room. That section contained the Peacock Room with its gorgeous wallpaper, in which so many of the club's membership had waited for the girls of their choice. Watching the Peacock Room roll by like a theatrical set suffused the members with such a flood of memories that they assigned one of their number to write a commemorative poem . . . not for publication.

The menfolk stayed in the shade of the Reading Room's piazza, literally and figuratively, and viewed with an amused tolerance the antic social competition of their wives and daughters. Male chauvinists to a man, they allowed their womenfolk to "reign" over the society they created, which they viewed with the same chuckling disdain as a child's tea party for her dolls. It wasn't real; not in the same sense of the Big Board down at the New York Stock Exchange. It was a foolish female game charted by the society pages, something to be paid for like a bill from Tiffany's. They knew where the real power lay—secured by purse strings, by the laws of property holding, which were still in male hands. So let the girls play High Society, the men still ruled the roost. "A fashionable resort," as Richmond Barrett, one of the most perceptive commentators on the power structure of the nineteenth-century resorts, wrote, "is popularly supposed to be a feminine world. The ladies do fill the foreground, it is true; and in the old days of the *grandes toilettes,* they all but obliterated the sober husbands and fathers from the picture." But in the background, puffing on their cigars and surveying the world from the piazza of the Reading Room, their menfolk were seeing to it that Newport stayed on a fairly even keel.

They were indulgent of the women's tempestuous moods, and quietly contemptuous of the willowy cotillion leaders who danced attendance on them, but they were determined to maintain Newport in its eminence as a summer resort. Many of them lived off inherited incomes and had the time to watch over Newport's prestige while others could devote consideration to such matters only between Saturday and Monday, when they were on leave from Wall Street. But no matter how many steel mills and railroads and mines they were operating, they always managed to reach Newport for the weekend on their private railway cars and their steam yachts.

Weekends for the working menfolk were rarely periods of relaxation, according to Barrett, but were occupied by board meetings of the Casino, the Reading Room and the Clambake Club, where the real business of the resort was conducted, excesses curbed and standards set. "With that sort of solid backbone," Barrett observed, "Newport was never in any real danger of going to the dogs. The fast set could do their worst. They were tolerated, they were even encouraged within certain limits . . . the final word was the clubman's every time."

The Titaness crouching on his mantelpiece, as in the celebrated James Thurber cartoon, was a creature to be placated. In the interest of domestic harmony, she would be allowed her social triumphs and consoled for her social disasters. Both, as he knew, were balanced on the knife-edge of his financial success. His luck made everything possible, his failure would remove her (unless she was agile enough to capture another husband quickly) from the scene as swiftly as the striking of a stage set. His business career, not her social intrigues, was the fulcrum.

Papa was still the essential factor and, unless he were entirely witless, was the repository of the family honor. "My father," Mrs. John King Van Rensselaer (*The Social Ladder*) recalled, "always escorted me to parties because the appearance of the woman of a family in any public place after dark without the convoy of the head of the house would have been a shock, almost amounting to scandal, to the social organization of that day."

So subtly pervasive was the influence of the masculine mystique, of the Victorian belief in justifying the male existence by doing something even if it wasn't financially necessary, that it even infected some of the professional dandies whose chief distinction was the grace with which they pirouetted through the figures of a cotillion. Such awakenings of the masculine spirit could have woeful consequences.

James J. Van Alen, for instance, was chiefly known for his old-family lineage and the fact that he had married one of the daughters of The Mrs. Astor. When his wife died, Van Alen was regarded as the most elegant—that is, useless, from the viewpoint of fellow males—widower in Newport society. He was stung into action by the genial contempt of his gender and contributed $50,000 to the Democratic national campaign fund in 1892. He also let it be known that, in return, he aspired to be the American ambassador to Italy.

A sojourner in the rival resort of Bar Harbor, Joseph Pulitzer, heard of Van Alen's aspirations and was horrified. Pulitzer was the publisher of the New York *World*, a Democratic organ that took a dim view of the bartering of ambassadorships for campaign contributions. He did not believe that Van Alen's career as a best-dressed man qualified him for the embassy in Rome and ordered his editors to send one of the sharper wits on his staff to interview Van Alen. The reporter destroyed Van Alen with a dozen paragraphs of uncharitable observation:

"He wears a single eyeglass with a heavy string attached. He speaks with a weird bastard cockney, which fills Englishmen with wonder. It is the sort of English accent that a man with no talent for imitation might get from hansom-cab drivers and Strand barmaids.

"A prize-fighting gentleman of the Bowery was brought to Newport to train the fat off Van Alen. The fighting gentleman, called One-Eye Connelly, said he had never met a man less fit to be on earth than Van Alen.

"Van Alen has all the vanities that an American ambassador could do without.

"He informs whoever will listen that he keeps English mustard in a mustard pot of English silver and French mustard in a French mustard pot.

"He entertains few convictions except those which refer to clothes, horses, and Scotch whiskey.

"He owns twenty pairs of breeches for hunting, this despite the fact that a Shetland pony could buck him off with a gentle shrug.

"If Abraham Lincoln could meet Van Alen his inclination would be to lift Van Alen up by the coat collar and duck him in a muddy pond as a graceful compliment to the Stars and Stripes. If Mr. Cleveland knew Van Alen, his inclination would be the same."

After that hatchet job in the *World*, Van Alen was scratched from President Cleveland's list of potential envoys and continued, happily enough, to survey the Newport scene through his monocle.*

Perhaps the happiest of Newport's chronically unemployable males was the unhinged former president of the Baltimore & Ohio Railroad, Robert W. Garrett, who believed that he was the Prince of Wales. Garrett had inherited the presidency of the railroad from his masterful father, John W. Garrett, on the latter's death in 1884.

* Confirmation of Van Alen's idiosyncrasies could be found in Elizabeth Drexel Lehr's memoir, which related that "He even carried his predilection for the Tudor period into his vocabulary, and his conversation was so flavoured with 'Egad . . . zounds . . . prithee' that one almost needed a special old English dictionary to talk to him. The highest praise he could bestow on any favoured lady was, 'A most delectable wench, forsooth,' while an impertinent railroad car attendant would draw forth an indignant, 'Yon varlet insults us.' "

The younger Garrett lasted only a few years at the head of the Baltimore & Ohio largely because of his heavy drinking and other excesses. One coup he failed to bring off, according to a financial historian of the period, was the purchase of the Philadelphia, Wilmington & Baltimore line. "The night before the final arrangements were to be made," it was recorded, "he invited a friend to celebrate the occasion. When bibulous from champagne, Garrett revealed the secret. The friend excused himself, went immediately to [Thomas] Scott, of the Pennsylvania Railroad, and informed that magnate. Scott at once filled a satchel full of bonds and hurried away to make an offer to the capitalists controlling the Philadelphia, Wilmington & Baltimore, outbid Garrett, and had secured the ownership of that railroad for the Pennsylvania system almost before Garrett had awakened from his drunken stupor."

The successful Scott soon worked himself to death while Garrett lost his reason through what was diagnosed as "softening of the brain," a somewhat imprecise term then in vogue, the effect of which was that Garrett imagined himself to be the Prince of Wales. His wife played up to the delusion despite the remonstrations of their friends, who urged her to commit him to an asylum.

"My husband has worked hard all his life to earn his large fortune," Mrs. Garrett, later Mrs. Henry Barton Jacobs, would reply, somewhat inaccurately. "He shall enjoy it in the way he wants. Why should I not spend it in giving him pleasure?"

Since Garrett had inherited a fortune of more than fifteen million, it was simple enough to cater to his delusion, though it required a costly supporting cast.

The Garrett summer home in Green Spring Valley was transformed into a reasonable, or unreasonable, facsimile of the Court of St. James. "A whole staff of actors," Elizabeth Drexel Lehr recorded in her memoir, "was hired to impersonate gentlemen-in-waiting, court officials, Cabinet Ministers and Ambassadors from other countries, and an expert was brought over from London to ensure that each of the costumes was correct. Robert Garrett was given copies of every order worn by

the Prince of Wales; he had the uniform of the principal
regiments of every country, so that he should greet each of his
visiting ambassadors correctly attired. Every day his wife would
come to him as the Princess of Wales, go through hours of tragic
farce in order that he might keep his cherished illusion."

Mrs. Lehr's husband once called on Garrett in the uniform of
a British field marshal, had himself announced as the Crown
Prince of Germany and "delighted the poor old gentleman by
talking broken English interspersed with German throughout the
afternoon."

6.

THE WAYWARD COMMODORE

NOT EVEN The Mrs. Astor or her successors, the Grand Triumvirate, or any other dowager who queened it over the Newport scene could equal James Gordon Bennett, Jr.'s imperious and high-handed manner or approach the intensity of his tantrums when his will was not obeyed. Nominally he was the publisher of the New York *Herald*, then the foremost American newspaper, and later the Paris *Herald*; the man who casually sent H. M. Stanley to find Dr. Livingstone in darkest Africa. He was also as prominent in Newport society, in his own hectic fashion, as The Mrs. Astor; the winner of the first transoceanic yacht race; the most spectacular profligate of the Gilded Age who spent an estimated thirty to forty million dollars on various lordly whims, one of which was the construction of the Newport Casino in a fit of pique over being kicked out of the Reading Room.

As a man whose bachelorhood lasted until his seventy-third year but who could never be persuaded of the virtues of celibacy, Bennett naturally had a polar attraction for trouble, scandal and controversy of all kinds.

He had begun sailing his yacht into Newport's harbor in the seventies, had acquired a fine old stone-walled villa on Bellevue Avenue called Sebastapol, and was a pioneer member of the New York phalanx that began invading Newport. Until early in 1875, he had been involved in a cozy and undemanding relationship with Miss Pauline Markham, a dark-eyed and statuesque English girl who was a star attraction with the Lydia Thompson Burlesque Company. Then he met Caroline May, the beautiful young daughter of a prominent Baltimore family that had produced a number of sprigs almost as high-tempered and erratic as Bennett himself. Caroline's father was Dr. William May, a sedate New York physician, but her uncle, Colonel Charles May, had commanded a regiment of dragoons in the Mexican War and once rode his charger up three flights of stairs in a Baltimore hotel to indicate his displeasure with the management. Caroline's uncle, Julian, had killed a man in a duel in Virginia. Her brother, Frederick deCourcy May, had become involved in a brawl with a New York policeman and the latter died of his injuries. Fellow members of the Union Club hid young May on the premises, then spirited him to South America and supplied him with remittances for a year until it was safe to return to their comradely embrace. Not, it seemed, a clan to trifle with, especially since its finances did not match the splendor of its social aspirations.

Bennett, however, could not be dissuaded from a headlong courtship of Caroline. In the summer of 1875 he invited her and her parents to spend the summer at his Newport villa, and soon found his bachelor establishment taxed to the utmost by an influx of Caroline's brothers, uncles, aunts and cousins. The resort's gossips noted that Caroline was given the "seat of honor" beside Bennett on the box of his coach when they went out driving. Their suspicions were confirmed during the next year when the engagement of James Gordon Bennett, Jr., to Miss Caroline May was announced.

Then Bennett began having his doubts about the charms of prospective domesticity. In the first place there was that importunate swarm of Mays he would evidently be marrying as well as the lissome bride-designate; he envisioned bibulous uncles and quarrelsome second cousins littering every corner of his homes, and was downright depressed by rumors that the May family was gloating over having snared the richest and therefore the most eligible bachelor in the country. Perhaps something of the caution of a long line of luckless Scottish ancestors—he was a first-generation aristocrat, his father having been a penniless printer until he invented the New York *Herald*—stirred deep inside him.

For some months he brooded over his situation and undoubtedly pondered various schemes for breaking his engagement
without being invited to a duel. Marksmanship, as well as
fecklessness, ran in the May family. Calculation was not
Bennett's long suit, however, and he usually solved his dilemmas
by outrageous action.

The flashpoint in his relations with the May clan occurred on
New Year's Day, 1877, when it was the custom of fashionable
New Yorkers to be driven in their sleighs on a round of calls
during which large amounts of punch and eggnog were swilled.
By nightfall the streets of New York would be a tangle of
erratically driven sleighs. Drunkenness would be endemic but
excusable on the grounds that even George Washington had
spoken favorably of the old Knickerbocker custom of getting
crapulously drunk on New Year's Day.

None had followed tradition that day more diligently than
young Mr. Bennett, and the brandy evidently only bolstered his
conviction that marriage would be calamitous. Naturally he was
expected to call at the May residence. He appeared at their door
in an uproarious mood, lurched into the drawing room, surveyed
the Mays and their friends through bloodshot eyes and proceeded to pour down more steaming punch. It was evident to
several of the Mays' guests that he was in a dangerous mood, and
they quietly called for their hats and coats. "He never stifled an
impulse," as one of his friends remarked.

What happened next is a matter of controversy, but it was
sufficiently scandalous to be gossiped about in New York society
for many years and ultimately to force Bennett to exile himself in
Paris. Accounts of such occurrences, as any traffic investigator
will testify, are likely to differ widely. There were almost as many
different versions as there were witnesses. One story was that
Bennett calmly unbuttoned his trousers and urinated on the
grand piano. By another account he mistook the fireplace for a
pissoir. He may merely have upchucked all over Dr. May's
brocaded waistcoat. Indubitably Bennett did *something* rather
awful to get himself thrown out of the May house; the Mays had
been prepared to put up with almost anything from such a

desirable son-in-law. Elizabeth Drexel Lehr, who was a later friend of Bennett's, may have been retailing his version of the incident when she wrote, "Any modern girl would have known how to handle the situation, and would have passed over the offence [the nature of which she did not describe]. But she [Caroline] belonged to another generation, and she was provincial to her finger-tips. She swooned in the classical manner of the 'nineties, and called upon her brother to throw her fiancé out of the house. Within a few hours the story, greatly exaggerated, had become a first-class scandal."

Possibly Bennett believed he had insulted his way out of the entanglement with the May family. Certainly if he had experienced any twinge of contrition—an entirely unfamiliar feeling—he could have done one of several things. He could have appeared on the May doorstep the next morning as a penitent and begged the family's pardon, or he could have boarded his yacht and steamed off to some remote island in the South Pacific, or he could have had himself committed to an asylum.

Instead he stayed under cover for two days, then ventured over to the Union Club to test the climate. His fellow clubmen, after all, were notorious for their tolerance; they had not only helped Fred May when he killed a cop but had refused to expel Judah P. Benjamin at the beginning of the Civil War when he joined the Confederate cabinet. Bennett was greatly relieved when he was allowed to enter the club and found that nobody turned his back on him when he appeared in the dining room.

Bennett lunched heartily and assured himself he would be able to ride out whatever storms of disapproval might be brewing. Just as he was leaving the club, the ominous figure of Fred May, horsewhip in hand, loomed before him. May began beating him with the whip—an instrument commonly used in those days for chastising errant editors, a custom many believe was abandoned too quickly—but Bennett would neither suffer the punishment as something due him, nor would he flee from his assailant. The two men grappled, punched, gouged and clawed like a pair of dockwallopers outside a Tenth Avenue saloon; they rolled down Fifth Avenue, and might have wound up in Washington Square if a couple of fellow members hadn't run out and separated them for the sake of civic dignity.

Bennett's *Herald* did not consider the encounter newsworthy, but the rival *Sun* was not reluctant to report that Bennett's blood had run into the gutter and added that Bennett "was to have sailed for England yesterday with his bride in the *Russia* but the marriage has been called off," indicating that Bennett misbehaved himself just one day before he was scheduled to lose his bachelor's freedom. Two days later the *Sun* happily reported Bennett had "fled to Canada." Actually Bennett just then was dispatching Charles Longfellow, the poet's son, with a challenge to Fred May. The latter agreed to meet Bennett over pistols the morning of January 7 at Slaughter's Gap, an old dueling ground on the Virginia-Maryland border.

The shootout was something of a fizzle by standards then established in Dodge City and other centers of gunplay. The duelists each took twelve paces and then turned and fired. Both shots went wild. Bennett and May, accompanied by their retinues, repaired to a hotel at Dover, Maryland, where they "betook themselves to their rooms," as the *Sun* joyfully reported, and "the proprietor mistook his guests for pickpockets and consequently sat up all night watching their movements." It was said to have been the last duel fought in the United States.

That may have settled accounts with the May family, but the leading hostesses of New York society were not satisfied that Bennett had purged himself of misconduct. They firmly crossed him off their guest lists. It was a different story in Newport, where the New York dowagers had not yet established themselves. The Newport *News* had risen to Bennett's defense without knowing just what he was accused of, and reported, "It is a well-known fact that Miss May's brothers, cousins and other members of the family spent the last season here, and that they were not backward in accepting Mr. Bennett's hospitality." *

* There was a farcical sequel to the Bennett-May duel. According to Mademoiselle Camille Clermont, intimate friend of Bennett's Paris exile, May appeared in Paris some years after the duel and the rumor sped around the American colony that he was planning to "shoot Bennett on sight. . . . J.G.B. valued his life far too highly to be thus

In Newport he would always be regarded as a legendary figure, a lordly dispenser of hospitality. "His entertainments were as fiery as himself," Maud Howe Elliott recalled. "At one ball, as night stretched into morning, some of the guests who could not be served fast enough cracked open the champagne bottles by knocking them together and striking off their heads. . . ."

The money that spawned such exuberances came from the efforts of James Gordon Bennett, Sr. to develop a new and more compelling form of American journalism. In the mid-1830's the New York *Herald* was merely one of fifteen newspapers struggling for survival in the competition of Park Row. Bennett Senior migrated from Scotland in his youth to thwart his family's determination that he enter the priesthood; he taught school in Maine, read proof in a Boston printshop and wound up in New York as a reporter, Washington correspondent for one journal and associate editor of another. In 1835 he established the *Herald* in a Wall Street basement, having decided that American newspapers were overstuffed with opinion and lacking in the human interest, the blood-and-thunder drama of daily events. Sensationalism put the *Herald* over; its pages dripped gore, clamored over various scandals, exposed the corruption on Wall Street and in City Hall, and avidly reported sexual misconduct.

A rather unhappy marriage with an Irish girl, which produced James Gordon Bennett, Jr. and his sister Jeanette, only increased the senior Bennett's devotion to his journalistic creation. Mrs. Bennett simply couldn't bear the ostracism, the violent assaults that were the portion of any vigorously independent, outspoken publisher of his day. She declared her intention of taking herself and their children "out of the sphere of calumny, misrepresentation and reckless wit" into which her hard-bitten husband daily flung himself with the joy of a Highland chieftain.

---

lightly disposed of, so he ordered a magnificent coat of mail to wear under his clothing, and with his long, lanky figure he looked supremely ridiculous. He wore that coat of mail for a month or so, until he tired of carrying the abnormal weight, so he sent two of his friends to Mr. May to ask what his intentions were, preferring the risk of a duel to the constant fatigue imposed by the medieval armour. Mr. May declared that he had no homicidal intentions, so, to his great relief, J.G.B. discarded the curaiss." Mademoiselle Clermont's memoir was one more proof that a rich man should choose someone illiterate for his intimate friend.

James, Jr., spent his boyhood in Paris, spoiled by his mother, despaired of by his tutors, who tried to acquaint him with some measure of discipline. He grew up firmly convinced that he was the center of the universe, and life rarely offered any correctives to that view until his last few years on earth. At the age of fifteen he was returned to New York to rejoin his father, who was simply too busy with the *Herald* to keep an eye on a youth who had already acquired a taste for alcohol and a seigneural attitude toward the female sex. Long before he reached voting age, he bore himself with the contemptuous manner of a Regency buck.

His father scorned society as something fit only for females and effeminate men, but Bennett Junior found the sporting element of the fashionable world to his liking. Generous with everything but paternal guidance, Bennett Senior indulged his son to the utmost; the power of the *Herald* enabled his son to join the exclusive New York Yacht Club at the age of seventeen and sail, with professional help, the sloop *Rebecca* and subsequently the 160-ton yacht *Henrietta*. His father's influence also persuaded the Revenue Cutter Service, a shore-patrolling adjunct of the Navy during the Civil War, to commission him as a third lieutenant and accept the *Henrietta* as an auxiliary in the task of blockading the Southern ports.

Meanwhile he was becoming the youthful satellite of a group of sportive financiers, the Belmont-Jerome clique of bon vivants, who spared as much time from moneymaking on Wall Street as possible to pursue in gentlemanly fashion the avocations of wining, wenching, yachting and coaching. (The three Jerome brothers included Leonard, whose daughter married Lord Randolph Churchill and produced the great Winston.) With August Belmont, the Jeromes founded the Coaching Club and popularized, for those who could afford it, the sport of driving a four-in-hand.

Young Bennett not only became a dashing "whip" but displayed some of the pathological traits that made his subsequent antics the talk of two continents. At coaching races he would sometimes race across the finish line and then continue careening down the road for miles. Speed intoxicated him to an alarming degree, particularly when combined with reckless amounts of alcohol. He often took midnight rides into the countryside, cracking his whip and driving his horses at a lunatic pace. Often he tore off all his clothes and rode the box stark naked because, as he explained, "I want to be able to breathe."

While only nominally the managing editor of the *Herald*, Bennett also imprinted his name permanently on the history of American yachting. The opportunity arose one evening over copious amounts of brandy in the Union Club. An argument over the merits of the centerboard *vs.* the keel in yacht construction led to a challenge: Bennett's keel-equipped *Henrietta* to race Frank Osgood's centerboard-equipped *Fleetwing* and Pierre Lorillard's similar *Vesta*, all the way across the Atlantic, though no yacht had as yet attempted such distances. The purse would be $90,000, all three boats to be skippered by their owners. On sober consideration of the perils of that winter crossing, Lorillard and Osgood decided not to accompany their yachts but turned them over to professionals. Bennett undeniably had the courage of his convictions, and was man enough to point out that he couldn't ask other men to take unshared risks for his sake. He would command the *Henrietta*, with Captain Bully Samuels as his sailing master. Three other amateurs were part of Bennett's crew, Charles Longfellow, Stephen Fiske, the playwright, and Lawrence Jerome.

The three contending yachts sailed off into the winter storms of the Atlantic. On December 19, 1866, they ran into heavy seas and *Fleetwing*, trying to drive through the storm, had six crew members washed overboard; the *Henrietta*, however, hove to under bare masts and survived without losing a man. *Vesta*, however, had sailed into the teeth of the gale-force winds and gained 222 miles on its competitors and was well in the lead when the three contenders sighted the lights of the Scilly Isles on Christmas Eve. Superior seamanship in negotiating the English Channel—thanks more to Bully Samuels than Bennett—resulted in the *Henrietta* sailing first into Cowes Roads several hours ahead of its rivals.

That feat greatly increased Bennett's standing with his father for a perfectly understandable reason. Bennett Senior made full use of the recently completed Atlantic cable to plaster the front page of the *Herald* with accounts of the victory in a proprietary manner. Nothing warmed the old man's heart faster than a boost in circulation.

Bennett Senior sensed in his son a growing maturity and urged him to take over partial control of the *Herald*. Bennett Junior agreed and at the age of twenty-six began appearing regularly at the *Herald* offices. His father was seventy-two and preferred to seclude himself in his mansion on Washington Heights. One day, six months after bestowing partial responsibility on his son, he studied the early edition of the *Herald* in his study and was astonished to note that Bennett Junior had changed the masthead to read "James Gordon Bennett, Jr., Editor-in-Chief and Publisher." Flaming mad, he hurried down to Park Row and ordered the page replated and his own name reinstated in command of the newspaper.

It became even more evident after Bennett Senior's death that his son had inherited several of his father's more valuable journalistic traits. Bennett Junior soon demonstrated a talent for picking extremely capable men, a flamboyant spirit of enterprise which was to electrify the world on occasion, and a sense of what people—especially those whose literary interests were confined to the daily press—wanted to read about. From the age of twenty-seven on, he was one of the moguls of the newspaper industry.

Now Commodore of the New York Yacht Club, a title in which he rejoiced and liked to be addressed by, he ran a tight ship on Park Row. All employees were required to write fitness reports on each other, which constituted a system of internal espionage. He was "too suspicious to trust his friends," wrote Stephen Fiske, who served as dramatic critic on the *Herald* for a time, and perhaps hoped that as a member of the crew in the transatlantic yacht race he would at least be favored with Bennett's confidence, "and he makes enemies unconsciously of those who would be, and have been, most truly devoted to him, by regarding all mankind as a band of conspirators organized to influence the *Herald* for their own purposes." That syndrome, too, he had inherited from his self-sufficient and solitary father.

The ten years between the time Bennett took charge and his exile to France following the imbroglio with the May family, during which he spent much of the paper's $750,000 annual net income on projects that enhanced its prestige as well as increased its circulation, the *Herald* acquired an international reputation, as a rival New York editor grudgingly admitted, "unsurpassed by any journal in the world." Other newspapers had to copy it or pass by news they could ill afford to ignore. His roving correspondents were not merely journalists but adventurers on the grand scale, ambassadors without portfolio, intrepid commanders of what were usually titled "The Herald Search Expedition."

His greatest discovery was the Welshman named Henry M. Stanley, raised in a workhouse as "a deserted bastard" (the Victorians could be blunt enough when dealing with the lower orders), who shipped out as a cabin boy and jumped ship in New Orleans. A swarthy, tough and energetic young man, Stanley journeyed to New York with a scheme for covering Lord Napier's punitive force in Abyssinia, using the funds he had saved up as a frontier correspondent to pay his own way if some newspaper would agree to publish his dispatches at space rates. The *Tribune* turned him down, but Bennett agreed to commission him as a special correspondent of the *Herald*. His accounts of the colonial campaign were so graphic Bennett put him on the payroll.

Bennett was vacationing in Paris when he was seized by one of those impulses that made the *Herald* celebrated for its enterprise and often brought it to the verge of ruin. He summoned Stanley from the Greek islands, where Stanley was writing some travel sketches. Both men were then twenty-eight years old. When Stanley appeared in his Paris hotel room, Bennett, without wasting words, announced that Stanley was going to Africa at the head of a Herald Search Expedition to find Dr. David Livingstone, the Albert Schweitzer of his time who, supposedly, was "lost." Never mind that he wasn't. Never mind that, after heroic effort, Stanley "found" Livingstone and the latter referred to the *Herald* as "that despicable newspaper." The understatement of the first Stanley-Livingstone exchange ("Dr. Livingstone, I presume?" "Yes.") still echoes. And the *Herald*'s circulation broke through the magic ceiling of 100,000. Bennett's reaction to his employee's worldwide fame was outrage. "Who was Stanley before I found him?" the Commodore demanded. "Who thought of looking for Livingstone? *Who paid the bills?*"

All the time, when he wasn't enlivening Newport or thundering orders around the *Herald* building in New York, he was traveling as widely as any of his roving correspondents. Bennett's high-handed eccentricity was never more in evidence than when he was sailing the Mediterranean on one of his yachts, which he always personally commanded in the style of Captain Bligh. Both crew and guests were subject to his imperious whims. One guest who incurred his displeasure was marooned on an uninhabited islet in the Mediterranean with food and water for a few days and a white shirt to wave at any passing ships. On another cruise he and his guests went ashore on an island off the Greek coast, the attraction of which was a monastery in which a votive flame reputedly had been kept burning for more than a thousand years. The flame fascinated the Commodore, and presented him with an unavoidable challenge. "Are you sure this thing has been burning for a thousand years?" he asked the monk who was escorting them. The monk assured him it had. "Well," replied the Commodore, leaning over and blowing out the flame, "it isn't now."

Aboard the last and lordliest of his yachts, the *Lysistrata*, which included a Turkish bath for the Commodore's use only and a miniature dairy outfitted for an Alderney cow to provide fresh milk for his table, he sometimes steamed as far as Turkey, where he struck up a friendship with another tyrant, the Sultan known in Western Europe as Abdul the Damned, and into the Indian Ocean to Ceylon.

He did not even hesitate to resort to kidnapping when he fancied company on a cruise, according to Consuelo Vanderbilt, later the Countess Balsan, who with her parents often visited Bennett at his villa at Beaulieu. Once three American beauties he had met in Newport during his salad days but who were now married—Lady Lily Bagot; Adele, the Countess of Essex; and a third whom Countess Balsan identified only as "the malaprop Mrs. Moore of Paris"—had lunch with him at Beaulieu. He invited them aboard the *Lysistrata* for dinner. Nothing untoward happened except that the Commodore seemed to be sluicing down an abnormal amount of champagne and brandy. When the ladies went out on deck after dinner, they found that the yacht had put to sea. Bennett had disappeared, locked himself in his cabin. The *Lysistrata* was heading into a storm and the seas were getting rough. Appealing to the first officer on the bridge, they were told, "I have Commodore Bennett's orders to proceed to Egypt." Not until the next morning could the Commodore be aroused and persuaded to return to Beaulieu, where the three ladies disembarked in their evening clothes to the snickers of bystanders on the dock.

Even after the Commodore expatriated himself to Europe and established the Paris *Herald* mainly for the benefit of fellow Americans expatriated on the Continent, he sometimes returned to the States for a whirlwind descent on the *Herald* building in New York, during which heads invariably rolled, and then sailed up the coast to Newport.

Such visits were awaited in the summer colony with a combination of delight and terror. Invariably they were accompanied by wild entertainments and outrageous incidents. "He had certain likable traits," as a Newport historian observed, "and was doing pretty well on the whole; but he was no sycophant. There was a streak of the devil in him, a love of dangerous practical jokes and a perverse desire to outrage even those people he was courting. Particularly when he was drunk, he was capable of feats of rebellious daring or mean little outbursts of spleen that threatened to prove his undoing. He belonged to the Reading Room, but was regarded by the other members as a sort of Peck's Bad Boy sadly in need of the birch-rod of discipline."

One summer the Commodore appeared there with an old friend, Captain "Sugar" Candy of the Ninth Lancers and a member of the British polo team. With Captain Candy's assistance, Bennett had introduced polo to the United States. In 1876 he had watched a polo game in England, where the sport was imported by officers of the Indian Army. One of the players was Captain Candy, whom he persuaded to accompany him back to the States, along with a collection of polo mallets and balls. Candy taught the rudiments of the game to Bennett and several of his friends, August Belmont, Frank Gray and William P. Douglas, first using a riding academy in Manhattan as their training field, then moving from the tanbark to a field at Jerome Park. Other members of the sporting element were recruited to form other teams, and the game began to catch on among people able to afford a string of polo ponies and made Bennett the undisputed Father of American Polo. Subsequently Bennett and his fellow sportsmen founded the Westchester Polo Club, built a clubhouse and engaged a member of the Delmonico family to take charge of providing the cuisine.

On this trip Bennett had whetted his appetite for social adventure by storming through the *Herald* building, with Captain Candy acting as his aide-de-camp, and firing anyone whose looks didn't appeal to him. Then Bennett and Candy steamed up to Newport in a mood to shake up the old place.

On a morning soon after their arrival he was irked by the senescent decay which, it seemed to him, had overtaken the Reading Room. All those old fossils, retired dandies and walrus-faced clubmen retired from Wall Street piracies gossiping away on the piazza. Place needed livening up. A gentlemen's club wasn't necessarily an old gents' nursing home.

So he challenged Captain Candy to ride a horse up on the piazza of the Reading Room. Candy took the dare, charged up the steps of the piazza as though leading the Light Brigade against the Russian batteries at Balaclava, clattered into the hall of the club, then out and away. Bennett was standing on the sidewalk and bellowing with laughter.

An emergency session of the Board of Governors was convened. Elderly members waved their canes and demanded that Bennett be cashiered. The shock waves went up and down Bellevue Avenue that afternoon.

"This was enough to set Newport agog," as Ward McAllister, a fossilized member of the club himself but one who evidently approved of Bennett's horseplay, recorded. "What sacrilege! An Englishman to ride in upon us, not respecting the sanctity of the place! It aroused the old patriots of that institution with the spirit of '76, and a summary note was sent to the great journalist, withdrawing the invitation the club had previously extended to his guest."

Although his own membership was not withdrawn, Bennett reacted violently to the club's rather mild reproof. He considered Newport as part of his fiefdom, like the *Herald*s of New York and Paris, his yacht and his French villa. He had been summering there long before those so-called society people from New York had ever heard of the place.

He thereupon consigned the Reading Room to the depths of social oblivion—despite which it survived, and still does—and announced plans to build his own playpen, something much grander and more attractive than the stodgy quarters occupied by the Old Club. It would be the Newport Casino and would include clubrooms, a tennis court, a restaurant and a theater.

Stanford White was engaged to design the Casino with orders to spare no expense. Undoubtedly White took on the task with trepidation. Bennett could be a demanding patron of architecture, and there was also his penchant for owls to be taken into consideration. The Commodore regarded the owl as his family's good-luck symbol, totem and an invariable part of the Bennett escutcheon; he was as superstitious about owls as any witch doctor assembling his magic kit. When White was commanded to design the new *Herald* building on what became known as Herald Square, he conceived a classic structure modeled after the Palazzo del Consiglio of Verona with an arcade supported by slender white marble columns. Bennett promptly ruined the cool classicism of the façade by demanding that two dozen bronze owls—equipped with electric eyes to blink over the square at night—be placed around the cornices; the exterior was further disrupted, to the artistic eye, by a huge $200,000 clock with two bronze figures trundling out to strike the hours.

On the Newport Casino project, White was allowed to follow the dictates of his own ornate fancy and the building survives both its designer and his patron, "a curious combination of Victorian grandeur and Chinese detail," as one critic of more austere tastes described it. Several generations have enjoyed its facilities, which became the center of Newport's social, athletic and theatrical activities. "It was the first thing of its kind in the country," wrote Maud Elliott, who was one of those who appreciated the Commodore's gesture, "and its building marks an epoch in Newport life. In the morning at eleven o'clock, the gay summer crowd assembled to play tennis or listen to Conrad's orchestra while they exchanged the news of the day. The theater was used chiefly for the biweekly dances that took the place of the Ocean House hops. Everybody attended them; the elders to watch, the youngsters to dance on that perfect parquet floor. . . . In the tangled web of memory many threads lead back to the Casino Theater where—besides the dances—concerts, readings and private theatricals were held." At the Casino balls even year-round Newporters, the "townies," were permitted to attend at a dollar a head and watch from the balcony as their betters swanned around the dance floor below.

The opening of the Casino in 1880, whether or not it was so intended by the Commodore, inaugurated the era of conspicuous and often outlandishly lavish spending in Newport. "The balls grew more elaborate, the hours longer," as Maud Elliott recalled. "At the ball given by Governor Levi P. Morton for the debut of his daughter, Lena, a dark-eyed beauty of the first-water, an outside ballroom was built and decorated with columns of glittering ice, festooned with smilax and roses. Thousands of lamps illuminated the pillars; the place looked like the cave of Aladdin. . . . Social life in every way showed increasing formality. The old high teas faded out of the picture, and late elaborate dinners took their place. Great emphasis was placed on gastronomy. The dinners were endlessly long, the decorations costly. A popular feature was a pond in the middle of the table, in which floated blue and pink water-lilies. These banquets now seem truly Roman in their gross exaggeration of the importance of eating. . . ."

In some part, at least, Bennett's construction of the Casino as a slap at the Reading Room and its stuffiness resulted in the transformation of Newport from the informality of the seventies to the growing ostentation of the eighties and the great-leap-forward of exhibitionistic spending and party-giving in the nineties. It was a contribution the Commodore made unwittingly; he was a determined enemy, as he had demonstrated, of formality and display for its own sake; his theory was that wealth ought to provide a liberation from the rules and conventions.

Newport would see less and less of him in the ensuing decades. He still retained an interest in the Casino as he would cling to his newspaper properties even when they became unprofitable and were close to bankruptcy at the end of his life. But the Casino was an undisputed success. "The place had an undeniable charm," as one local historian wrote, "that had soon awakened the civic pride of the colonists; for all its bigness, it was somehow snug and cozy-looking, with a quality of unassuming hospitality about it." All those who yearned for acceptance in resort society schemed to become a Casino stockholder. Even after he transferred himself to Paris permanently, Bennett clung to his thirty-two shares of Casino stock, which comprised the largest block of all. Otherwise he had no further connection with the institution he had established.

Even as an absentee the Commodore was almost a palpable presence on the Newport scene, not only for his visible works but for the memories he left behind of a hectic and often mischievous personality.

Who could forget the Bennett clambakes, especially the one at which the Duke of Beaufort was served a forty-pound sea bass that he had caught himself?

Or the strenuous nature of his companionship on land or sea, as Michael Strange learned when she asked what had happened to her Uncle Harry (Oelrichs) when he returned home an ashen-faced invalid from a cruise with the Commodore, and was told that "Uncle Harry had gone around the world on the

Lysistrata with Mr. Gorden Bennett, and it seemed I must accept the fact that no one could survive, unscathed, a trip around the world on Mr. Bennett's yacht."

The old gentlemen maundering over their ancient escapades on the Reading Room's piazza would certainly never forget Bennett's Domino Ball, which was held in a huge tent behind his house and illuminated by the newly introduced electric lights. Even the deadly prose of Ward McAllister could not muffle the excitement of that occasion:

"At this ball appeared a Blue Domino that set all the men wild. Coming to the ball in her own carriage—her servants, she felt, she could trust not to betray her—she dashed into the merry throng and gliding from one to the other whispered airy nothings into men's ears. But they contained enough to excite the most intense curiosity as to who she was.

"She was the belle of the evening; she became bold and daring at times, attacking men with the inmost secrets of their hearts, so as to alarm them, and when she had worked them all up to a fever heat, she came to me to take her to the door that she might make good her escape. A dozen men barricaded the way, but with the rapidity of a deer she dashed through them, reached the sidewalk, and her coachman literally threw her into the carriage. Her coachman, well drilled, dashed off at a furious rate."

Blue Domino's identity was never discovered, but there was little doubt in many minds that Commodore Bennett had hired and coached her in the spicy indiscretions that enlivened his party.

7.

THE TERRIBLE COLONEL

BROODING over the gaieties of the summer season, the unseen eye and ear at every festive occasion, the catchpole who smartly rapped the most august skulls if they participated in behavior, was one of the most picaresque rascals of the Gilded Age. He was Colonel William d'Alton Mann, inventor of the gossip column and publisher of the scandal-dripping *Town Topics*. The Colonel never set foot in Newport but the resort was continuously conscious of his ominous interest in its activities; his journalistic power was narrowly based but it took the daughter of a President of the United States, inadvertently and indirectly, to bring him down.

With heavy heart and heavier hand, he offered correctives to the excesses, gaucheries and missteps of Newport society in the years when its admissions policy was, by mossback standards, a little more than liberal. As he explained his role—no, his mission, for he could convince one in a flash that he was the reincarnation of an Old Testament prophet warning that real estate values in Gomorrah were about to be severely damaged—he was high society's self-appointed conscience and moral watchdog.

"My ambition," he told a reporter, laying a fatherly hand on the young man's shoulder, "is to reform the Four Hundred by making them too deeply disgusted with themselves to continue their silly, empty way of life. I am also teaching the great American public not to pay any attention to these silly fools. If I didn't publish *Town Topics*, someone else without moral responsibility would do so. I am really doing it for the sake of the country."

The Colonel's rhetoric was sadly at variance with his performance as editor and publisher of *Town Topics*. His real purpose was to terrorize by publishing or threatening to publish the most scurrilous gossip to further what was essentially a blackmail operation. Anyone willing to subsidize his extravagant tastes in food and drink could barter his way out of any predicament that came to the Colonel's attention through a pervasive network of backstairs spies.

The arrival of the *Town Topics* in the post every weekend was awaited with terror by those who had failed to insure themselves against its omniscience. "Nobody who did not live in Newport when the *Town Topics* was in its virulent prime," as Richmond Barrett observed, "can have any idea of the sensation it created. Even today [he was writing in 1941], an old Newporter has only to look at that black and white cover, with the two pretty ladies whispering their eager secrets, and straightaway his blood runs cold in his veins. Colonel Mann was a brilliantly resourceful person; his tactics of alternate threats and cajolery, and of devious diplomacy, have a curious resemblance to those that Hitler immortalized in *Mein Kampf*."

Mann acquired *Town Topics* in 1885 from an innocuous fellow named Louis Keller, who founded not only *The American Queen and Town Topics*, as the weekly was originally known, but the *Social Register*. Keller, it is evident, would have been shocked if he had known to what purposes the Colonel would direct his periodical. He was one of those anomalous figures on the fringe of New York society, who would have dearly loved to displace Ward McAllister as a censor of guest lists and choreographer of cotillions.

Keller was obsessed by society, but it was the obsession of a wistful outsider peering through the lighted windows of the Fifth Avenue mansions. A sandy-haired man with hangdog eyes, a droopy mustache and a squeaky voice, he had tried and failed at a number of occupations, including that of gunsmith and dairy farmer. Finally he found an opening wedge when golfing was imported from Britain and he laid out the Baltusrol Golf Club on his New Jersey farm. Providing a new distraction for the wealthy was always a way to attract their interest, and they began joining his club in larger numbers.

Keller established *The American Queen and Town Topics* with the hope that respectful reporting of society's activities would win its patronage. He was certain that "journalism can be clean and decent and yet thrive," but he was proved mistaken, at least in that instance. *Town Topics*, with its innocent prattle of balls and dinner parties, soon foundered; you had to offer something besides sycophancy to attract either society or the lesser orders. It was on the verge of bankruptcy when Keller, who a few years later established the *Social Register*, disposed of his magazine to Colonel Mann, his brother Eugene, an occasional journalist, and Paul Potter, a former dramatic critic for the New York *Herald*. Potter soon sold his third interest to the Manns and eventually Eugene Mann, having failed to discover the formula that would make *Town Topics* a scandalous success, turned over the whole operation to the Colonel. Soon enough after the Colonel took the helm the society weekly stopped prattling about Mrs. Ogden Goelet's latest dinner party and began dealing in gossip, dishing the dirt, invading private lives with gusto, and proving that personal journalism—of a peculiarly unethical sort—could still be successfully practiced.

The Colonel was, in a kinky way, an original genius, a man of considerable accomplishment who found his ultimate satisfaction in bedeviling the rest of his species. That he did not find his most spectacular role until late in life was not for lack of trying; he had been everything from a cavalry colonel to a railroad magnate, and he bore little resemblance to the traditional practitioner of gutter journalism in his backstreet printshop.

Mann was a blackmailer, yes, but on a heroic and picturesque scale. Not the sort of sneak who approached his victim with a grubby packet of letters—no, the Colonel had style, wit, energy, and a flair for showmanship, a character of Dickensian paradox. He exuded a "buoyant animalism from every pore," as one reluctant admirer wrote. His curious business was conducted, not in a furtive rendezvous but at a table at Delmonico's. A prospective victim, having approached the Colonel over his

bottle of Mumm's, often felt as though he had acquired Friar
Tuck as his father confessor.

A jolly fellow despite the squalor of his calling, he was a large
portly man with a mop of grandfatherly white hair, whiskers that
splayed out like an untrimmed hedge, twinkling blue eyes, a
large red nose, and the belly of an alderman with lucrative
connections with the street contractors. His costume only enhanced the impression of an elderly bon vivant and included a
black plug hat, a frock coat, a pleated white shirt with a flaring
red bow tie and vest to match, and striped pants. His pockets
were usually full of sugar lumps, which he distributed, with
benevolent chuckles, to the horses en route from his Fortieth
Street office to his table at Delmonico's. His appetite was not at
all diminished by the suffering and penance in which he dealt,
and his customary lunch included six mutton chops, a heap of
candied yams, two heads of lettuce drenched in salad dressing, a
basket of biscuits, the quarter of a chocolate cake, two bottles of
vintage champagne, and a dollar cigar.

In the lengthy gallery of nineteenth-century rascals, Colonel
William d'Alton Mann stands out as perhaps the most effulgent,
picturesque and ingenious. The briefest résumé of his career
limns a character no novelist would have dared invent. He was
born on an Ohio farm in 1839, claimed to have been educated
and to have practiced as a civil engineer, and when the Civil
War started, he flung himself into the Union cause with
Napoleonic energy. Although many people thought his title was
self-bestowed, he won his colonel's eagles legitimately, first by
organizing the Fifth Michigan Cavalry, then organizing, training and taking command of the Seventh Michigan Cavalry.
There was no doubt of his military courage and accomplishments. At the age of twenty-four, he led the 407 sabers of the
Seventh Michigan, part of Custer's brigade, against Stuart's
Confederate cavalry at Gettysburg, and helped to rout the
plumed cavalier of the Confederacy. He also invented a number
of pieces of cavalry equipment and accoutrements, on which he
obtained patents.

His postwar career provided a case-history study of the sort of intelligent and imaginative man who also has a natural affinity for crime. Given the choice of an honest million and a similar amount gained through outwitting his fellows, and thus satisfying some deep psychic compulsion, Mann would always choose the latter. Instead of seizing one of the honest opportunities available to him, Colonel Mann plunged into the first recorded oil-stock promotion fraud. The discovery of the Pennsylvania oilfields and their growing possibilities provided him with the inspiration, which developed into what the newspapers headlined as "The Great Petroleum Swindle." Oil-bearing land was eagerly sought then, and he founded the U.S. Petroleum Company on the basis of the old family farm in Ohio and one acre bought in Venango, Pennsylvania, and persuaded the celebrated Major General Winfield Scott Hancock to accept the presidency. He collected $57,500 from various investors, including many old army comrades, and shortly thereafter was arrested on charges of obtaining money under false pretenses. The case was dismissed because the charges were brought before a New York court but the offenses had occurred in Washington, D.C.

His subsequent career was equally innovative and slightly more respectable. Despite his scrape with the law, he wangled the post of federal assessor of internal revenue in Mobile, Alabama, then still under occupation by federal troops. Somehow some of the money supposed to be forwarded to the U.S. Treasury was diverted to Colonel Mann's pockets and he was enabled to become owner and publisher of the Mobile *Register*. Despite the fact that he had been a Yankee officer, Mann became a popular figure in Mobile, acquired a rich Alabama accent, was elected to Congress (but the election was nullified on the grounds that Negro votes had been trifled with), bought a cottonseed oil refinery and joined the Ku Klux Klan.

Mobile, however, was too provincial and distant from the great cities to contain his imperial ambitions. He went back up North with a new inspiration. Railroads just then were being built in all directions and some thought was being given to the comfort of the passengers. He developed the Mann sleeping car, the first refrigerator car and the vestibule, which allowed passengers to cross from one car to another. George Pullman monopolized the American sleeping-car market, so Mann took his business to Europe, where his eight-compartment *wagon-lits*, designed for the privacy of the well-heeled, were more appealing than the egalitarian Pullman berths, and soon his cars were in service on railways in half a dozen European countries. The sleeping cars of the fabled Orient Express, in fact, were built according to his original specifications. Mann spent a decade in Europe promoting the affairs of the Mann Boudoir Car Company.

He turned his innovative mind to society journalism on his return to the United States. The genesis of his interest in a field that must have seemed rather parochial, if exotic, to a man who had flourished in so many more important arenas, apparently occurred during his sojourn abroad. He became acquainted with Edmund Yates, formerly European correspondent for the New York *Herald*, and Henry Labouchere, when they decided to establish the British social journal called the *World*, and claimed to have helped them out with funds when needed. The *World*, which the *Times* of London described as having "set us all listening at the keyhole," certainly awakened in Mann ambitions to do for American society what the *World* was doing for, or to, the English. He must have been fascinated by the terror the *World* created, too; Labouchere's biographer recounted that when the gossip sheet made its weekly appearance, there was a quiver of apprehension from "every institution from the Crown to the Treasury, from the Church to the Army." He was undismayed by the fact that in 1883 his friend Yates spent four months in prison after being convicted of criminal libel.

When he took over full control of *Town Topics*, he made it plain that his coverage of society would not be of the forelock-tugging, bootlicking kind to which American society had become accustomed except for a few years during which the society pages of the New York *Herald*, largely for circulation-pulling reasons, took a hostile and sardonic attitude.

The Colonel came not to praise and comfort society but to criticize its lack of values and chastise its baseless pretensions.

Not only did he realize that a lickspittle attitude didn't attract the respect of the people he was writing about, but his posture as a reformer and a moralist, coinciding with a flood of new money and parvenu behavior, served as a cover for his real purposes. First, he persuaded society to subscribe to *Town Topics* by leading off with a ten-page "Saunterings" column, which served up gossip as spicy and steaming as his legal adviser and right-hand man, Judge Joseph M. Deuel, would permit.

He served notice almost immediately that a harshly revealing spotlight would be beamed on the Four Hundred and its candidates. A little essay on the general unworthiness of that group of the elect, written in the Colonel's southern-editor style, appeared in *Town Topics* shortly after he took over its direction: " . . . How many of the swellest of the swell today were anything at all twenty years ago—fifteen years ago even? Where were the Vanderbilts, socially, even five years ago? The Astors had just fifteen years the social start. The Vanderbilts in fifteen more will come up to an equality, and I prophesy they will eventually lead, partly because there is more gold on the young male, and more brass on the young female side of their house. Where, indeed, are the Knickerbockers now? . . . "

The main gun in the Colonel's battery was that pioneer gossip column innocuously headed "Saunterings." Every Tuesday, just before the magazine went to press, the Colonel and his staff of rewritemen would winnow the sheaves of reports received from official and unofficial correspondents, the latter mostly tipsters who made a sideline of peaching on their employers, and assemble it in a leeringly suggestive, highly readable form. Most of "Saunterings" was devoted to New York socialites and their naughty behavior in Manhattan townhouses, Broadway cabarets, Newport (or Tuxedo Park, Saratoga Springs, Bar Harbor) cottages or on their floating fun houses called yachts. The relentless malice of those paragraphs that made up *Town Topics* columns year after year, their utter lack of charity or compassion, would do more to win sympathy for their roguish subjects than anything a publicist could concoct. They may have been a greedy and self-centered lot, but they must have deserved a

kindlier Father Grundy than Colonel Mann and his quilled
assassins.

The Colonel's method of omitting names in his more scurrilous
paragraphs, then tipping off the identity of the culprits in the
following items, was explained by his biographer Andy Logan:
"The Saunterer's social scene was populated by individuals who
gave receptions, tea dances, and tennis parties, and got married
and engaged as much as they did on the town's other society
pages. It was also populated by charlatans, transvestites, adulter-
ers (often incestuous), nymphomaniacs, lesbians, and cuckolds. It
was the Saunterer's custom to run news of routine social
engagements, of his weekly cast of characters directly after
reports of their indictable pursuits, which usually left out names
but provided such do-it-yourself clues as the subject's precise
address or such information as, 'The young man's last name,
incidentally, is the same as the title of the leading primate of the
Church of Rome.' With the help of this literary counterpoint
Town Topics' subscribers had no difficulty identifying the bride of
the season who had once born twins out of wedlock, the cotillion
leader down with syphilis, or the prominent Philadelphia matron
against whom divorce proceedings were brought because of her
passionate friendship with a female librarian." As the Colonel
had warned at the outset of his monitorial career with *Town
Topics*, it was not a periodical for "babes, prudes, idiots or dudes."

The Colonel did not always resort to blind items in "Saunterings" or shy away from inflicting personal humiliations,
perhaps in the belief they would delight or titillate more people
than they offended. Thus: "Seldom does a brunette make a
pretty bride, and Miss Maria Arnot Haver was no exception.
. . . Miss Van Alen suffers from some kind of throat trouble—
she cannot go more than half an hour without a drink. . . . Mrs.
Belmont dyes her hair. Though covered with diamond rings, her
hands are wrinkled like a washerwoman's. . . . Mrs. Frederick
Nielsen has aged a great deal lately. Her complexion has become
almost blue, and the crow's feet are visible at a distance. . . ."
Obviously the Colonel did not have the Southern gentleman's
manners to match his Alabama accent.

Mann also regarded himself as the arbiter of fashion and was outraged by the appearance of Griswold Lorillard, the young son of Pierre Lorillard V, at the Autumn Ball in October, 1886, in a tailless dress coat—that is, a dinner jacket, as it was known to the well-bred, or tuxedo as it was known to the lower orders. Its origins are lost to sartorial history—though some said it was adapted from the Prince of Wales' smoking jacket, others that it had been introduced by a visiting Anglo-Irishman attending one of the Chowder and Marching Club's dances in the Bowery—but it was greeted with loathing by traditionalists. Young Lorillard gave further offense by having his pioneer dinner jacket tailored with scarlet satin lapels.

To the Colonel, Lorillard was an apparition signaling some sort of social revolution and "looked for all the world like a royal footman," as *Town Topics* commented, adding that Lorillard and his frolicsome young friends "ought to have been put in strait jackets long ago."

On press day, it was said, the Colonel customarily trotted off to Delmonico's clutching a batch of galley proofs of stories and paragraphs about to appear in *Town Topics*, or in the occasional special editions issued for the delectation of Wall Street and replete with accounts of financial skulduggery and speculative conspiracies. Certain gentlemen who had been advised that the periodical would shortly publish something of interest to them would approach the Colonel's table. They would be shown a proof of the story concerning them, blanch, reach for their well-stuffed wallets, and pay handsomely for the Colonel's agreement to stifle his editorial conscience and spike the damaging item.

Later, as the deadline approached and midnight struck, there would be a rush of last-minute supplicants for editorial mercy. There would be a pounding on the door to the editorial room, as one chronicler has described those midnight incursions, and "whoever opened it would be nearly trampled down by unscheduled visitors, who had got word from one source or another that a certain factually accurate but hideously inconvenient report was about to be dispatched to the printers. These invaders (after dark no one seems to have come alone) would take a sweeping look around the outer editorial room and . . . would advance through the open door of Mann's private office. By this time the old Colonel, suddenly agile as a stripling, would have sprung to his feet, reached out one hand for his Scotch fir walking stick—'a weapon that might have floored a mule,' as one employee described it—and with the other hand have grabbed the pistol from his top desk drawer. So far as the record shows, however, no blood was ever shed on such occasions. The high drama was swiftly transformed into a business negotiation. At its conclusion a check changed hands, marked down as a loan or stock purchase or perhaps an advertising contract, the offending item was removed from the next week's edition (though not from the *Town Topics* files), and the visitors retired, sighing the long sigh of the reprieved."

No doubt about it, Colonel Mann was combining blackmail with journalism—and he got away with it for two decades. Society never struck back. The list of his victims included practically every gilded name in society, high finance and industry. They submitted regularly, without a protest, to the leeching; much more frightened of *Town Topics* than of any grand jury or congressional investigating committee.

One of the Colonel's boldest and most lucrative inspirations was the publication of a heavy, fancily bound volume titled *Fads and Fancies of Representative Americans*. For payment of a sizable fee, each of the Colonel's patrons would receive a flattering mini-biography and photographs of his favorite possessions. Some coughed up to avoid exposure of their various misdemeanors in *Town Topics*, others were eager to be included in the roll call of eminent names. Some paid more than the going price, including (as the subsequent investigation showed) Ogden Armour of the Chicago meat-packing family; James W. Gerard, the corporation lawyer; Thomas Walsh, the Colorado silver king, who was trying to make a splash in Eastern society, and Mrs. Potter Palmer, the Chicago society queen. Charles M. Schwab, the steel magnate, paid $1,500 to have published what he insisted was the correct version of his attempt to break the bank at Monte Carlo.

That well-publicized foray had got him in trouble with J. Pierpont Morgan, the czar of the steel industry, who placed a high value on discretion. "I didn't do anything behind locked doors," Schwab protested to Morgan. "That's what doors are *for*, Schwab," Morgan replied. With such names as Duke, Vanderbilt, Astor, Huntington, Flagler, Whitney, Lorillard, Ryan, Hyde, Belmont and Fleischmann heading the list of subscribers to *Fads and Fancies*, the Colonel cleared $90,000 in profit on the venture.

The only irksome incident connected with that enterprise was that President Theodore Roosevelt sent him a stiff little note protesting his inclusion in the volume, which he had not sought. The President also publicly denied he had ever joined the list of *Fads and Fancies* subscribers. Colonel Mann took umbrage—a fearsome sight, with his eyes blazing, his cheeks purpling and his blood pressure skyrocketing. He swore he'd get even for that snub from the White House. But an editor in his delicate position, balancing extortion with exposé journalism, loses his temper at considerable risk; he can't afford feuds based on affronts to his dignity. Indirectly that grievance, nursed for several years, would prove disastrous.

In the main, however, the Colonel presented himself as a benevolent figure. Social betterment, the sanctity of the upperclass home, the guardianship of society's manners and morals, the preservation of decorum on all occasions were, he insisted, his greatest concerns. No one could scold a debutante for overuse of cosmetics with more paternal authority than the Colonel; none could be so shocked at reports of loose living at Newport or Palm Beach as he and his fellow moralists on the *Town Topics* staff. "Scandal!" he would bluster when anyone accused him of operating a gossip sheet. "Harumph! Harumph! Nothing of the sort. We're only pointing a moral. *Town Topics* stands for moral purity. Written by gentle folk, for gentle folk, on topics of interest to gentle folk."

The gentle folk of Newport's summer colony were not convinced of Colonel Mann's benevolence. Too often had one of the matron's been stung by an item in "Saunterings" describing

her thirst for champagne and brandy cocktails. Too often had
the head of one of the summer households had to hasten back to
New York, checkbook in hand, to prevent the Colonel from
detailing the presence of a chorus girl on his yacht or reporting
on his daughters' escapades.

Summer after summer fashionable Newport quivered under
the Colonel's lash. It could bear up under ridicule, it could
withstand his barbed comments on social gaffes, it could shrug off
his remarks on the missteps of the newly rich feeling their way
toward acceptance. It could not suffer lightly his blabbing of
sexual misconduct and extramarital alliances; the rich could
afford them, but it could not afford to have them revealed.
Cotton Mather and Mother Grundy were still influences in the
land, and there was always the self-conscious duty of "setting an
example" for the lower classes, which, it was feared, would turn
to all sorts of licentious conduct—and possibly even demand a
better wage than eight dollars a week—if they got the wrong
ideas about the higher levels of society.

Town Topics, as one Newport historian suggested, "could not
have wielded the power it did if all the paragraphs had been
made up out of whole cloth; the sad truth is that there were
many guilty consciences in Newport in those days. Even the Age
of Innocence had been no golden age of virtue . . . the double
standard of morality had been the accepted and effectively
standardized order of the day." (*Privately* accepted, of course, as
an "understood" thing that needed no public comment.)

Colonel Mann and his *Town Topics*, of course, broke that
taboo. They did not hesitate, out of gallantry or old-fashioned
chivalry, to report in detail on a society woman's extramarital
affairs or her daughter's seduction. Their menfolk, as a result,
were forced to face up to it that the handsome and attentive
young men who clustered around their wives were not always
courtiers but might be rendering other services besides flattery.

The terrifying aspect of *Town Topics*' invisible presence, not
only at every social function but outside boudoir doors and
peering from behind the hedges of formal gardens by moonlight,
was the Colonel's spy system. His agents, it seemed, were

everywhere, supplementing their income by passing along information to the *Town Topics* editorial rooms.

"Nobody," according to the chronicler quoted above, "could be sure that the butler or the personal maid wasn't a spy, that the charming but penniless young cousin *wasn't* selling his rich relatives down the river. To make confusion worse confounded, the *Town Topics* reporters weren't above spreading propaganda to the effect that some of the spiteful ladies in the inner circle were betraying the secrets of their deadlier rivals. Harry Lehr himself was once under suspicion as a sort of roving ambassador for Colonel Mann. [Lehr had taken over Ward McAllister's functions as a grand vizier to the reigning dowagers.] There wasn't the slightest justification for the charge; but at that particular time it was thought that Lehr was slipping from grace and might be using *Town Topics* to pay off certain grudges."

A rash of poison-pen letter writing broke out as a result of the *Town Topics'* incessant snooping. Inevitably, in that atmosphere of constant suspicion and uneasiness, anonymous letters began appearing on breakfast trays, threats that unless the recipients mended their ways the *Town Topics'* espionage service would be alerted. The manager of the Casino was warned that the magazine's spies were ubiquitous. "You should tell your subscribers to watch their words when their week-end friend Mr. C. is within earshot. . . . It is high time you learned that two of your doormen are paid hirelings of *Town Topics*. . . ." And so forth. The anonymous letters were not inspired by Colonel Mann, but they served his purposes; they made his prospective victims all the more eager to buy immunity.

The Colonel's chief operative in Newport, it later developed, was Robert Rowe, whose presumed full-time occupation was as a telegraph operator. Obviously he was placed in an excellent position to intercept information of value to the Colonel, no matter that the privacy of Western Union's communications was flagrantly breached. Rowe was an ambitious young man, with energy for his avocation as a *Town Topics* spy after leaving his key at the telegraph office.

Rowe, at subsequent legal proceedings, testified that in various disguises, employing stratagems worthy of a Sherlock Holmes, he often peered through a screen of potted palms to observe Newport society disporting itself. Once, he admitted, he attended a ball in honor of the Duchess of Marlborough in the guise of a tambourine player.

Though he was apparently invisible to the older people, a self-effacing quality he cultivated by always wearing pale gray suits to match his colorless personality, Rowe and his nefarious activities were well known to the youth of Newport. Michael Strange (Blanche Oelrichs) recalled that she knew Rowe and other *Town Topics* snoopers by sight and "with sardonic amusement would watch them sitting behind the dowagers (especially old Mrs. Kernochan whom we called, with that veracity that children have, 'The Sitting Bull') taking notes of her gossip which, starting out as it did on a strong note of vituperation, could very likely be printed straight off the reel."

One morning during Tennis Week Jack Rutherford and Blanche were standing outside a jeweler's display window on Bellevue Avenue and arranging a bet on one of the matches, a gold bangle to a leather cigarette case. Out of the corner of her eye she saw Rowe lurking nearby. He wasn't taking notes but he was observing—and misunderstanding—the transaction between them. The result was a long paragraph in *Town Topics* detailing how a "precocious racketeer" had been "testing the powers of extortion before a jeweler's window upon a green youth." She was not named but was described well enough for everyone in Newport to identify her.

She had forgotten the incident until a week later when her father, Charles Oelrichs, "stormed into the house from the Reading Room, that natural harbor of stiff drinks, crying out that my virginity had been called in question in the public print, my reputation ruined, and my chance of marrying any decent young man annihilated."

"If I knew who wrote that," Oelrichs thundered, "I would kill him."

"Well," his quaking daughter replied, "I can tell you just who it was, and his name and address as well."

Oelrichs summoned a cab from the livery stable and hastened over to Robert Rowe's residence. An hour later he returned to report, "I saw the wretched little creature, I shook him like a rat. He admitted the article, but claimed he hadn't meant anything by it. He crawled on his knees before me and I hadn't the heart to beat him up. He has promised never to say another derogatory word about you in his filthy sheet in which I told him you preferred not to be mentioned."

Rowe, however, did his best to make amends in a series of paragraphs in which "Blanche Oelrichs, 'the precocious racketeer,' gave way to 'a girl so in advance of all other girls in good looks, that not since the days of Ava Willing had anything been seen to touch her.'"

She frankly enjoyed the attention that resulted from those paragraphs in *Town Topics*. "It was said that my entrance at Freebody Park, a vaudeville show changing its bill once a week, and to which even girls who were not 'out' were allowed to go, had caused a sensation. . . . These paragraphs of forensic praise were cut out and pasted into a scrapbook by my mother, and did me a great deal of good with the boys, who were quite pleased to be seen around with me."

Sometimes Rowe went further afield on orders from Colonel Mann's headquarters. He once spent several days snooping around a prep school, Exeter, while posing as a visiting professor of mathematics. His purpose, he explained subsequently at Colonel Mann's trial, was not only to report on the manners and morals of the "preppies" but to sound them out on the sexual availability of the girls at Miss Ely's nearby finishing school.

Rowe's testimony on his career as a keyhole journalist and backstairs spy was amusing enough for Alan Dale, the New York *American* dramatic critic assigned to cover the trial as though it were a Broadway instead of a Fifth Avenue production, to describe it as "a delightful little intimate domestic society comedy, quite on a par with *Man and Superman*. It achieved the rarest of all combinations, for it was vulgar and funny at the same time."

For some time a group of aristocratic clubmen in New York had been discussing how to deodorize Colonel Mann's brand of skunk journalism. Foremost among them was William Travers Jerome, the crusading district attorney of New York County, whose office walls were covered with the scalps of Tammany miscreants, crooked police officials, gamblers and Tenderloin figures.

Other members of the anti-Mann junta included Robert Collier, the son of the founder of *Collier's Weekly*; Harry Payne Whitney, Charles Dana Gibson and Mark Sullivan. Young Whitney and young Collier both had personal reasons for detesting the Colonel. Whitney's father had been forced to help subsidize Mann and so had the younger Whitney himself (a $13,000 loan for unspecified reasons). And Collier's father had been grossly affronted by a "Saunterings" item which claimed that he had once sold Catholic Bibles to innocent Protestant bumpkins in the Catskills.

For several years that group had been reading every issue of *Town Topics*, line by line, hoping to catch the Colonel in the act of criminal libel, but Mann had his associate, Judge Deuel, by his side to prevent him from falling into that trap. Jerome and his friends could only bide their time, meanwhile watching the Colonel's bank account and real estate holdings swell by the year.

In 1904, not long before the twentieth anniversary of Colonel Mann's taking over *Town Topics* and the attendant duty of monitoring its readership, he was particularly vexed with the current occupant of the White House. Mann had acquired a large parcel of real estate on West Thirty-eighth Street and Ninth Avenue, which he was offering, in his usual vigorous fashion, to the government as the site for the new main post office. The government nevertheless decided to build four blocks to the south. Mann, a Democrat ever since his Alabama days, was convinced that President Roosevelt had intervened in the decision simply to thwart him as a matter of partisan politics.

About a month after he learned that his real estate scheme had fallen through, the Colonel alerted his Newport secret service to keep a close watch on the President's daughter on her late-summer visit to the resort.

Alice Roosevelt, then twenty, was America's sweetheart of the moment, a lively and independent young woman (and later renowned as one of the few resident wits of Washington society, one of her more devastating shafts being the comparison of presidential candidate Thomas E. Dewey to the "little man on top of the wedding cake").

The adoration of Princess Alice, as the newspapers called her with undue deference, had reached a cultlike proportion not to be equaled until Jacqueline Kennedy's years in the White House. Everything she did, everything she wore, everything she said was breathlessly reported. Her Alice Blue gowns inspired a Tin Pan Alley tune. Her choice of an escort, her changes of coiffure, the names on her dance card were front-paged in the bulletin style otherwise reserved for ax murders and South American revolutions.

Alice Roosevelt was not only glamorous but had a merry disposition that rebelled at the stuffier conventions. She journeyed to Newport for her first visit to that summer colony in a mood to enjoy herself; apparently no one had warned her of Colonel Mann's ubiquitous spies. And she did have a gay time that week as the guest of Grace Vanderbilt, Robert Fulton Cutting and other Newporters.

In his most sorrowful manner, as though pondering the misdeeds of a favorite granddaughter, the Colonel commented in "Saunterings" that the daughter of a man at the summit of the national life—he did not name her—was the talk of Newport for her uninhibited conduct, that "from wearing costly lingerie to indulging in fancy dances for the edification of men was only a step. And then came a second step—indulging freely in stimulants. Flying all around Newport without a chaperone was another thing that greatly concerned Mrs. Grundy. . . . If the young woman knew some of the tales that were told in clubs at Newport, she would be more careful in the future. . . . I was really surprised to hear her name mentioned openly there in connection with certain doings that gentle folk are not supposed to discuss." It was one of those blind items, in which Alice Roosevelt was identified—clearly enough for most of his readers —as the guest of a man "named after a distinguished American to whom the world of steam navigation is deeply indebted [Robert Fulton Cutting]."

Talking about the innocent adventures of that week in Newport years later, Mrs. Alice Roosevelt Longworth would recall, "When I danced the hootchy-kootchy on Grace Vanderbilt's roof at Newport, you would have thought the world was coming to an end."

No one in Newport ever admitted to subscribing to or reading *Town Topics*, so the shock of the Colonel's disclosures was initially muffled. Everyone had read it and accepted it as just another of Mann's outrages. The White House did not, as later administrations might, dispatch a squad of federal investigators to harass the Colonel. (That handy investigative device, the federal income tax, had not yet been imposed.) One man who admittedly read the *Town Topics* paragraph was Robert Collier. He was so enraged that he kicked over a basket of firewood. The following Monday morning, after a weekend of fuming, Collier returned to New York, stormed into his magazine's offices and ordered his editor, Norman Hapgood, to lower the boom on *Town Topics* forthwith. The result was a scorcher:

"The most degraded paper of any prominence in the United States is a weekly of which the function is to distribute news and scandal about society. The mind which guides such a publication tests credulity and forces one to take Swift's Yahoo as an unexaggerated truth. The editor in question leads a somewhat secluded life, and well he may. . . . A recent issue of his sewer-like sheet contains as its leading feature an attack on a young girl who happens to be the daughter of the President of the United States. . . . It charges her with all the errors that hurt a woman most, and it makes these charges in a most coarse and leering way. . . ."

Hapgood ended by declaring that "the editor's standing among the people is somewhat worse than that of an ordinary forger, horse-thief or second-story man."

For some months *Collier's* and *Town Topics* engaged in a duel of editorial artillery. The Colonel was confident that when it came to invective he could outdo any of *Collier's* Ivy Leaguers, and his performance was indeed worthy of an editor who had learned his craft in Alabama during the Reconstruction era. His principal target, perhaps because he was more vulnerable, was old Pat Collier, whom Mann described as a dirty old man who, because he had taken up foxhunting, was "the first man to ride into the heart of swelldom behind a pack of hounds." Collier was referred to in *Town Topics* as Pat Fagin because *Collier's Weekly* was serializing the British best seller, *Raffles*, which dealt romantically with the adventures of a society jewel thief. Collier, Mann insisted, was encouraging American youth to take up a life of crime. And when jewelry was stolen from a house party at Newport, Mann urged the police to collar Pat Collier and examine the new scarf pin he was wearing.

During the summer of 1905, smarting under those barbs, Robert Collier, his editor Norman Hapgood and District Attorney Jerome conferred on how to put the quietus on Colonel Mann. Jerome advised that Mann and his legal eagle be forced into a position in which they had to file charges of criminal libel. *Collier's* published a Hapgood editorial describing *Town Topics* as a blackmail operation and Mann and Deuel as a pair of scoundrels. The two men then sued Hapgood and *Collier's* for $100,000 in a civil suit and in October, 1905, obtained Hapgood's indictment on charges of criminal libel.

Jerome and his group of clubmen chuckled over plans to turn the Hapgood trial into a barbecue pit in which Colonel Mann would be roasted, though Peter Finley Dunne warned Hapgood that given the public's short and confused memory "ten years from now people will think you were arrested for writing an article in *Town Topics* libeling Alice Roosevelt, and many of them will remember your name without being sure whether you were the editor of *Town Topics* or the man who jumped off the Brooklyn Bridge."

In the delicate task of turning the prosecution of Hapgood into an inquisition in which Mann and Deuel would be exposed in all their lurid infamy, Jerome was greatly assisted by the fact that *Collier's Weekly*, by offering higher salaries, lured a number of the members of the *Town Topics* staff away from the Colonel and encouraged them to bring sheaves of memoranda with them.

The highlight of the Hapgood trial was not the testimony of the nominal culprits who had been indicted, but the appearance of Colonel Mann who took the witness stand, as the New York *Herald* remarked, "with the air of one who is about to accomplish great things." Instead he fell head-first into the district attorney's trap. Jerome produced a memorandum signed W. D. M., which ordered that pressure be applied to certain persons unwilling to have their private lives illuminated by the *Town Topics* style of reportage. Mann denied having inscribed the initials. Jerome then summarily dismissed him, summoned a handwriting expert to the stand, and permitted himself a feline smile as the expert testified those were indeed Mann's initials. Mann was then recalled to deny—and thereby lay himself open to perjury charges—that he had ever extorted money from people to "keep unpleasant things about them out of *Town Topics*."

The Colonel's denial was quickly riddled when Oliver H. P. Belmont was summoned to testify on just how the Colonel operated in the privacy of his Fifth Avenue offices. There was a full house when Belmont appeared, society turning out to cheer on the champions of its honor. One corner of the courtroom, called the "royal box," was reserved for society women, shepherded into the enclosure by Mrs. Robert Collier (a granddaughter of The Mrs. Astor, who demonstrated in her person how high and how fast the descendants of an Irish bookpeddler could rise, now that an enlarged edition of the social studbook had been issued). The New York *Times* remarked on the fact that the young matrons behaved as though the trial were an entertainment staged for their delectation. "Dressed as if for the theater, they would drop their lorgnettes and gasp in unison at indelicate references in the testimony and after each recess would pose for newspaper photographs whose captions dwelt on their fashionable costumes."

Belmont's testimony as a state's witness clinched the case, not for the state but for the defense. He told how he had been summoned to Mann's office and listened to the Colonel's suggestion that he buy $5000 worth of *Town Topics* stock. Belmont demurred, upon which Mann suggested a loan of $5000. Once again Belmont refused. Mann lowered his sights to $2000 and again was turned down. "It would be well for you to think it over," Mann advised him. Belmont then received unfavorable attention in the magazine's columns, he testified, though his brother Perry, who had knuckled under to Mann, was "kindly treated."

It took the jury only seven minutes to return a verdict acquitting Hapgood of criminal libel.

Within twenty-four hours Mann was arrested on a perjury charge. He would now be forced to spend much of his tainted fortune on keeping himself out of prison. Yet his insouciance was undiminished; he was the boyo, after all, who had faced Stuart's cavalry at Gettysburg. James Gordon Bennett's Paris *Herald* loyally denounced Mann and published a letter describing *Town Topics* as the enterprise of "a gang of blackmailers." The Colonel won a suit against Bennett in a French court, which directed the Commodore to publish a retraction and pay 200 francs in damages. The Colonel donated the money to the *Herald's* charity fund. And the commander of the Seventh Michigan kept on attacking the commander of the Rough Riders, constantly referring to President Roosevelt as a "professional cowboy" and charging that he was being persecuted on orders from the White House.

At his perjury trial, only nominally concerned with the matter of that memo he denied having signed, Mann was forced to admit that he had extracted almost $200,000 from such towering contemporaries as James R. Keene, William K. Vanderbilt, Thomas Fortune Ryan, John W. Gates, William C. Whitney and Collis P. Huntington. But he had perhaps the ablest lawyer in the country as his defender, Martin Littleton, with his cellolike voice. Littleton did not bother erecting a defense against the state's charges but, his voice throbbing in the summation to the jury, he detailed the Colonel's military services almost saber stroke by stroke and claimed for him the laurels of Gettysburg. "Send this gallant old hero from this courtroom a free man," he begged the jurors. They did just that.

The old rascal's fangs had been drawn, however, and *Town Topics* had lost its "power to terrify." Several years later he admitted in "Saunterings" that his advertising revenues had disastrously declined because of what he called "the Roosevelt-Collier conspiracy," but he clung to his editorial roost until his death in 1920.

Newport could breathe easier, all because Alice Roosevelt had "danced the hootchy-kootchy on Grace Vanderbilt's roof" one summer night, but there were many of the staider members of the colony who would regret there wasn't someone around to chasten the livelier spirits.

8.

SCENES FROM SPORTING LIFE

THE PRINCIPLE of exclusivity, and the expensiveness thereof, has always governed the wealthy in their pursuit of sport. The late Brendan Behan epitomized the Anglo-Irish aristocracy, perhaps a bit too pithily, as "Protestants with horses." He was illustrating the principle that to the upper classes any sport that requires nothing more than an open space, a ball and some implement to propel it with is not likely to become fashionable. A man of substance inclines toward a sport requiring equipment or travel or considerable leisure not available to the lower orders: shooting wild game in Africa, yachting, lawn tennis, fox hunting, steeplechasing, trapshooting, all endeavors in which a certain amount of grace and elegance are required.

"You can do business with anyone," was J. P. Morgan's famous dictum, "but you can go sailing only with a gentleman."

(The riposte of Leonard Jerome, the grandfather of Winston Churchill, is not quite so famous. "Right," he crisply commented on Morgan's dictum, "although it depends on what you mean by a gentleman." He was thinking, according to his kinswoman and biographer, Anita Leslie, of the stouthearted crew of James Gordon Bennett's *Henrietta*, all rankers, who won the first transatlantic yacht race for him, "crouching half-frozen in the lee of weather cloths during long hours of watch, and putting all their heart into the handling of canvas in shifting freezing winds, and of *Fleetwing*'s six sailors lost in the roaring ocean." A gentleman, in Leonard Jerome's view, wasn't simply the fellow who owned the yacht or possessed the social credentials to which Morgan evidently referred.)

131

In Newport and elsewhere, the masculine sector of American society was adopting the attitudes of the English sportsman as their wives, consciously or not, modeled themselves after the remnants of the French aristocracy. Sports became important in Newport because they were the preoccupation, even the obsession, of English county gentry. "All New York aped the British," as one perceptive lady wrote in her memoirs. "New York society men, especially sportsmen, were slaves to the Prince of Wales to the last button on his coat. . . . The improvement in ocean transportation in the Eighties made it possible for many more Americans to acquaint themselves with the traditions of English country life, and having found it the most delightful existence in the world decided to fashion their own upon it. . . . The flamboyant New Yorkers of the Eighties, the bankers and the empire-minded railroad owners who were the economic power behind the new leisure class, looked for their fashion not to the old Dutch aristocratic customs, nor to the intellectual and political traditions that permeated fashionable New England, but to Britain. And Britain gave them sports."

Newport in the summer months abounded with sporting activity until at times it looked like a vast panel of those steel engravings that covered the walls of men's clubs, Broad Street offices and the studies of private houses, and were usually captioned "scenes from sporting life." For many years Newport would be the capital of the more exquisite sports in which the lower classes could not participate and which thereby acquired the benchmark of exclusivity: polo, yachting and lawn tennis.

While their womenfolk pursued careers of social domination, the wealthy male Newporters strived for the title of "prominent sportsman," the American equivalent of being knighted. Their yachts, polo ponies and racks of English-made rifles and shotguns were more than expensive toys; they were investments in prestige, certificates of acceptance by their peers, as ennobling as a seat on the stock exchange and a decent rating in Dun & Bradstreet.

For those too infirm, too lazy or too ill-coordinated for the rigors of the sporting life on land and water, there was always the pursuit of gentleman-farming and fanciful estate-building. The construction of extravagant simplicities became a Newport art form. Whether they were conscious of it or not, the avocation was a throwback to the English aristocracy of the eighteenth century, when country gentlemen, bored with wining and wenching and yearning for at least a vicarious taste of austerity, built moss-covered "ruins" on their estates and then advertised for men to impersonate hermits and inhabit them. One of the thriftier squires, Sir Richard Hill of Hawkstone, bought a stuffed hermit to serve as his surrogate for sampling the joys of poverty.

Arthur Curtiss James was a commodore of the New York Yacht Club but in his later years, with all that money rolling in from his family's Anaconda copper mines, he began to yearn for the simplicities of the pastoral life. Oh, to be a simple Swiss shepherd yodeling to his flock. Instead of simply moving to Switzerland he re-created an Alpine setting for himself on his estate in Sunrise Valley.

His Swiss farm certainly would have startled any visiting Helvetian. Among the fifty outbuildings was a piggery in which each porker had his own sty and pig run, possibly with imported mud, along with a signboard detailing his pedigree and analyzing his personality. Not only the swine were pampered, but James' stables had leaded windows. The Rosina Daintymouth henhouse was also deluxe but bore a sign picturing an ax and a roast chicken, along with the ominous legend, "From happy egghood/ Through pullet age/ Up to the Inevitable END."

For some reason pigs, whether or not it was due to their swinish charms, were the favorites of the gentleman farmers. Their fate was a long and pampered life, not to provide a platter of pork chops for their owners. Mrs. Edward Spencer kept a pig in her drawing room, it was alleged, and another gentleman farmer's wife took one of their pigs for an airing on Bellevue Avenue every afternoon in her victoria.

A whole squirearchy of frivolous farmers sprang up around the summer colony. William Fahnestock, an orchardist supreme, hung fourteen-carat gold apples, pears and peaches on his trees.

To most full-blooded millionaires, however, stables and outbuildings were not for cosseting pigs and cooing over baby lambs but for housing their sleek and well-groomed horseflesh. Fox hunting was the first sport to have caught the Newporters' fancy, its social qualifications verified by the view-hallooing in the English county society. That pursuit, undeterred by Oscar Wilde's frosty epigram about the unspeakable harrying the inedible, would engage the gentry of Newport for many decades.

Fox hunting began as far back as Bishop Berkeley's time, when he wrote in a letter to England, "We heard the confused noise of the opening of the hounds, the winding of horns, and the shouts of the country squires."

And one of those colonial squires, a Mr. Hazard, recalled that "every member of the family had his own particular horse and servant, and rarely rode unattended by a servant to open gates and take charge of the horse. Carriages were unknown, and the public roads were not so good, nor so numerous as at present. The fox chase with hounds and horns, fishing and fowling were objects of enchanting recreation. . . ."

Shortly after the Civil War, when all the new war-profit money began rolling into Newport, the social aspects of fox hunting were rediscovered. To those unacquainted with the hot pulsations of sporting blood, there may seem something a trifle one-sided about a horde of pink-coated people on horseback following a pack of fifty hounds to track and harry one small fox to his den; something nauseating about the trophy of the chase being a bloodstained brush detached from the body of the object of that unequal contest. Such considerations would not weigh heavily on a man who had made his millions selling leaky vessels to the United States Navy or faulty rifles to the Union army. Anyway the arbiters of such matters insisted that fox hunting was the premier sport of the English and European aristocracies, and what was good enough for a duke ought to be good enough for an American millionaire.

Undeniably there was a pageantry, a pictorial gloss to fox hunting that made it more esthetically appealing than kicking a soccer ball around a muddy field. Maud Howe Elliott recaptured the spectacle in 1883 in a letter to her raffish Uncle Sam Ward:

"We all went up to the great hill behind the house and watched the hunt sweep by. At the rendezvous we found a large group of riders, all well mounted and well got up, the majority wearing pink coats. The huntsmen were busy with the hounds, a fine pack imported from Buckinghamshire; the hunters talking and laughing, walking their horses or tightening their girths for the long run. In the open space of the grove, hundreds of carriages filled with spectators were assembled; more were arriving every moment. The horns of a coach sounded merrily in the distance, and presently a drag, driven by an injured polo player, his crutches conspicuously displayed beside him, rolled into the grove." All that colorful pageantry across field and stream, over stone walls and through the woods, ended with the small terrified figure of the fox standing in bewilderment on a hillside. "When the pack was close upon him he realized what it all meant—that it was to take his miserable life that all these brave men, delicate women, hounds and horses, had come out on this bright summer afternoon. He realized it, but too late even to try to escape. He looked about him over a strange country with fields on either side, and, seeing how hopeless it was, stood quite still, looking at the pack. He gave one great cry as the teeth of the foremost hound fastened on his throat. All was over, and in something less than sixty seconds the belle of the day hung the brush of the fox on the pommel of her saddle."

It was not the newly organized Society for the Prevention of Cruelty to Animals, or any humane revulsion at blood sports, that brought fox hunting to an end around Newport but the local farmers. They were no docile yeomanry such as in England and Europe who watched their fences ripped down and their fields of growing crops trampled by the gentry. A Rhode Island farmer, with all the "stubborn Rhody" tradition behind him, did not merely tug his forelock and grin bashfully when the hunters rode over his fields. To him they were not the lords of creation but a pack of rich idlers. "This aristocratic pastime," as Maud Elliott wrote, "is a forced importation, not a natural development, and will, I think, die like an exotic in an unfriendly soil."

The farmers around Newport soon demonstrated that they

weren't going to put up with a sport no better, to them, than
organized trespassing. One farmer who was reminded that
members of the Newport hunt had undertaken to compensate
him and his fellows for any damage done his property replied,
"That's so. They undertake to do it, but they don't undertake to
pay you for the time it takes to get the money out of them. I don't
want to have my daughter's flower bed and the bit of lawn that
the children keep green and clean in front of the house all trod
down. I haven't time to go after them a dozen times to get the
money to repair the damage, and when I do, it don't pay me. It
don't make the flowers grown again. Do I want them on my
grounds? I told them no, civilly, but they come twice—paid no
more attention to me than if I hadn't spoke at all."

. The summertime gentry were, however, given pause when the
farmers organized and announced they would take counter-
action, not necessarily in the courts, against mounted trespassers.
The ardor of the chase was cooled by visions of a hunter
confronting, not a bewildered fox dumbly awaiting the coup de
grâce, but a ring of enraged smallholders armed with pitchforks
and brush hooks—that would have been adding a dash too much
of the spice of danger.

By then, in any case, the summer colony had turned to
another and even more spectacular pastime. Coaching was much
more expensive too; you had to be able to afford a coach, four
trained horses, with attendant grooms and stable boys, not
merely a horse and a pink coat. It was brought to Newport by
James Gordon Bennett and members of the Belmont Clique who
introduced others to the niceties of the sport. Being a good
"whip" meant you had to observe the proper form, it wasn't
simply a matter of sending four horses and a coach bucketing
down the road. You had to wear a silk topper, a large
boutonniere, bright green coat with gilt buttons, yellow-striped
waistcoat and patent-leather boots like Mr. Pickwick. If you were
a "howling swell," you also fastened a bunch of artificial flowers
to the throatlatch of each horse.

Soon the roads around Newport were churned into dust clouds
as reckless coachmen raced each other and made strollers leap

for their lives. Soon the farmers around Newport, often driven off the pike by speed-maddened coachmen and their plunging steeds, were as outraged by them as they had been by the fox hunters. Commodore Bennett, of course, outdid everyone else in breakneck driving; once he seriously endangered the future birth of Winston Churchill. Leonard Jerome's daughter and Churchill's mother, Jennie Jerome, went out coaching with Bennett one afternoon and came home to confess that "we came to grief and were nearly killed" when Bennett took a corner on two wheels and overturned the coach.

Most wealthy Newporters, however, took to milder versions of coaching in the belief that display of one's possessions was more pleasurable than risking your neck. Coaching of the sedate variety reached the height of its appeal during the nineties, long after Bennett and the more sportive "whips" had retired or expatriated themselves. One longtime resident of the resort recalled how "Newport assembled at noon to watch the gay four-in-hands clatter by with the tooting of horns, the cracking of whips, the jingle of chains. It was a brave sight."

The horse, as Richmond Barrett pointed out, was an integral part of the fashionable scene, "as important as his mistress's Paris gowns and jewels in the lavish parade of fashion." No latterday Rolls Royce or Duesenberg, it was boasted by the resorts' old-timers, could match in splendor one of those beautifully crafted carriages with four perfectly drilled horses between the shafts and stepping out with a pride that equaled their owner's.

What had been a rather daring sport had been tamed to a ritual as intricate and tradition-bound as an evening with one of the crustier empresses of Byzantium. From the marble cottages on Bellevue Avenue and Ocean Drive, through the immense wrought-iron gates, would issue the carriages of the Astors, Vanderbilts, Goelets and their satellites bearing the ladies of those houses, eyes glazed from long and formal luncheons, out on their afternoon calls. There was the incredibly solemn routine of leaving one's calling cards at residences qualified for the honor; *your* footman gave *her* footman a bit of pasteboard; you swept on to the next great house, and the social contract was maintained.

To at least one young Newporter, Cornelius Vanderbilt, Jr., it was puzzling that most of an afternoon had to be wasted "showering the colony with our calling cards when we had already nodded and spoken to our friends several times since breakfast."

Yet he and his sister, along with his equally disgusted father, had to join Mrs. Vanderbilt in the dress parade every day. "How vividly I can recall the tedium of those occasions when, proceeding at a snail's pace in a shiny black victoria and clutching our hateful card cases in spotless white gloves, we accompanied Mother on this sacred ritual. At each imposing entrance, a Vanderbilt footman would step off the carriage and deliver our cards to the front door. We seldom alighted ourselves, as it was considered a *faux pas* to be found at home—everyone was out dropping cards at everyone else's house.

"For two hours in the velvet-upholstered carriage we were not allowed to lounge, or slump, or cross our legs. My cards, at the age of nine, read 'Master Cornelius Vanderbilt Junr.' Nor would Mother ever tolerate my changing the English abbreviation of 'Junior' to the American 'Jr.' . . . Father's boredom on these expeditions matched my own. However, he soon developed the habit of disappearing to his boats or club just before the calling hour began. . . ."

Exchanging bits of cardboard kept the ladies out of mischief for about an hour, then the coaching parade began. A wide array of equipages was on display, some of the summer people having as many as twenty different kinds of horse-drawn vehicle in their carriage houses. Clip-clopping up Bellevue Avenue and out along Ocean Drive were *demi-daumonts*, dogcarts, victorias, landaus, phaetons, barouches, four-in-hands; just about everything on wheels except droshkies and Conestoga wagons. The afternoon drive-cum-exhibition was a stately occasion, patterned as precisely as a quadrille, down to the last liveried footman. The Vanderbilt crew wore maroon coats; The Mrs. Astor's coachmen, her personal shade of blue, which may or may not have been made by Central European elves. Coachmen sat stiffly in their boxes with expressionless faces, as though each held a royal flush; the ladies bowed to each other if such recognition was warranted by social standing. One Newporter recalled:

"The entire fifteen-mile circuit of the afternoon drive was a sort of horse-shoe ring where the summer colony exhibited themselves and their equipages; the competition was just as keen as at the Casino, too, though there was no distribution of blue, red, yellow and white ribbons at the close of the daily event and no prize money for the footmen to pocket. Every entry in the unofficial show was of pristine splendor. The ensemble was perfect, down to the last minute detail—the short manes braided just so, not a hair of a clubbed tail out of place, every crinkled rosette in its time-honored position."

To the onlooker it appeared that the whole coaching parade on a sunny afternoon had been unpacked from a bandbox. It looked like a set of toys. Everything from the polished hides of the horses to the black boots worn by the coachmen had a glittering sheen. The phaetons and victorias were so perfectly waxed and polished they were almost blinding. And the toylike illusion was maintained by the stiffness, the almost lifeless composure with which servants, masters and mistresses displayed themselves. The idea was to appear as aloof, as haughtily disinterested in the spectacle as if you had joined the procession by accident.

"Newport fairly reeked of horseflesh," as one resident remembered. Particularly from the direction of Coggeshall Avenue, a back street which served as the mews of Newport. The stables belonging to the various estates were no mere barns but large, solidly built piles of brick and stone, some of them the size of railroad terminals, all dedicated to the proposition that the horse would always be the linchpin in the transportation system. They were inhabited by the handsomest horseflesh in the country and attended by a swarm of grooms and stableboys.

The horse bought by one of the wealthier summer residents was a fortunate animal. He was fed and quartered in a style fitting his owner's station. Zoophilia, it is evident, was rampant among Newporters, whose animals fared better than, say, many of the occupants of slum tenements they owned and managed as absentee landlords. After a visit to the horse-fancying O.H.P.

Belmont's estate Belcourt, Julia Ward Howe wrote one of her daughters:

"It is a most singular house. The first floor is all stable, with stalls for some thirteen or more horses, all filled, and everything elaborate and elegant. Oh! To lodge horses so, and be content that men and women should lodge in sheds and cellars!"

True enough, the ground floor of Belcourt was given over to stables because Belmont couldn't bear not to have his horses under the same roof with him. The stalls had been designed by Richard Morris Hunt, with all modern conveniences laid on. The horses were provided with changes of equipment for morning, afternoon and evening, and at night they bedded down on white linen sheets embroidered with the Belmont crest in gold thread. On the floor above, in the salon, were two of Belmont's favorite horses stuffed by a taxidermist and mounted by two figures in armor.

Not all Newporters went to such lengths of cossetting their horses, but one of the Vanderbilts' stables did have gold name plates over each stall.

One of the great events late in the season was the annual Horse Show at the Casino for three days in September. Here, too, the principle of exclusivity prevailed. The nabobs and their families sat in boxes above the tanbark of the arena and seemed, according to one observer, to be "hermetically sealed" off from the hoi polloi in the grandstands. The price of the boxes tended to keep them exclusive, $100 for one in the front, $75 for one in the rear. The boxes would be noisy with the chatter of people who had little more to concern them than the imminent return to country houses up the Hudson, town houses in Manhattan, autumnal retreats to Hot Springs or White Sulphur, or hunting lodges in the Carolinas.

A certain amount of distant cordiality was permitted two classes of nonsocialites that constituted a necessary auxiliary to the breeding and showing of horses. One was the dealers, sharp little men who all seemed to have been ex-jockeys, who lounged against the white fence enclosing the oval ring of the arena. The other was the professional horsewomen, not quite accorded the status of ladies but treated with a "sort of blurred unfocussed friendliness" because they showed off the accomplishments of the Newport thoroughbreds. The horsewomen, of course, rode side-saddle and many were such graceful figures swaying on their mounts as they rode around the ring that they were regarded as temporary possessions as admirable as an old master.

Two special favorites of the horsey set were a Mrs. Beach and her daughter Belle, who were wittier and more entertaining than most people the wealthy met in their great houses. They had devoted their lives to riding. Late in life Mrs. Beach fell critically ill and was said to be dying; it was during the Madison Square Garden horse show, in which Belle, for once, was riding a mare the Beaches had acquired and trained themselves. Belle won a blue ribbon, her mother recovered within three months and returned to the tanbark arenas for twelve more years.

Another horsewoman, almost socially acceptable, was the beautiful Mrs. Rasmussen, who caught the eye of a Providence brewer named Walter Hanley. The new Mrs. Hanley then acquired a large stable of her own, but if she hoped for recognition as a social equal, she was disappointed. The moment she stopped being a professional rider she became a nonperson as far as fashionable Newport was concerned.

Yachting, of course, was foremost among Newport's sporting activities. With the reaches of Narragansett Bay and the open sea beyond, and a fine roadstead shared with the less frivolous craft of the U.S. Navy, Newport was regarded as the finest yachting harbor on the Atlantic coast. Into its harbor sailed such lordly vessels as James Gordon Bennett's *Lysistrata*; the Commodore's conversion to steampower made it respectable not to sail entirely under canvas. Other oceangoing floating palaces included J. Pierpont Morgan's *Corsair*, the Astors' *Nourmahal*, the Leeds' *Noma*, the Wideners' *Josephine*, the Drexels' *Sultana*, Arthur James Curtiss' *Aloha*. Almost at once, it seemed, the Newport harbor was full of yachts riding at anchor, spreading their white wings out on the bay, joining in competition for the cup offered by Commodore Bennett in 1871 for an international race on a course off Benton's Reef Lighthouse. Various other moguls offered cups, Newport eventually became the scene of the America's Cup races and the yachting capital of the world. Mainly because of the annual yacht races the Newport dateline still appears in the world's newspapers.

From the beginning, the sport was encrusted with gentlemanly tradition; a caste system was firmly established, and rules promulgated that no sportsman would break any more than he would tread a polished desk in riding boots. And yet it was often difficult to keep out the muckers. Soon after the yachts of the mighty appeared in Newport harbor, according to a yachting historian, "Mr. Thomas Dolan's houseboat also worked her way along the shore to be with the anointed."

The Irish surname, and the fact its owner had ventured from proletarian Providence, alerted Newporters to the danger of pushy vulgarians intruding into their yacht basin.

To maintain gentlemanly standards, therefore, the cost of anchoring among Newport's yachting elite became prohibitive for all but millionaires. Even some of the wealthiest objected to the fees charged for anchorage. Mrs. Richard Cadwalader of Philadelphia could afford the largest yacht in the world, the 407-foot *Savarona*, with its Persian rugs, tapestry-hung cabins, gold-plated faucets and full-sized pipe organ. But you didn't stay rich by throwing your money around, and Mrs. Cadwalader was affronted by the Newport yacht basin's fees, always anchored outside the harbor and maintained her yacht in ports abroad where the tariffs were lower.

Other summer people spared no expense in showing off their vessels during the Newport season. Pierre Lorillard, one of the pioneer yachtsmen, built a pier over the reefs so he could bring his yacht *Rhoda* right up to the bottom of the lawn of his estate, stroll out of his house and board the boat.

Yachting became an obsessive pursuit with some of the summer sailors, not least of all William Douglas, who had taken up the sport under the tutelage of Commodore Bennett. Mrs. J. Borden Harriman was particularly impressed by his devotion. "Once," she recalled, "in a half gale of wind and rough seas, in a

Goelet Cup race off Newport, when all hands on his yacht *Arrow* were recruited to haul on the mainsheet, he stuffed into his pocket without reading some telegrams from his broker that had come just as he was leaving the anchorage. Not until the race was over did he pull them out of his pocket—damp, undecipherable wads. By the time he had telegraphed to New York 'repeat,' the market had broken and he was the loser by many thousands of dollars. 'A great race. Worth it. Couldn't be bothered, with a wind like that,' was all he said, chuckling."

In the summertime it seemed that most of the mightiest figures on Wall Street were aboard their yachts riding the gentle surf in Newport harbor, that almost every man who owned a seat on the stock exchange also wore the white cap and blue blazer of the seasonal skipper.

This confluence of speculative finance and maritime elegance caught the attention of William R. Travers, the "stammering wit" of the Belmont clique and himself a wealthy stockbroker. Sometimes Travers' remarks were a trifle too close to the bone for the comfort and self-esteem of his colleagues.

Once at a Newport yacht race, Travers cocked his head attentively as the winners of the various events were announced.

"B-b-but where," he innocently inquired, "are the *customers'* yachts?"

Despite such occasional intrusions as that of Mr. Dolan's houseboat, the Newport yachtsmen managed to maintain social standards as lofty as those of their wives. It wasn't enough to own a yacht. The money to buy the vessel had to be sanctified by having been "in the family" for a generation or two. Self-made men were not welcomed. Thus, Sir Thomas Lipton, the persistent British yachtsman who contested unsuccessfully for so many years for the America's Cup, was roundly snubbed. As a tea merchant, he was "in trade"; groceries lacked the cachet of railroads or coal mines, and The Mrs. Astor's famous writ proscribing people who had enriched themselves in the homelier commodities ran right down to the Newport docks.

The Newport sportsmen became so secure in their social exclusiveness that eventually they could afford a little satire at

their own expense, and they organized a mock-yacht club called
the Kat-Bote Club with a fleet of seventeen imaginary vessels
and an anthem whose last stanza went:

> There goes the *Myrtle*,
> And here goes the *Turtle*,
> And now comes the *Thirsty Maud*.
> They never will be sunk
> While the owners keep drunk;
> And so let us praise the Lord!

The Kat-Bote Club's forty-nine members included some of
Newport's leading sportsmen. One of its bylaws read: "Uniforms
shall consist of a kilt, a tam o'shanter, and a life-preserver;
officers of the highest rank may wear spurs." William Hunter
was the Fleet Captain, Winthrop Chanler the Cabin Boy,
Frederick Garrettson the Powder Monkey, Neilson Howard the
Able-bodied Seaman, Pierre Lorillard the Whistling Boy, Isaac
Townsend the Ballast, Daniel Gearing the Fog Horn, E. J.
Berwind the Coal Heaver, Oliver Belmont the Captain of the
Horse Marines, and Herman Oelrichs the Lord Chief High
Steward.

Aside from yo-ho-hoing over rum bottles, the members of the
Kat-Bote Club took a serious interest in deep-sea fishing.
Oelrichs' prowess in landing huge fish was celebrated among his
fellow clubmen, particularly after he claimed that he could land
a man as easily as a marlin. One member challenged that claim,
and a wager resulted. The challenger, an expert swimmer, was
fitted out with a special cap to which a swivel and ring were
attached, and swam out from Bailey's beach. Oelrichs stood on a
raft and angled for the challenger, whom he gaffed in short order
and hauled to the raft.

With experts like that available, the outings of the Clambake
Club, to which most members of the Kat-Bote Club belonged,
were succulent affairs. "It was indeed a delight," as one nostalgic
survivor of those outings on the shore recalled, "to sit and pick
from the seaweed the clams, lobsters, fish (wrapped in cheese-

cloth), corn, sweet potatoes, and all the other good things that were contained in the big round oven. . . . A very distinguished soldier of the Civil War rode out to the bake many years ago. In the course of the afternoon he ate so many clams, etc., that he could not mount his horse. We had to bed him down on the clamshells. . . ."

Tennis Week in August, however, was the highlight of the sporting scene, if only because of the fact that the game had more interest for spectators than watching bits and pieces of a yacht race from the shore. More formally it was the United States National Lawn Tennis Tournament, which was held at the Newport Casino. The smooth well-tended turf of its courts—so much more elegant than hard-packed clay, therefore more exclusive, therefore the form of tennis favored by Newport— served as the birthplace of lawn tennis in America. The first tournament was held shortly after James Gordon Bennett built, then gave up personal direction of, the Casino.

The players in the first tournament match played in 1881 were Richard D. Sears and Dr. James Dwight of Boston. "They wore knickerbockers, blazers, caps, belts, woollen stockings and rub-ber-soled canvas shoes," one survivor of the occasion recalled. "There was no grandstand. The spectators—we were not a gallery until later—sat on camp-stools in a space roped off outside the courts. The figure that stands out clearest in my memory is that of Dicky Sears, an endearing youth who had the curious habit when he played of letting his tongue hang out of his mouth like a little dog's!"

Usually held in the third week of August, Tennis Week was a brilliant occasion, not only *pour le sport* but—as always in Newport—as the stage setting of a fashion show, an arena in which social aspirations could be tested, promoted or deflated, a place to display one's prominence.

Lawn tennis, of course, was a game for gentlefolk then. There were no professionals such as were a necessary part of the Horse Show. That some slum kid who happened to have the coordina-tion, the painfully acquired skills to swing a racket in competition would appear on the courts of the Casino was starkly unthinkable. The proper pedigree was the first, if not the only qualification. Thus, the impeccable Sears family of Boston long held sway at the Newport tournaments, Dick Sears winning the championship eight years in succession, the celebrated all-around sportswoman Eleanora Sears also a star of Tennis Week. Sears would always stand for tennis in its most genteel phase, and as an obituary on his death in 1943 put it, he "represented the era of ruffles and parasols, roped-off lawns and sunny afternoons, lopsided tennis bats and the genteel pat of the ball against languid strings."

By 1890 the Newport tournament had attained national fame and the Casino's board of governors had to buy a grandstand from the Barnum & Bailey circus to accommodate all the spectators. It was a rickety affair, and the Casino's membership protested that it would never do, that it was all too easy to imagine some brittle old dowager plunging to her death through the open spaces. To one observer it looked like a giant typewriter with people perching on its keys. At least some of the premonitions were justified, according to Richmond Barrett. "Women were forever dropping their long white kid gloves into the wide-open spaces beneath them. The trips up the narrow aisles—and down again—were hazardous adventures. One morning Mrs. John Jacob Astor caught her heel at the very top of the grand-stand, lost her balance and fell the whole length to the ground. . . . Mrs. Astor happened to be the most beautiful woman of that period of beautiful women . . . before she was thirty she had been unofficially deified." A lesser female would have been severely shaken, if not physically then in her morale, by cartwheeling down a crowded grandstand. But breeding, as the well-bred insist, will tell. Mrs. Astor simply picked herself up and strolled nonchalantly toward the exit as though nothing had happened.

Within a few years the tournaments at the Casino had obtained the imprimatur of the resort's social rulers, and year after year the Belmonts, the Astors, the Goelets, the Vanderbilts occupied the same seats, which they claimed by right of birth.

"Indeed," as Barrett recorded, "the seats in the Casino grandstand had soon become as much a part of the family tradition as the red plush parterre box at the Metropolitan, the pew at Trinity and the shaving mug at Merker's barber shop. Not that a block of seats cost an outrageous sum of money. . . . The question was, not how much a man must pay but how under the sun he could get hold of one of those rare collector's items."

During the years in which the tournament became more of a national event, though kept strictly under the patronage of the Casino's board of governors, the Casino opened up its entry lists to some extent and admitted what were called "carpetbaggers" to the Tennis Week competition. Most of them were college boys, not yet generically typed as "tennis bums," and so the sport was not entirely abandoned to the democratic spirit. There were a certain roughneck tendency to be observed among the outsiders who came to Newport only to participate in the tournament. Gladiatorial traits cropped out one year when it rained a solid week before the tournament was scheduled to begin. The court on which the championship matches were to be played had turned into a small lake, which had to be pumped out by the Newport fire department. And day after day the start of the tournament was delayed until it was judged the court was fast and dry enough.

The players had to make the best of the delays, but the drumming rain apparently got on their nerves. Alcohol helped relieve the boredom but made the players a trial for the Casino's board of governors, who quartered them at the Casino. The best players, it seemed, were also the most rambunctious drinkers. A local historian admitted his bewilderment over how few compound fractures resulted from the drinking bouts that occupied most of the players while they waited for the court to dry out. The governors watched in horror as players tumbled down the staircase into the entrance corridor. One day a National Doubles champion leaped out of the window overlooking the courts and landed astride an iron lantern below.

A squad of masseurs was enlisted to knead the alcohol out of the players and the kinks out of their muscles. Somehow the visiting athletes were pounded into shape equal to their tasks on the tournament court, though it was noted that the play that year lacked some of the championship style. Treasured around Newport for years was a newspaper clipping that obliquely reported on the reason for the players being off-form. "So-and-so was not up to his usual form yesterday," it observed. "He was suffering from a recurrence of an old elbow complication."

Despite such opportunities for wassail, the young men who traveled the tennis circuit eventually began to resent the Newport atmosphere. Tennis Week in Newport had assumed the aspect of a command performance. Players newly rising from the middle class wondered why it should be deemed such an honor to display themselves before the quality folk, and resented the patronizing attitude of their hosts. They began to clamor for a change of venue for the national championship matches, to campaign for the Forest Hills (Long Island) West Side Tennis Club as the site of the tournament. The New York City suburb would provide a more egalitarian atmosphere and better accommodations for the thousands of people who came to Newport from the "outside" and found no hotel rooms available. Tennis as a mostly social occasion, as a summertime distraction for the very rich, was passing out of style.

Other symptoms of disorder were to be noted by the patrons of lawn tennis in its most elegant phase when the urchins from Newport's meaner streets who served as ball boys at the Casino went out on strike for higher wages. On the morning of a championship match they marched in a column of twos to the Casino and delivered their ultimatum: more money or an immediate strike. "Get the hell out of here this minute or we'll have the cops put you out," the manager told their spokesman. The Casino management then put in a rush call to the parish priests who recruited their ball boys and asked for a new, less unruly batch to be sent over. The new "shackers" were hastily drilled in their duties and the championship play was not disrupted. Yet that afternoon it seemed to fashionable Newport as though they were hearing echoes of the violent clamor for social change heard elsewhere in the land from the Knights of

Labor, the socialist and anarchist firebrands, and radicals of every hue. It didn't contribute to the joy of the occasion when the lazy afternoon air was rent by cries of "Scab, scab!" from the striking ball boys who sat on the wall of Commodore Bennett's estate across the street from the Casino. The Casino's patrons could only attribute the unmannerly demonstration to the fact that the striking ball boys were Irish and therefore not properly respectful to their betters.

The ball boys' uprising, however, was a feedback from greater events stirring in the land—a symptom of the feeling that the rich and powerful had been overexercising their privileges. Even such a perfectly insulated enclave as Newport could, and increasingly would, become aware of a disgruntlement that would result in a federal income tax, child labor laws, legislation protecting the unions, and other threats to the serenity of those long carefree summers on the Rhode Island strand.

If the coming of twilight was sensed by the more aware summer people, it could always be dispelled by another dip into the sporting life. There were always plenty of distractions, new toys, new games. If Tennis Week began to lose its luster, there was that new and more spectacular pastime—automobiling—to be considered. At the turn of the century, of course, the automobile was a sporting machine and there were only a few hundred in the whole country. No one suspected what the internal combustion engine would do to such graceful interludes in daily life as the afternoon carriage drive.

Automobiling rapidly became a craze when O. H. P. Belmont imported an automobile from France, Harry Payne Whitney stocked his stables with several of the machines and John Jacob Astor began selling his horses to make room for his horseless carriages. Within a few years the more dashing Newport males were competing in races on the beach at which they sometimes attained speed above ten miles an hour. The obstacle race held on the grounds of the Belmont estate on September 7, 1899, was long remembered, mostly for the distinction of the contestants. The course was laid out at Belcourt with flags marking the route between dummies of horses, children, nurses, maids, policemen. The idea was to make the best time possible without running over any of the dummies.

O. H. P. Belmont piloted the first automobile with Mrs. Stuyvesant Fish at his side. They were followed by James W. Gerard and Mrs. Belmont in a vehicle smothered in blue hydrangeas. Even The Mrs. Astor participated in a third car with Harry Lehr at the wheel. Queen Caroline brought her lapdog along as their mascot. Belmont, Gerard and Lehr all performed rather poorly and knocked down dummies right and left, but a fourth car with Colonel John Jacob Astor, who thirteen years later might have wished he was steering the *Titanic* the night it was gored by an iceberg, was piloted with a skill that gave Astor the honors of the day.

9.

NAVAL NEWPORT

FROM EARLY in the nineteenth century on, Newport figured in larger national considerations than mere social strategy. The cerebrations of admirals may be less complex than those of a society leader plotting her conquests, but they can be of greater moment. Certainly that was the case of the Navy's small intellectual core, which was located in Newport after the establishment of the Naval War College. It was not too much to claim, in fact, that America's imperialistic role, particularly in the Caribbean and the western Pacific, was charted in Newport, in the classrooms and offices of the large gray stone building that housed the war college, while all around the most frivolous, the most thoughtless people in America engaged in their summer frolics.

Newport hostesses would complacently remark that the Navy established itself there to provide "extra men" for their parties. Young officers were presumed to be gentlemen, were usually presentable and often came of "good" families. They were more socially adaptable than other spare parts available on the summer scene. Navy and society did not quite fuse, because of the disparity in earnings between a lieutenant and a steel magnate, but they were on an amiable footing. Each gained from the other. Young officers found their social lives made livelier and hostesses could always find plenty of recruits for their stag lines.

It wasn't social considerations but Newport's location on Narragansett Bay that had long attracted the attention of military and naval planners. A fort designed by a French engineer was built on the site of Fort Adams in 1799, to be replaced a quarter-century later by the larger installation. During the Civil War, the Naval Academy at Annapolis was deemed too close to the swaying battle line and was evacuated to Newport for the duration. Both the Army and the Navy kept sizable contingents in Newport, the Army at Fort Adams, the Navy at increasingly important installations nearby. Mrs. Maud Howe Elliott recalled that in the 1870's Fort Adams was an important part of the town's social life. "On Thursday afternoons the *beau monde* gathered there to watch the drill, to promenade the ramparts, to dance with the officers. We wore large Gainsborough hats and carried parasols. Girls in full white muslin dresses flitted about the grim cannon like gay butterflies. We were still so near to the Civil War that soldiers and sailors were the most desirable escorts. . . . On special occasions the officers hired the ferryboat *Jamestown* to carry us back and forth. It was impossible to get the girls to go home until the sunset gun boomed, the bugle sounded retreat, and the colors were lowered."

But it was the Navy rather than the Army, given Newport's maritime history, that the resort took to its heart. The heroic brothers, Oliver Hazard Perry ("We have met the enemy, and they are ours") and Commodore Matthew Perry, whose tiny black-hulled squadron opened the ports of Japan to Western trade, were "Newport boys" and Newport never forgot it. Matthew Perry's daughter married the financier August Belmont, an early comer to the Newport scene, and it was Belmont who erected the statue of Perry in Touro Park that was sculpted by J. Q. A. Ward and placed on a pedestal designed by Richard Hunt. But it was Oliver Hazard Perry whom Newport considered the greater hero, for his exploits on Lake Erie during the War of 1812, and several of his sailing masters were also Newport natives or residents.

About 1880 the Navy began moving into Newport in force. The Naval Torpedo Station was established on Goat Island, not far from the graves of twenty-six pirates who were captured by the British in pre-Revolutionary days, tried, convicted and hanged on one day between low tide and high tide. In 1881 Coasters' Harbor Island was ceded by the city and state to the federal government for the establishment of the Naval Training Station. Four years later came the establishment of the Naval War College.

A long line of distinguished naval officers, including most of the fleet commanders of World War II, would remember Newport and their duty at one or the other of its three installations as one of the gayer phases of their careers.

Most of Newport's naval importance was credited to Commodore Stephen B. Luce, whose chief professional interest was not in fighting great sea battles but in training and educating the officers and enlisted men who would fight them. Luce, it was justly written, "taught the Navy how to think."

As first commander of the training station, in 1881, he drilled newly enlisted men on the three vessels of the Training Practice Squadron, *Constitution*, *Saratoga* and *Portsmouth*, in their sea duties. Though not a professional educator, he saw that it took more than rigorous discipline to make a first-rate sailor. "Mental stimulus is necessary," he wrote, "to complete muscular development. A boy gladly expends much heat and energy in a game of baseball as would be required to saw a cord of wood; the latter would disgust him."

Commodore Luce not only improved training methods by viewing enlisted men as human beings rather than anonymous, faceless jack-tars scoured from the slums by recruiting officers, but displayed a civilized sense of humor not ordinarily associated with the quarterdeck. "Whenever Luce's squadron was maneuvering in the Bay," one of his admirers recalled, "he was solicited by the Smart Set to let his officers attend their big social functions. This irritated him, and when such an invitation came, he would anchor his ships far up the Bay and give orders that no officer could go beyond signal distance. Once, however, he was caught between two fires, for in running away from a Newport function he anchored within reach of another—in Providence. The humor of the situation appealed to him so, that he let everybody off duty go to the party, even going himself, and

entering the spirit of the occasion allowed his usual dignity to
give way to a boyish mood of fun."

Noting that Commodore Luce seemed to be shifting champagne into his bunkers as though refitting for a long dry cruise, a
friend of his declared, "Stephen, I believe you're tight."

"My dear fellow," the Commodore drawled, "if Stephen B.
Luce, how can Stephen B. Tight?"

The Commodore retired from active service at the age of
sixty-one but by then had persuaded the Navy Department to
establish the Naval War College in Newport with himself as its
first director. Annapolis, he had observed, succeeded in turning
out officers who could command a ship but few, if any, who could
maneuver squadrons, fleets and task forces against an enemy at
sea. A postgraduate school was needed to fit selected officers for
high command.

His concept of educating the fittest officers for high command,
of seeking out the Nelson type more scientifically than through
the hugger-mugger of naval politics, was sound enough to be
copied assiduously in succeeding years.* It developed just at the
time the United States was beginning to flex its muscles and
consider the possibilities of Manifest Destiny far from its own
shores. Under a drumfire of propaganda from the Navy League
and the then-omnipotent steel industry, succeeding administrations in Washington were bedazzled by the idea of whole fleets of
steel-hulled, heavy-gunned ships ranging the world as rivals of
the British navy. America had been at peace for twenty years
and was getting bored with it. Pacific archipelagoes and eastern
Asia beckoned.

Soon enough the U.S. was building its dreadnoughts and
searching for an imperialistic mission on which to employ them.
The rationale would come from its first consciously designed
think tank in Newport; the bureau chiefs in Washington would
operate the fleet-in-being while the intellectuals in Newport
pondered its future role, under all possible combinations of
circumstance, in their new hothouse on Narragansett Bay.

* The U.S. Army established its own war college in 1901, the Royal Navy a year
earlier. Germany, Japan and France followed suit with similar war colleges.

The first of Luce's classes met in the old Newport poorhouse in 1885, a humble setting soon to be replaced by a large new stone building. Among his first instructors were several notable men. Major General Tasker Bliss was borrowed from the Army; he served as American representative on the Supreme War Council during World War I. William McCarty Little was a retired Navy captain—"railroaded to the retired list," as one of his friends put it—whom Luce tapped for his faculty. It was Little who developed the "war game," in which large-scale naval operations could be conducted on a table with model ships, the modest beginning of the "games theory" that enchanted Washington during the 1960's. Many of the Navy's future leaders would learn the principles of deploying a fleet on Little's massive war-game table and would develop the tactics governing the great sea battles in the Pacific during World War II in the naval college's classrooms.

Luce's most striking choice for his faculty, however, was an obscure captain who had been relegated to routine commands on the China Station and elsewhere, in which he had failed either to distinguish or to disgrace himself. He was a dry-mannered, humorless, rather pedantic fellow whose habit of reading incessantly in his sea cabin won him the suspicion of his heartier fellow officers—Captain Alfred Thayer Mahan. Few men have registered such an impact on American history. His theories of how America should expand, must expand into distant areas through the employment of seapower, fired up Theodore Roosevelt, Henry Cabot Lodge and other political figures who provided the opportunity to test them in practice.

The seminal influence of the series of lectures which Captain Mahan delivered under the title of "The Influence of Sea Power upon History" can hardly be exaggerated. They provided the intellectual basis and political rationale for American expansion, the seedling from which grew the seizure of Cuba and Puerto Rico, the building of the Panama Canal, the conquest of the Philippines, the encroachment on the Asian mainland.

Their influence, however, grew slowly. The steel magnates who summered at Newport for many years were unaware that

only a short distance from their villas and yachts a deadly serious
man, dusted with chalk, gesturing with his pointer at the
methods by which Rome and Byzantium conquered their world
through the exercise of naval power, was going to make them
vastly more wealthy through the manufacture of armor plate and
gun barrels. Mahan's influence was purely local at first. Then
President Luce urged him to publish his lectures. His first book
was largely ignored in the United States, but was quickly
translated and became a strategic bible for the British sea lords,
the German Kaiser (who was inspired to begin building his own
High Seas Fleet), the Japanese admiralty. Only after Mahan
made triumphal tours abroad was his worth as an apostle of
geopolitics widely recognized in the United States. Captain
Mahan, who was to succeed Luce as president of the Naval War
College, rapidly became the darling of the Republican expan-
sionists, the inspiration of the Navy League and other pressure
groups urging the "expand or perish" doctrine.

The more influential Mahan and the shorebound intellectuals
at Newport became, the more jealousy and suspicion they
aroused in Washington. Old sea dogs, now encrusted with gold
braid, snorted indignantly at the idea of another Horatio Nelson
or John Paul Jones emerging, diploma in hand, from such an
academic atmosphere. You learned your business on a bridge, at
sea, not in a classroom mooning over Mercator's projection or
playing with toy fleets on a map table. The Navy Board, mostly
composed of sclerotic old admirals, denounced the Naval War
College as "too highbrow," and that was only the politest phrase
they used.

It managed to survive, however, largely owing to Mahan's
prestige and the roll of prophetic thunder that seemed to
underscore his pronouncements. They sent a quiver of apprehension through the nation's military and political establishments
when they pointed with increasing urgency to the danger of an
onslaught from newly awakening East Asia. Semi-Westernized
Japan, "opened up" by Matthew Perry's squadron, was gazing
across the Pacific with envious eyes on America's material
prosperity. "The history of the present century," Mahan wrote

from his ivory conning tower in Newport, "has been that of increasing pressure of our own civilization upon these older ones, till now, as we cast our eyes in any direction, there is everywhere a stirring, a rousing from sleep, drowsy for the most part, but real, unorganized as yet, but conscious that that which rudely interrupts their dreams of centuries possesses over them at least two advantages—power and material prosperity—the things which unspiritual humanity, the world over, most craves." Christianity, as well as battle fleets, must be reinforced. Twenty years before the Russian Revolution he was pointing in alarm to "the strength of Communism as an aggressive social force."

With Mahan as its intellectual figurehead, the Naval War College would survive through the decades and provide the theories for the sea battles which would engage the American Navy in two world wars. Most of the great naval leaders passed through its halls and lecture rooms. Ten years before he led the U.S. naval task forces in the Pacific a younger Captain William F. Halsey studied there and would recall that "few years in a naval officer's life are more pleasant than this one. It is restful because you have no official responsibilities, and it is stimulating because of the instruction, the exchange of ideas, the chance to test your pet theories on the game board. . . ." For the wives of married officers, apparently, it was less charming. When a young Navy bride asked her what impressed her most about Navy life, Mrs. Halsey snapped, "Buying and abandoning garbage cans all over the world."

During that same period, Fleet Admiral Ernest J. King, the Navy's member of the Joint Chiefs of Staff and therefore chief architect of the strategy employed against Japan in World War II, was also a captain being groomed for higher command at the Naval War College. In 1933 he and members of the Senior Course were preoccupied by the annual strategic maneuver, which climaxed their studies. They coolly, and prophetically, assumed that Japan would seize the Philippines and plotted on the war-game board how American forces would strike back. King, again prophetically, favored a flanking maneuver north of the Marshalls and Carolines and an all-out drive through the

Marianas. Thus, with the sounds of summer-colony frivolity all around them, the future leaders of the U.S. Navy would meditate on how to defend that sanctuary of pleasure, not on the yacht-strewn waters of Narragansett Bay but on horizons comfortingly distant, the length of a continent and an ocean away.

Newport continued through the years to be the Navy's favorite place for shore duty. Jonathan Daniels, who accompanied his father (Josephus Daniels, Secretary of the Navy in the Wilson administration), on a tour of the Atlantic bases, recalled in a memoir that Newport was a sailor's idea of heaven. "Naval officers were almost as welcome as diplomats at the big parties in the palaces along Bellevue Avenue and Ocean Drive. Most important, Narragansett Bay was the base of the fleet during the summer months. The intermarrying Navy brought its daughters to Newport to be near the congregation of young officers. Old admirals often went to Newport as they were later to move to California." *

Daniels suggested the reason why society and the Navy coexisted so amiably on the Newport shore. Each group was proud and rank-conscious; neither wanted anything from the other except a little casual socializing; they were parallel hierarchies with their own pecking orders. The Navy families married within their service, without trying to invade the palaces on Ochre Point in search of husbands or wives. Mrs. Rear Admiral felt quite as secure socially, with her respectful bevy of commodores' and captains' wives closed around her, as Mrs. Astor and Mrs. Fish with their attendant dowagers and debutantes. Her husband, with the sense of mission inculcated by Captain Mahan and the Navy League propagandists, felt himself quite as important and a hell of a lot more respectable than a Wall Street plunger or a Fifth Avenue clubman. Thus sustained, they could meet and mingle on roughly equal terms.

---

* Mrs. Harry Lehr recalled that her husband would call the naval base and ask the commanding officer, "Can you let me have five bridge players for tommorow at Mrs. Hamilton Twombley's?" or "Will you send a dozen dancing men for Mrs. Oliver Belmont's ball?"

Occasionally the Newport establishment would feel itself threatened by interference from Washington, where there was a lingering impression that the Naval War College was an expensive frivolity, that the Navy should concentrate on producing gunnery experts instead of strategists and geopoliticians. In 1893 President Grover Cleveland's Secretary of the Navy, Hilary A. Herbert, descended on Newport with the intention of closing out the war college, but Mahan and others equally eloquent persuaded him not to do so. Some years later Secretary of the Navy George von L. Meyer, in the Taft administration, grimly set out on the same mission. Fortunately for the war college, he traveled up the coast on a yacht. The voyage took three days. During it, some friend or agent of the war college suggested that Meyer relieve the tedium of the journey by reading Captain Mahan's *The Influence of Sea Power upon History*, a copy of which was produced with suspicious ease. Meyer was converted to Mahanism before the yacht docked at Newport.

In the Wilson administration, Secretary of the Navy Daniels also considered elimination of the war college from the naval budget. By the time he arrived in Newport, he had already knocked off a naval coaling station up the coast on Frenchman's Bay.

Daniels was a notorious teetotaler, who had forbidden liquor aboard all warships except for medical reasons. No more tots of rum, no more splicing of the main brace. His name was more than adequately cursed in the Navy's wardrooms. During his tour of the installation, he was escorted through the library and into a large alcove in which, as he would recall, "a bar was fitted up in a manner that would do credit to any saloon. A bartender with the regulation apron stood behind the counter."

The senior of a group of six escorting admirals asked Daniels what he'd like to drink.

"White Rock," the Secretary of the Navy replied.

Each of the admirals was asked a similar question.

"White Rock," each of them dutifully replied.

Daniels expressed amazement that the Navy, which had always associated grog with glory, had become so widely temperate. One elderly admiral who always had a triple ration of whiskey before lunch later explained his sudden preference for White Rock in Daniels' company: "I was damned if I was going to let any of you other fellows appear more temperate before the Secretary than me."

Naval and social Newport combined forces in 1917 when the United States joined the Allies and a sudden expansion of the Navy was required. Both factions were proud that Admiral William S. Sims, a graduate and former president of the Naval War College, and therefore regarded as a Newporter, took command of U.S. naval forces in European waters and conceived the convoy system, which successfully combatted the U-boat terror in the Atlantic. Society got a new thrill out of demonstrating its patriotic feelings. In the Preparedness Parade, one chronicler wrote, "all the active Red Cross workers marched in their uniforms, led by Elsie French Vanderbilt—a vision of grace and beauty, with her kindled face and gorgeous Titian hair." When the Army and Navy installations in and around Newport were flooded with recruits, "parish houses were turned into barracks; private houses were filled. Everyone who had a spare room took in a boy. Do what we could, not all could be comfortably housed. They suffered from the unaccustomed exposure. There was a serious epidemic of grippe; many of our boys died of it. . . ."

A bit later on, however, naval/social relations were strained quite severely when word reached Washington that morally "awful conditions" prevailed in Newport. Local homosexuals, it was reported, were preying on the servicemen—this at a time when only the most sophisticated people had any understanding of homosexuality or even any belief that such a thing existed.

The matter came to the attention of Secretary of the Navy Daniels and his undersecretary, Franklin D. Roosevelt. Daniels conferred with the governor of Rhode Island on the situation. As Daniels' son and biographer recorded, "Undoubtedly, the vice conditions there were bad but local officials, Daniels noted, were inclined to blame the Navy for conditions caused they thought by crowding and lack of adequate quarters. That conference may have been responsible for a note Daniels made a little later that a 'Secret Service man in Newport wrote a report quoting a gambler saying everything would be open soon for Governor Beekman had bought up Secretary Daniels.' "

Young Mr. Roosevelt was vastly amused that his puritanical chief should have been reportedly bribed to allow the "awful" conditions at Newport to continue.

His amusement soon evaporated when Daniels ordered him to assist in the cleanup around the naval stations. "Daniels had told him to stop and investigate conditions when he went in June to Cambridge to become a Harvard overseer. Franklin not only went but he was charged with approving the use of some sailors as decoys for the entrapment of homosexuals, a charge which was greatly to embarrass him later."

The war was soon over, and the amiable relations between Newport's two establishments were resumed, never to be disrupted again. The girls in their summer dresses, the young officers in their summer whites again promenaded on the long lazy afternoons; admirals and admirals-to-be fleshed out guest lists and agreed with their hosts that America, on recovering from the distractions of a European war, must resume its westward course and live up to the dictates of two of Newport's most distinguished residents, Bishop Berkeley and Captain Mahan. Newport looks out on the Atlantic, but it was the intellectual staging-area for the American incursions into the far Pacific and the Asian mainland.

Part Three

THREE QUEENS AND A JOKER

10.

THE PERILS OF SOCIAL CLIMBING

From the nineties to the first year of the First World War, the competition in Newport for social acceptance was so intense the resort sometimes seemed like an arena full of bloodied female gladiators. First there was the struggle to get in, socially, a process so intricate and full of potential disasters that Ward McAllister in his waning years advised aspirants to spend a few seasons in one of the lesser resorts as a training period for the ultimate test. Then there was the struggle to attain recognition as an equal, and finally the long hard climb toward a position from which you could dominate others. In her memoir of that quarter-century in Newport, which often resembled the autobiography of a general looking back over his wars, Mrs. John King Van Rensselaer shook her head sadly over the aspirants who spent "thousands of dollars for the mere privilege of writing their names in the membership book of a shabby old Casino."

The influx of new money and heightened aspirations around the turn of the century only intensified the competition for admittance to the dress circle. "Never before in Newport's history," wrote a society reporter in the summer of 1901, "have the lines between the smart set and the others been more closely drawn. A few women seem to lead the concourse like sheep and there is an almost riotous struggle of getting in and keeping other people out. Everyone is waiting to see if they will be asked to one of Mrs. Astor's dinners, the acme of social success. On the other hand, there is the hostess who, despite an unlimited supply of money and the backing of three influential women, seems to have met with nothing but disaster from the very commencement of her campaign. She is almost forced to go into the highways and byways to gather in her guests."

When Mrs. Cornelius Vanderbilt began her career as a notable hostess—at the height of which, it was estimated, she entertained 37,000 guests at her Newport and New York homes in a single year—she was thirty-one years old and, as the former Grace Wilson, knew just how to go about attaining supremacy. One art she practiced with finesse, as her son recalled, was that of dis-invitation. Cornelius Vanderbilt, Jr. would remember her spending several hours in bed every morning, during which the telephone "never stopped its shrill ringing. Mother had several numbers, both public and private, as well as a complicated set of signals which her secretary rang on the house phone from downstairs. 'No, no, I don't want to talk to her,' Mother would instruct the secretary. . . . Climbers were always trying to break into Mother's charmed clique; Mother dealt with them politely, but decisively. If the butler came out to announce someone she didn't care to see, Mother would tell him graciously, 'Please say that Mrs. Vanderbilt regrets that Mrs. B_____ is not on her calling list this afternoon.' "

The crushing effect of such a rebuff on an aspirant already trembling with the fear of rejection may easily be imagined. On those gloriously sunny afternoons, in that setting of incomparable ease and luxury, there was a long sequence of microscopic tragedies as hopeful ladies, dressed as carefully and elegantly as new money could buy, groomed for hours by hairdressers and ladies' maids, trouped from one great house to another to submit their petitions for acknowledgment of their social existence. One casual cuff from one of the lionesses whose favor they sought and they were sent sprawling back among the nonentities.

Grace Vanderbilt, as her son admitted, "could be very cold and stuffy when she chose." Like most women born to her queenly role, she felt no sympathy for the strivers, no compassion for those who sought to share what she acquired as a birthright. Her assertion of the divine rights of a society queen even extended to the President's daughter. Alice Roosevelt, whose hootchy-kootchy exhibition on the roof of Mrs. Vanderbilt's house, Beaulieu, had attracted so much attention, was one of her closest friends. Yet even Miss Roosevelt had to submit to Mrs. Vanderbilt on occasion. "Once they had a big row while Alice Roosevelt was at Beaulieu," her son wrote, "and Mother refused to speak to her until, at tea time, the President's daughter came crawling across the piazza on her hands and knees, like a contrite puppy." Lesser creatures, obviously, would be treated with even less consideration. The maintenance of the pecking order was of supreme importance.

Obviously it was difficult for the wife or daughter of a newly rich and important man to acknowledge the realities of the social process, the need for patiently standing in line, the realization that there were some things that would not yield to the sheer weight of a fortune. There was a veritable stampede of applicants for admission to the dress circle of the social theater in those years. At the time of the Civil War there were reportedly only three millionaires in the United States. By 1900 there were nearly four thousand, their millions acquired in the newer industrial areas such as steel, oil, railroads and mining. Like latterday Visigoths, they clamored under the walls and brandished before patrician eyes their yachts and carriages and jewelry and private railroad cars and game preserves, all of what Constance Cary Harrison termed "the very carmagnole of display that in earlier days was supposed to be the appanage of royalty alone." And there was genuine grief when they were informed that earlier claimants to social position had waited two or three generations for the family money to cool off, to stop giving off noisome whiffs of the methods by which it was acquired.

There was nothing frivolous about the selection process, as McAllister had informed his readers. An intense mental earnestness was required of those who presented themselves. For the postulant, as the New York *Times* remarked in its review of his book, "No suspicion that he is making a continental laughing stock of himself must disturb his mind." The social climber, though a figure of satire in the nineties and soon to be more crudely limned in the comic strips of the popular press, was engaged in a deadly serious business. He, or more likely she, provided a windfall for the neurologists, as the forerunners of psychoanalysis were known; "nerves" was the polite code name for melancholia and other forms of psychic disorder resulting from the strain and frustration of social competition. A social historian of note has remarked on how "Mrs. Astor and an extraordinary number of other Newport ladies" lost their minds at the end of their strenuously artificial lives.

Even for those families that had gained entry before the influx of new money, there was the constant strain of putting up a front, especially after the heads of those families, ill-equipped to deal with the new tigers on Wall Street, suffered reverses on the stock exchange. Michael Strange would recall the "strain and exhaustion and final indifference" that came over her father, Charles Oelrichs, when he fell among the losers and "we lived our increasingly nervous life—always in Newport in the summer" but in small rented houses or hotel rooms in Manhattan during the winter. "Oh, those cheap hotels to which we resorted on the fluctuations of the market! How dreadful were the rooms when we arrived with our bags in the evening, before Mama had time to order in palms from Waldey and Smythe, and throw charming tea-cloths over the tables and set out the *repoussé* silver tea service." She would also remember the bills from provisioners, dressmakers and other tradesmen "kept in neat stacks tied up with pink ribbon" and how her father "never knew how much he was in debt."

There was the anguish of the old families, with their feeble grasp of financial affairs, never having had to struggle for their money or concern themselves about where it came from, over their seeping resources, matched only by the agonies of the well-heeled but excluded. In Newport, she recalled, "Social ambition began to rear its perennially ludicrous visage on every side; and one morning shortly after breakfast I found a lady actually crumpled up on the stairs outside Mama's door, weeping bitterly because my good-natured mother had failed to procure for her an invitation to somebody's ball. 'How pretty she was,' I thought, crouched in the abandonment of her grief, and wearing

a lovely morning gown of pink taffeta and lace. . . . I began
take in the fact of 'failures' in Wall Street, and some puff of fev..
seemed to enter with my tired father on Friday evenings when we
met him at the Wickford boat . . . from the moment he stepped
wearily in the cab, there would be arguments heightening into
disputes, so that riding backwards on a small seat at my parents'
feet, I was filled with dejection."

The intensity of social pressures was compellingly recalled by
Edith Wharton in *The House of Mirth* from her memories of a
girlhood spent the year around in Newport. She ironically
conceded the intellectual poverty of that small fashionable world.
At the same time she conveyed the fascination of the kind of life
money, used with some taste, could buy. Even while sounding the
moralistic theme of the Biblical quotation that "the heart of the
fool is in the house of mirth," Mrs. Wharton brilliantly
recaptured the allure of possessions graciously preserved and
well-rubbed by time.

As she described the Gus Trenor's summer retreat Bellomont,
"The library was almost the only surviving portion of the old
manor house of Bellomont; a long spacious room, revealing the
traditions of the mother country in its classically-cased doors, the
Dutch tiles of the chimney, and the elaborate hob-grate with its
shining brass urns. A few family portraits of lantern-jawed
gentlemen in tie-wigs, and ladies with large head-dresses and
small bodies, hung between the shelves lined with pleasantly
shabby books; books mostly contemporaneous with the ancestors
in question, and to which the subsequent Trenors had made no
perceptible additions. The library at Bellomont was in fact never
used for reading, though it had a certain popularity as a
smoking-room or quiet retreat for flirtation. . . ."

Beneath the surface of those aristocratic lives, however, Mrs.
Wharton perceived the intrigue, envy, rivalry, and obsession with
position. *The House of Mirth* is a clinical study of Lily Bart, "blown
hither and thither with every wind of fashion," who is searching
for a rich husband. She makes her way through a Balzacian
throng of hostesses made secure by their husbands' wealth and
therefore capable of occasional generosity toward the adven-

turess; the thick-skinned climbers, the old Knickerbocker families stolidly assured of their social impregnability, the people on
the fringe who have neither been accepted nor rejected by the
inner circle. The literary fascination of Lily's quest for an
impregnable position of her own is heightened by her innate
taste, her awareness that this can't be the best of all possible
worlds. There are moments of revelation as when she sits at the
Trenors' long dinner table, almost smothered in orchids, with
Mrs. Trenor at one end in a multicolored blaze of jewelry and
her husband at the other greedily plunging his knife and fork
into a jellied plover—"and between the two, what a long stretch
of vacuity!" Lily acknowledged to herself the vulgarity of display,
the inevitable dangers of surfeit, but "she felt an affinity to all the
subtler manifestations of wealth."

There were many Lily Barts on the summer scene, not in
reality quite so perceptive as Mrs. Wharton's heroine, many of
them less secure in birth or beauty and lacking Lily's suppleness.

The cruelty with which "pushiness" could be punished was
illustrated by the case of a lovely young woman who had married
money but not social position. She managed to sublet a front-row
box at the Horse Show from a family in mourning. One
afternoon she sat alone and ignored in her box while other box
holders called to each other and chattered away over her head,
as though she were invisible. That night she was giving a party at
Berger's open-air dance pavilion just behind the Casino.

As newcomers entered their boxes, she rose from her seat, went
out in the aisle and buttonholed each one, plaintively asking,
"Are you coming to my party tonight?"

The politer ones she invited merely smiled noncommittally
and stepped past her, but the majority stared at her as though
she had invited them to feast with cannibals.

Not one person accepted her invitation, and she spent the rest
of the afternoon smiling brightly in her box and pretending to be
unaware of the outraged glares she received whenever she caught
the eye of her neighbors.

The lady left Newport shortly thereafter, but she was resolved
to return in triumph. The magnetic attraction of Newport's

social arena for women of a certain type was quite as strong as Wall Street's financial bearpit for their menfolk. She would not be dissuaded by the actual dullness of much of the resort's social discourse, nor dismayed by the views of a journalistic prole who visited Newport and reported in the New York *Morning Telegraph* that "This seaside Valhalla of swaggerdom is dull—dull as a Presidential message or a 'Punch' joke. It is also as hot—hot as a conning tower in a sea fight, and even dinner dances, barn dances and other species of hops, including the kind that comes in a mottoed stein at the Dutch pavilions, are boresome even to the death."

No, this lovely young woman persevered—she got rid of her first husband, who lacked both the sufficient wealth and the social qualifications that might have assisted her assault on the citadel, and remarried. Her second husband was the "most resounding catch in the entire summer colony," and when she returned to a front-row box at the Casino for the Horse Show she was smilingly greeted on all sides.

Richmond Barrett took note of another case which illustrated the pathos of ostracism, which was the method used to punish an erring female member of society with all the cruelty of a wild-dog pack against an offending bitch and her whelps. No matter what their transgressions, Barrett noted, men were rarely punished in a similar fashion. "A man who had become involved in a scandal was usually let off with a suspended sentence. Men in a summer resort have always been something of a luxury; to plow them under would hardly lead to the more abundant life."

As an example of what could happen to the woman who transgressed the standards of conduct imposed by her peers, he cited the case of a famous beauty who remarried when she was in her forties. Her second husband was one of those ambiguous self-styled noblemen from the Balkans, actually, as it later developed, a horse dealer. For that mésalliance, she was grudgingly forgiven because it was conceded that every woman was entitled to one misstep. When the marriage broke up, however, the ungallant horse coper took the stand and made lurid allegations about his wife's conduct. The social powers in

Newport agreed that his charges were undoubtedly baseless, but
they were spread over the front pages of the newspapers. The
lady had not willingly incurred the publicity, but she was
charged, however inadvertently, with having let her class down,
subjected it to the ridicule of the lower orders, which must always
be encouraged to believe that their betters led lives of impeccable
order and dignity.

Retribution was dealt her in the sunlit clarity of Tennis Week,
on the grounds of the Casino, where her humiliation would be
apparent to everyone and future transgressors warned. She
entered the Casino leading her Pomeranian, with her handsome
grown son on one side and her daughter on the other, both the
children of her first marriage. She walked to the steps of the
tennis court, then, as Barrett described the scene, "turned and
retraced her steps up the grounds, carrying herself with the
indolent floating grace for which she had been famous from
childhood. They made an arresting group . . . the mother,
indeed, was smiling; but it was a fixed smile, and there was a
look of almost feverish agony in her wide-open eyes. All around
her were the people who had been her friends for years; many of
them had been her playmates when she was a child. But not a
single person in the crowd had spoken to her! . . . One and all,
they slowly pivoted on their heels till their backs were squarely
turned to the transgressor. . . ."

To at least one disillusioned veteran of Newport summers, the
struggle to stay afloat on those frequently turbulent seas was
hardly worth the effort, if associating with millionaires was your
main purpose in life. Socially they were dullards, even if their
wives were capable of a certain amount of malicious wit. "The
Newport millionaires," wrote Elizabeth Drexel Lehr, "were for
the most part dull companions at a dinner table. They might
give evidence of brilliance of mind in Wall Street; in their homes
they gave none. They might hold up the market but they could
not prevent conversation from slumping heavily at their own
tables. They either talked of business or sat silent and apathetic
through course after course, too nerve-wracked by the strain of
building a fortune to be able to relax. They were prepared to

spend their last cent in gratifying the whims of their womenfolk, but they were incapable of amusing them themselves."

If the men found themselves on a sort of Procrustean bed of ambition that destroyed their ability to provide enjoyment for themselves or anyone else, and their wives were hag-ridden by observing the rules of the social competition, the lives of their female children were equally constrained and anxious. Even for a child of the Vanderbilts, there was nothing carefree about girlhood. Consuelo Vanderbilt recalled in her memoir:

"When I was seventeen my skirts almost touched the floor; it was considered immodest to wear them shorter. My dresses had high, tight, whalebone collars. A corset laced my waist to the eighteen inches fashion decreed. An enormous hat adorned with flowers, feathers and ribbons was fastened to my hair with long steel pins, and a veil covered my face. Tight gloves pinched my hands and I carried a parasol. Thus attired I went to Bailey's Beach for a morning bathe.

"There, clad in a dark blue alpaca outfit consisting of a dress under which there were drawers, and black silk stockings, with a large hat to protect me from the sun, I bobbled up and down over incoming waves. Needless to add that I was never taught to swim. Tennis and golf played no part in my education, but lessons in deportment cultivated a stately and measured walk. How full of tedious restraint was this artificial life! . . .

"As I grew older, discipline increased. I then saw little of my contemporaries, and spent my days at my studies. My mother disapproved of what she termed silly boy and girl flirtations, so the picnics at the farm ceased and my governess had strict injunctions to report any flighty disturbance of my thoughts. . . ."

The highlight of her day was having lunch with her mother and her friends, but she was repelled by the "arid social gossip women talk when in each other's company."

Even those gilded daughters of the rich who weren't kept virtually in purdah until they reached debutante status lived under a constant censorship of their elders.

Miss Emily Shaunberg, who was criticized for overrouging her face, coquettishly asked the visiting Lord Napier, "Isn't it disgraceful for people to say that I paint my face, Lord Napier?"

"If you would let me try," Napier crisply replied, "I think I could get a little off with my handkerchief."

11.

THE GREAT TRIUMVIRATE (I)

ON THE strength of their names—Tessie, Mamie and Alva—
they might have been three amiable upstairs maids. None of
them was a great beauty and only one inherited the manner of a
grande dame. Only one of the three was attached by marriage to a
really mammoth fortune. But together, as the Great Triumvirate,
as society-page writers referred to them, or as the Newport Board
of Social Strategy, as they sometimes playfully called themselves,
they dominated the quarter-century of Newport's golden age
from 1890 to 1914.

Tessie was more formally known as Mrs. Herman Oelrichs,
Mamie was Mrs. Stuyvesant Fish, and Alva was first Mrs.
William K. Vanderbilt and later Mrs. O. H. P. Belmont.

There were other contenders for the role Mrs. Astor had
played in solitary majesty for so many years, but none of them
attained the discretionary powers held, in usually amiable
concert, by the Great Triumvirate, which ruled less arbitrarily
than Queen Caroline and looked more to the fun-and-games
aspect of society and less to the stuffiness of grand balls and
endless reception lines.

There were "five or six grand duchesses" who vied for
dominance, as Mrs. J. Borden Harriman recalled in her memoir,
but none of them managed to displace the Great Triumvirate. It
took more than money or determination to reach the heights.
Tact, for one thing, now that even the Four Hundred was
becoming less autocratic. Mrs. Harriman remembered one of the
contending "grand duchesses" who came to a reception at her
grandfather's house with the explanation, "I meant to go to the

Vanderbilts but on the way I decided I wasn't dressed well enough and so I came here." That gaffe somehow was wafted across the Atlantic and figured in a celebrated *Punch* cartoon.

And there were others with the financial reserves, the position and the charm to achieve social leadership, but who lacked the ambition to dominate or even the taste for high living that was absolutely essential. There was Mrs. James R. Keene, for instance, whose husband was shudderingly known as "The Silver Fox of Wall Street," a plunderer whose operations on the stock exchange caused a long series of violent tremors. His speculative fortune grew by geometric proportions after he arrived from California with four million dollars acquired as a plunger on the San Francisco exchange. His own style fitted his robber-baron methods; he owned a large stable of racing horses, and instead of taking the Fall River boat as most weekend Newporters from New York did, he weekly chartered the steamer *Aeolus* to meet him at the rail terminus and take him back Monday morning. His wife, however, simply couldn't adapt herself to Keene's aspirations and yearned for the simpler life she had known before, as she inelegantly put it, "Jim made his pile." In defiance of the prevailing notion that a wife should spend her husband's money just a little faster than he made it—if possible—she would sigh, "Oh, for my little cottage at the foot of Mount Shasta, when I had my husband and children to myself."

There were other "duchesses" whose personal style was off-putting, too haughty for the lustier tastes of society in the nineties and after the turn of the century. Mrs. Ogden Mills, whose husband would become Secretary of the Treasury during the Republican administrations of the 1920's, was a "perfect hostess" and the "leader of a small young-married set," as Mrs. Harriman observed, but she was a "great stickler for form." Their house parties in Newport were stately affairs during which, Mrs. Mills boasted, she could give a dinner for a hundred guests without calling in extra help. But Mrs. Mills was too haughty to gain adherents. A friend once asked Ogden Mills if he'd had a pleasant weekend, and the latter replied, "Oh, yes, we entertained eighteen valets and maids."

Newport "summer cottages" facing the Atlantic. The largest structure (center) is the Vanderbilt mansion, The Breakers

(*Photograph by John Hopf*)

The dining room in The Breakers

(*Newport Historical Society*)

The Newport Reading Room on Bellevue Avenue
(*Newport Historical Society*)

The Newport Country and Golf Club
(*Brown Bros.*)

James Gordon Bennett, Newport wit and powerful newspaper publisher

(Brown Bros.)

August Belmont in the driver's seat, 1899
(Culver Pictures, Inc.)

A view of Bailey's Beach
(*Brown Bros.*)

Sailing off Newport
(*Brown Bros.*)

Mrs. Stuyvesant Fish
(*Culver Pictures, Inc.*)

Virginia "Birdie" Fair, sister of
Tessie Oelrichs, at Bailey's
Beach, *c.* 1894
(*Newport Historical Society*)

Harry Lehr and Mrs. John Jacob Astor in a parade of decorated
cars, *c.* 1899

(*Brown Bros.*)

A tennis match at the Casino, c. 1905
(*Newport Historical Society*)

Mrs. O. H. P. Belmont (right) and her daughter Consuelo Vanderbilt (Duchess of Marlborough) in front of Belmont's "cottage," Marble House, before a suffragette meeting

(*Brown Bros.*)

None of the contending "duchesses," nor even the members of the Great Triumvirate, could equal the grace of Mrs. Paran Stevens, who was credited with having created the only European-style salon, glowing with wit and erudition, such as enlivened Paris and London society. But Mrs. Stevens was one of those who lacked the will to dominate; she didn't want to lead society, merely to keep it from expiring from boredom. She would always be lovingly remembered in Newport as one of the more imaginative great hostesses. Even after certain disasters connected with the importation of a celebrated chef from Paris who considered himself as much a maestro of the saucepans as any Escoffier or Brillat-Savarin. "His sauces were priceless," it was recalled, "and his temperament also. Once during a tennis tournament, Mrs. Stevens had asked a hundred people for luncheon. They came. They sat. But nothing happened. Downstairs the chef was saying that unless he had three bottles of a particular champagne he couldn't go on with his sauce. People left. Finally three starving young men found six bottles, made their way to the kitchen and laid them on the altar. . . ."

Certainly Mrs. Stevens had a consideration for the feelings of others rarely to be found among the dowagers who cultivated a glacial exterior, who strove endlessly to make aspirants for their favor feel ill at ease. She could understand that even visiting nobility, particularly those woebegone specimens who had lost their princely standing in their native countries, had to be spared discomfiture. One season she played hostess at her Newport home for Don Carlos, the pretender to the Spanish throne, and his tatterdemalion suite, including the Marquis de Ponce de Leon (breezily known to Americans as Pounce Lion) and the Marquis de Montsarratt (who had won himself the sobriquet of Mountain Rat). "Don Carlos," one of Mrs. Stevens' admirers recalled, "was travelling incognito as the Duke of Madrid. For some days, while waiting for a full set of American false teeth, he wouldn't be entertained. Society was quite agog from waiting when he finally came forth to be presented to Mrs. Stevens. Just as he started to bow, a slippery rug undid him and he fell flat upon his back. She was as quick to make excuses for him as when she was the social unfortunate herself. Once when she was fifty minutes late at a dinner in New York, instead of making the convenient excuse 'the horse fell down,' she came in with a rush, 'Really, my dear, my memory plays me tricks. I told the coachman to drive me to the Waldorf, and before I knew it I was being shot up and down the sixteen stories in the lift inquiring for you at every floor. Then I suddenly remembered that you lived across the street.' As the Waldorf at that time was only a hole in the ground with its future wonders constantly cried in incredible advertisements, her fantasy delighted both hungry guests and hostess."

Mrs. Stevens lacked the extra glandular thrust for making herself the leader of the pride of lionesses, and besides she had too elfin a sense of humor to consider the role worthy of the effort. Other great ladies were simply too self-engrossed, such as the first Mrs. John Jacob Astor, the former Ava Willing and the future Lady Ribblesdale, who was as stunned by her own willowy beauty as any of her admirers and who apparently lived in her own narcissistic little world. Even her foot was so gracefully proportioned that, as Michael Strange remarked, "sculpted and isolated in a lit-up cabinet, it might have passed for an extreme sample of breeding." The great beauties like Mrs. Astor and the moon-goddess Whelan twins, Mrs. Robert Goelet and Mrs. Craig Biddle, lived in a self-enchanted state that required no sustenance from the pleasures of rivalry and competition.

The Great Triumvirate, however, did not attain its position through default. Its members were willful women, each strikingly individualistic, who got what they wanted and wanted what they got. And they obeyed one of the last dictums of The Mrs. Astor, who left them with the injunction to "discountenance the undignified methods employed by certain women to attract a following."

Perhaps the least known of the trio was the one who had traveled furthest up the social scale, considering the fact that her father was a penniless Irish immigrant. That was Tessie, Mrs. Herman Oelrichs, the former Theresa Fair, a tall, fair-skinned woman with raven black hair. She was no less queenly in attitude than the other two members of the Great Triumvirate, though her manner was oftener compared to that of a drill sergeant than that of a lady of fashion.

Tessie's fortune came directly from that fabulous breeder of millionaires called the Comstock Lode. Her father, James G. Fair, born in 1831, was a Dubliner who migrated to America with his family as a boy. In his youth he continued westward alone and joined a wagon train to the California goldfields. Fair was one of those swaggering, black-Irish buckoes on the outside, but inwardly he was more complicated and devious. Also, unlike many of his compatriots, he believed more in hard work and thrift than hard drink and frolic. Behind the hail-fellow exterior was a calculating and ambitious brain; he believed in "keeping his eyes and ears open and his purse-strings drawn tight," as a California chronicler observed. He toiled in the creekbeds of northern California without striking it rich but accumulating a competence in mining methods. For years he superintended other men's mines and managed quartz-stamping mills, building up his nest egg and waiting for a real opportunity. Just after the Civil War, scenting that chance, he joined the stampede to the silver mines of Nevada.

Eventually, through a process more interesting to a financial than a social historian, he linked up with three other Irishmen (John W. Mackay, James C. Flood and William S. O'Brien) to become the "bonanza kings" of the Comstock Lode. Fair supplied the technical brain, the practical miner's expertise, to complement his partners' financial and business acumen. Soon the quartet had bought up claims, dug new shafts and tunnels, and begun producing large quantities of the soft bluish ore, which had been washed away in the tailings by the gold miners who preceded them. They struck what was described as the "richest hoard of gold and silver that ever dazzled the eyes of a treasure-seeker," thick veins of ore rich in silver chloride. The deeper they dug, the more impressive the bonanza they had uncovered. "The wonder grew," as a contemporary mining historian wrote, "as its depths were searched out foot by foot. The bonanza was struck at a point 1167 feet below the surface. . . .

One hundred feet deeper, and the prying pick and drill told the same story. . . . When, finally, the 1500-foot level was reached and richer ore than any before met with was disclosed, the fancy of the coolest brains ran wild. . . ."

Within a few years Jim Fair and his partners were catapulted to a position dominating not only the silver-mining industry but the financial world of San Francisco, which then rivaled New York's. They were taking three out of every four dollars of profit being extracted from the Comstock mines, a total estimated at more than a quarter-billion dollars split between them. In a dizzyingly brief period, they were thrust into "positions of vast influence and power . . . and every prospect of colossal fortunes lying just ahead."

The impact of all that wealth on Fair, his wife and four children was predictable. In Fair himself it exaggerated most of his worst qualities, his greed and ambition. When he died in 1894 there was hardly an obituary that did not denounce his career and the man himself. "Since James G. Fair died last week," wrote one of the more charitable editors, "his name has been on everyone's lips. I have yet to hear a good word spoken of him. . . . Never did I meet a man of good intelligence who had dealings with him of any sort who did not detest him. . . . The common estimate of Fair, though spoken freely, is not printable." This obloquy extended to his brief political career, which began and ended with one term in the Senate, the seat in which he obtained through $350,000 spent on a Nevada election campaign.

The smiling Irishman, oozing charm when it profited him, had acquired a wife early in his career in the California foothills. In Angels Camp, where he managed a quartz mill, his dark and rather sinister eye fell upon a comely and amiable young widow named Theresa Rooney. Already a notorious womanizer, he decided to marry Mrs. Rooney in hope that she would provide him with the children to inherit the fortune he was certain would be his. Thus Tessie—along with her sister Virginia (Birdie) and brothers, Charley and Jim—was born in the mining camp of

Angels Camp, which Mark Twain made lastingly famous with his short story about the jumping-frog contest of Calaveras County.

With his fortune not only made but increasing daily without his having to lift a finger, Fair found time for philandering. Mrs. Fair might have overlooked an occasional infidelity but Jim was almost as tricky and ill-mannered a husband as he was a business associate. Twenty-one years after they were married, in 1883, Mrs. Fair sued him for divorce on charges of adultery. He publicly denied the charges, blandly telling newspapermen that he was being framed by political enemies. A rather weak defense for such a supple intelligence, since Fair had no intention of returning to the U.S. Senate (which he had expected to find an arena of political thunder and rhetorical lightning but which he considered no more interesting than a south-of-Market bar room).

Mrs. Fair got her divorce, custody of their two daughters and a third of his fortune as a property settlement; the care of their two sons was entrusted to her husband.

It soon became apparent that the two girls, Tessie and her sister Birdie, got the best of the parental bargain. Or possibly they had innate qualities of character their brothers lacked. "Mrs. Fair," as the biographer of the four Comstock kings commented, "devoted herself to the training of the young women, giving them the benefit of a genteel Christian home and engaging the best of tutors to instruct them in the deportment and accomplishments suitable to their time and station. Fair, immersed in the management of his involved affairs, had little time or inclination to hold an equally tight rein on the boys. . . . Jimmy and Charley, with too much time on their hands and too much money in their pockets, developed tastes that must have pained their well-bred sisters. . . ." The boys fell victim to hard drinking, and Jimmy was sent to a sanitarium to take the Keeley Cure before he reached voting age. A few years later, having set some kind of local record by consuming twenty cocktails one after the other, he committed suicide. Charley also took to drink and compounded his affront to respectability by marrying a blond woman identified in one of the San Francisco newspapers as having operated a "questionable resort."

Contemplating the wreckage of their brothers' lives—Charley would die in an automobile smashup in France while driving at a speed of more than 100 kilometers an hour—Tessie and her sister were determined to live more sedate and useful lives. That, of course, would include "sensible" marriages. Tessie waited until she was in her mid-twenties before accepting a proposal of marriage, having weeded out from various fortune hunters, playboys and alcoholics the amiable figure of Herman Oelrichs. Intermarriage between Irish and German-Americans was popular among all classes, amateurs in eugenics having determined to their own satisfaction that the imaginative but flighty Celtic blood should blend well with the earnest but turgid Teutonic. Aside from that pseudo-scientific conclusion, Tessie was attracted by Herman's amiable disposition—her own was somewhat commanding—and his impeccable lineage. The Oelrichs clan had long been established in Bremen as ship owners. Herman's father migrated to the United States before the Civil War to become North German Lloyd's agent in New York just before the transatlantic passenger traffic became the great prize of the maritime world. Henry Oelrichs married one of the lusty, quarrelsome Mays of Baltimore. Thus, his son Herman was half German and half hot-blooded Southerner.

Herman was thirty-seven, all but a confirmed bachelor, when he fell for the female centurion. Perhaps he was attracted by her wit, which was of the abrasive type she apparently inherited from her father. (When his old partner Flood, a former bartender, built his mansion down the peninsula from San Francisco among the homes of a number of aristocratic Southerners, Fair blandly remarked, "Flood should be popular in Menlo. There's not a bartender on the Coast who can make a better julep than him.")

The Fair-Oelrichs marriage in the fall of 1890 made a tremendous splash. It took the San Francisco *Examiner* twenty-four columns of type to convey the magnificence of the occasion, the stature of the wedding guests, the brilliance of the costumes.

Among the hundreds invited to attend the reception, old James G. Fair was not to be found. Reporters sought him out and asked why he hadn't attended his daughter's wedding. "I wasn't invited," he replied with a rare candor. Had he sent a wedding present? Yes, a check for a million dollars. That claim was received with skepticism among those who had experienced his tightfisted attitude toward money.

Herman Oelrichs allowed that he liked San Francisco better than the Eastern cities and resorts in which he had been reared, but Tessie wouldn't have any of that. Her clear blue eyes were fixed on New York and Newport, and she was determined to claim the social standing conferred by her marriage. And she not only packed up her bridegroom for the trip East but her sixteen-year-old sister who, she asserted, would also make a brilliant match. From then on, the short, plump, easygoing Birdie, her character resembling her brother-in-law's more than her sister's, was maneuvered into the matrimonial market by her willful sister.

During the next several years Birdie was reported engaged to various suitors, the Polish Prince Poniatowski, John Mackay, Jr. and others—and the speculation only increased when their mother died in 1891 and their father in 1894, and their financial worth accordingly increased. In the case of their father's will, complications arose immediately, as might have been expected in probating the estate of a lusty and persistent womanizer.

The court fights over Jim Fair's will during the nineties frequently distracted Tessie Oelrichs from the pursuit of social prominence. They also enriched what the San Francisco *Chronicle* called the "most brilliant galaxy of legal luminaries ever seen in the West." Jim Fair's estate attracted almost as many would-be heirs as the Tichborne Claimants case in England. It took several years and two million dollars to oppose the claim of Mrs. Nettie Craven, a school principal, that Fair had written a new will and named her the chief beneficiary; she finally accepted a small cash settlement. But that was only the start of a litigous stampede. THE CROP OF NATURAL HEIRS TO THE DEAD MILLIONAIRE NOW MAKING AN APPEARANCE," the San Francisco *Examiner* headlined it. They were a rich assortment of females claiming to have been "his last sweetheart," common-law wives, fiancées. A half-dozen entered the lists with assertions that Fair had seduced them by promising to marry them, or had taken them on long buggy rides. An eighteen-year-old Los Angeles girl named Sarah Gamble, who operated the flower stand in a hotel, and who was picturesquely known as Sarah the Flower Girl, sued the estate on the grounds that Fair had proposed to her and she had accepted. Several ladies with children they claimed had been fathered by Fair joined the parade, along with Miss Phoebe Couzins, identified as "the world-famed women's rights advocate," who stated that Fair had courted her accompanied by an entourage that included his nurse, two secretaries and his nephew. A half-dozen years passed before all the claimants were legally weighed and disposed of, leaving the estate greatly diminished, and the name of Slippery Jim Fair garlanded with the reputation of having left more widows than one of the livelier sultans of the Ottoman empire.

By then Tessie had managed to arrange the brilliant match she wanted for her tomboyish younger sister Birdie. In April, 1899, Birdie was married to William K. Vanderbilt II, great grandson of the Commodore and generally conceded to be the most eligible bachelor in the country. High society and its doings were then so fascinating to the public—much like Hollywood a generation later—that the newspapers were filled with column after column reciting the plans for the wedding; the bride's trousseau was a matter of such compelling interest that it called for banner headlines and extra editions. The bridesmaids were the daughters of houses so rich, as one excited journal reported, that their combined fortunes "exceeded that of half the royal families of Europe."

The details of the wedding were reported in incredible detail. The bride, as one society editor gurgled, remained the same unaffected girl as she had been when "in simple calico she had romped about the streets of Virginia City." If so, she was an extraordinary creature not to be impressed by Vanderbilt's wedding gift, a $75,000 pearl necklace, or the two orchestras that

played during the reception, or the wedding breakfast in the
Oelrichs' mansion at Fifth Avenue and Fifty-seventh Street
attended by "just the *upper half* of New York's Four Hundred."

Although Herman Oelrichs gave the bride away at that
ceremony, he and Tessie weren't hitting it off too well. Like
many easygoing husbands with assertive wives, he solved his
marital problems by sideslipping away from them. There was no
formal separation, but Tessie presided alone over their Newport
mansion Rosecliff while Herman lived in San Francisco, the
informality of which pleasingly contrasted with the stiff ceremo-
nial existence in which Tessie imbedded herself and their son, or
sailed back and forth on the Atlantic aboard one of the family's
North German Lloyd liners, standing on the bridge with a huge
tankard of Wurzburger in his fist.

Although Tessie achieved a professional gaiety as one of the
lionesses of Newport, she seemed to those who knew her
intimately to keep herself busy from morning to night to fight off
melancholy. She kept up a brave front and always maintained
that she and Herman were on the most affectionate terms, she
pretended that her career as a member of the Great Triumvirate
was completely satisfying, but it all seemed a glittering façade to
her niece Blanche Oelrichs (Michael Strange), who wrote: "My
aunt Tessie, attired in white elbow-length gloves, princess lace
dresses, and towering picture hats, seemed always starting for
another point, in her victoria or electric brougham. And I
fancied she must ever appear out of glittering hallways—from
between lanes of potted hydrangea plants in their spectral
August bloom. . . .

"But I thought that my aunt, between her outbursts of
laughter and a delightfully cool manner she had of swearing,
seemed restless and unhappy, and perhaps this was the reason
that, as I heard, she flew into such rages when the servants
exceeded their weekly allowance of tea. And I learnt that before
she had married my uncle she had been Miss Fair, of a famous
mining family recruited from the Forty-niners, and I would
repeat to myself, Mackay Flood Fair O'Brien and picture the
Forty-niners to myself as four gigantic men in sombreros with

beards like Buffalo Bill's, striding over the blue dreamlike foothills of the Sierra Nevadas armed with pick axes, cracking off the surface of the earth to lay bare sheer plains of gold. The result of all this good fortune was that already in our childhood, Aunt Tessie, with her Irish beauty, classic nose and extraordinary humor too, had decided to remain amicably separated from her charming husband with his noticeably high blood pressure. And well do I remember the strain it was to sit at their luncheon table on one of my uncle's rare visits, listening to their pretense of intimacy. . . ."

Tessie managed Rosecliff like the proverbial Dutch housewife. Every morning at eight she rose and dressed her own hair (refusing to have a personal maid on her staff) and then made a first-sergeant's inspection of every room in the mansion. Every bed had to be made up with fresh linen daily, no matter whether anyone had slept in it or not. If she found the marble floor in any of the rooms improperly cleaned, she bawled for a mop and bucket to do the job herself. "When I die," she frequently said, "bury me with a cake of Sapolio in one hand and a scrubbing-brush in the other. They are my symbols."

Her passion for cleanliness and order even extended to the stables and outbuildings. Once the house had been inspected from cellars to attic, she called for her electric runabout and toured the rest of her property. A careless groom or a sloppy stableboy was reprimanded in phrases that would have made a Seventh Cavalry sergeant cover his ears.

Her attention to every detail concerning her summer retreat brought about a tragic mishap. One day carpenters were working on an upper story of Rosecliff, and Mrs. Oelrichs, of course, appeared below the scaffolding and began shouting commands. One of the workmen dropped a tack—presumably by accident—and it struck the pupil of one of her beautiful eyes. After that she was blind in one eye, but little escaped her good one.

But half-blindness wasn't the worst of her afflictions. Tessie had always prided herself on a lithe and slender figure, rightly believing it was her best feature. Then just after the turn of the century she began putting on weight, no matter how she disciplined herself at the table; apparently, she was told, it was a glandular condition. In the past decade, of course, a full-fashioned figure in the style of Lillian Russell, with a shelflike bosom and hips curved like a cello, was the height of pulchritude. Recently, however, fashion had decreed a willowy figure, society aping the stage, everyone trying to look like one of the Floradora Girls.

With Tessie Oelrichs that ideal seemed unattainable. She called in a succession of masseurs and masseuses to pound away at her aldermanic corpulence. She tried diets that would have wrung tears from a Chinese peasant. When those measures failed, she turned to the artifices of the corset-making industry. She wore a corset so confining it resembled one of the nastier inventions of the Inquisition and required the services of her strongest male servant to lace up. Those who knew the ordeals she endured to present a more compact figure to the world easily forgave her for her sulphuric tongue and quick temper. The results, as Tessie saw it, were worth the agony. As one summertime observer noted, Mrs. Oelrichs in her concealed armor of whalebone and steel presented an almost girlishly supple figure. "No young athlete ever had hips of so compact span; except for the almost tidal sweep of her bosom, Mrs. Oelrichs in her aggressive tailored simplicity of her princess gowns took up no more room than a slip of a girl in a Misses' model. She and her sister Birdie used to make an interesting study in contrast when they entered the Casino grounds together . . . Tessie superbly handsome, carrying herself with the regal sweep of a Nike of Samothrace in spite of her harness; and Birdie so tiny and alert in her natural and unrestricted slenderness, with something about her big black eyes and broad tilted nostrils suggestive of a charming toy Boston Bull puppy."

Tessie and Herman had been married for sixteen years and for most of them had been separated by the width of the continent or the Atlantic Ocean when, in 1906, the San Francisco earthquake occurred. She was overcome by anxiety. Despite their long separations, she was still in love with Herman, even if she couldn't restrain her drillmaster's temperament for the sake of domestic harmony. When she learned that Herman had survived and was returning by train to New York, she resolved to become a different sort of wife; no more devoting herself to being the Great Hostess; no more domineering over her husband; no more obsession with the fripperies of the fashionable world. She would slip comfortably into the role of Mrs. Herman Oelrichs. While awaiting his arrival and memorizing her new resolutions, she ordered a new wardrobe for Herman from Brooks Brothers and hastily had his room in their Fifth Avenue mansion redecorated. She filled the house with flowers and planned a supper for two, over which she would complete their reconciliation by promising to devote herself to him and let the Great Triumvirate find a new member.

She was sitting in the entry hall the day of Herman's arrival, ready to leap up and embrace her husband when he walked in.

The door opened but it was only Herbert, her butler. Herbert reported that he had seen Mr. Oelrichs strolling up Fifth Avenue a few minutes earlier. Instead of coming home, Herman had repaired to his club.

So there was no reconciliation, despite what Tessie had regarded as the timely intervention of the San Francisco earthquake, and she returned to the distractions of her social life.

Herman, however, had one more unpleasant shock for her. That was revealed after he died of a heart attack aboard a North German Lloyd liner while returning from taking the cure at Carlsbad. The bad news was contained in his will. Herman considered that the Fair millions should be enough to take care of Tessie in luxury, and left his paltry half-million to his brother Charles, who for years had been unsuccessful at making a stylish living in a Wall Street brokerage. Tessie liked her brother-in-law and presumably revered Herman's memory, but she was not so overcome by sentiment as to allow her husband's will to be probated without challenge. Tessie had a decent respect for money and long experience in fighting for or against wills. By California law, furthermore, a husband could not disinherit his wife. "So naturally," her niece Blanche Oelrichs wrote, "with her right smart feeling about money, Aunt Tessie was not prepared to pass up what she had a legal right to, and after some flying mud had been gathered up for public consumption in the dailies, Papa was advised by his lawyer and brother-in-law, William Jay, to compromise for half the amount. Of course, Uncle Herman had never dreamed that his wife would want the money; he was probably no better judge than my father of people unlike himself."

Tessie's afflictions only grew with the years, and there was nothing her money could do to cure them. She became increasingly deaf as well as blind in one eye, and eventually, like The Mrs. Astor, she lost her mind. And like Mrs. Astor—so great, apparently, was the emotional impact of the social wars in which she had engaged—she lived in a ghostly world of dinner parties and balls forgotten by everyone else. Her niece left a touching memory of her last years when "she would wander, a fragile and still incredibly beautiful person, her raven hair with its deep wave gone snow-white, through the rooms of her immense marble copy of the Villa Trianon, reseating her guests over and over again, pressing them to take just another ice, one more glass of champagne!"

Tessie's fellow triumvir Mrs. O. H. P. Belmont was a lady of equally firm mind and assertive personality, older but of greater durability, and had been plain Alva Smith, then Mrs. William K. Vanderbilt before she married into the Belmont family. It was her son, William K. Vanderbilt II, who married Birdie Fair, a match arranged by Alva and Tessie at least partly in testimony to their friendship.

She was a doughty woman with dyed red hair, and eventually she would work as hard for women's suffrage as she would labor over the affairs of the Newport Board of Social Strategy.

"I always do everything first," she was proud of saying. "I blaze the trail for the rest to walk on. I was the first girl of my set to marry a Vanderbilt. Then I was the first society woman to ask for a divorce, and within a year ever so many others had followed my example. They had been wanting divorces all the time, but they had not dared to do it until I showed them the way."

Socially, too, she showed an independent spirit, as when William B. Leeds, scornfully known in Newport as The Tinplate King, and his wife built Rough Point, a gray stone Tudor house with an imposing Gothic hall and lawns running down to the cliffs, and tried to make time with the resort establishment. Then Alva announced that "I like those Leeds people"—despite the fact they came drably from Indiana—"and I am going to take them up and put an end to this silly nonsense about them." Other social powers had ruled them out and the Leedses were ready to decamp after two dismal summers in Newport, but Alva prevailed and the Leedses joined the in-group. She accomplished that by giving a dinner and ball "in honour of Mr. and Mrs. William B. Leeds." The invitations caused a tumult of mixed emotions among their recipients. "Many of them," as Elizabeth Drexel Lehr noted, "had been strenuously opposing the advance of the Tinplate King and his wife. . . . On the other hand, if they declined the invitation, Belcourt with all its lavish hospitality would be closed to them for the rest of the season. . . . Their letters of acceptance were carried into Belcourt in shoals. The light of victory shone in Mrs. Belmont's eyes as she stood in the entrance of Oliver's enormous armour gallery to receive her guests on the night of the ball. By her side stood Mrs. William B. Leeds, then young and imperially beautiful in her white satin dress. Her charm was more potent than her husband's millions. Society took her to its heart from that moment." And that, apparently, was what the lady meant by social strategy.

Like the other members of the triumvirate, Mrs. Alva Smith Vanderbilt Belmont ruled the Newport scene not so much through beauty or charm as an imperious will. Her daughter Consuelo ascribed to her a "towering ambition," of the sort made familiar in American fiction, the queen-bee type, from *Gone with the Wind* backward to the memoirs of the Confederate ladies who did more to keep the Civil War going than any number of cavalier generals. Alva did not exercise any Scarlett O'Hara charm, if she had any, but opted for a directly overbearing manner. "Her combative nature," as her daughter, one of its chief victims, wrote, "rejoiced in conquests. She loved a fight. A born dictator, she dominated events about her as thoroughly as she eventually dominated her husband and her children. If she admitted another point of view she never conceded it; we were pawns in her game to be moved as her wishes decreed. I remember once objecting to her taste in clothes she selected for me. With a harshness hardly warranted by so innocent an observation, she informed me that I had no taste and that my opinions were not worth listening to. She brooked no contradictions, and when once I replied, 'I thought I was doing right,' she stated, 'I don't ask *you* to think, *I* do the thinking, you do as you are told,' which reduced me to imbecility. Her dynamic energy and her quick mind, together with her varied interests, made her a delightful companion. But the bane of her life and of those who shared it was a violent temper that like a tempest at times engulfed us all."

Nobody could deny Alva's courage, whether it was in assaulting the social battlements then held by Mrs. Astor and her cohorts, crusading for a cause unrelated to social precedence, or acting quickly in a domestic emergency. Consuelo would always remember the day she was out driving in her pony cart, when she was nine years old, and the pony made a dash for a water hydrant. "My cart would undoubtedly have been overturned; but without the slightest hesitation my mother who was standing near by threw herself between the hydrant and the racing pony and seized his bridle, thus preventing a serious accident."

Matched against that memory were others more painful of her mother lashing her and her brother with a riding crop when they misbehaved.

Alva Smith was born on an Alabama plantation where the whip was a familiar domestic tool employed with vigor down among the slave cabins. She always believed that her background was as much or more aristocratic than the people she would meet in New York or anywhere else. She was, as she frequently proclaimed, "a Desha of Kentucky." If few people had ever heard of the Deshas, that was merely a symptom of their ignorance and stupidity. Undeniably Alva was as bright as she was ambitious; she would always be discontent with things as they were, even when she was possibly the most envied woman in America, because her sharp intelligence was always comparing them with more ideal possibilities. It was probably significant that she was fascinated by the Medici and would have propelled herself back to their era in Mr. H. G. Wells' time machine if it had been possible.

Educated in a French boarding school, which provided her with a veneer as hard and glossy as polished ebony, she made a trip to that most fashionable of waterholes, White Sulphur Springs, in 1875, when she was twenty-two. The daughters of the plantation aristocracy, which would never recover from the Confederate war and Reconstruction, trekked there in simpering droves to place themselves on display. The spa, with all those Yankee millionaires traipsing around, was a first-class hunting ground, a place where family fortunes could be revived by a rich son-in-law.

Alva did her best by the Smiths and Deshas and snared the richest bachelor on the scene, William K. Vanderbilt, the grandson of the old Commodore.

And she did her best by the Vanderbilts, too, by propelling them into the upper branches of the social tree. All her maneuvering to compel the acknowledgment of the Vanderbilt qualifications from Caroline Astor culminated in 1883 when she gave the fancy-dress ball that Mrs. Astor's daughter simply had to attend. Mrs. Astor's calling card was the Old Guard's white flag; the bastion had fallen, and the Vanderbilts, aggressively led by Alva, were *in*.

Newport was the next citadel to be stormed, and up went the eleven-million-dollar Marble House. Still there were worlds to be conquered. "Now firmly established as a social leader," her daughter recorded, "my mother, wishing still further to dominate her world, assumed the prerogatives of an arbiter elegantarium, instructing her contemporaries both in the fine arts and the art of living. Ransacking the antique shops of Europe, she returned with pictures and furniture to adorn the mansions it became her passion to build. She thus set the fashion for period houses, which at that date was little known in this country."

Alva was a perfectionist when it came to her surroundings, was constantly rebuilding, and, as her friend Harry Lehr observed, "she loved nothing better than to be knee-deep in mortar." In one of her houses she had a new wing built with a bedroom for her that was certain to be free of ghostly presences. Her mammy down in Alabama had instilled a fear of ghosts and she was especially fearful of sleeping in a bedroom in which anyone had died. The day the new wing was completed, one of the masons fell off a ladder, was carried to the new bedroom and died of his injuries. "It really does seem," she sighed after signing a check for his widow, "as though Fate had decided I am never to sleep peacefully at night."

Alva would not allow her reputation for expertise in all matters concerning architecture and interior decoration to be challenged. Elizabeth Drexel Lehr recalled an occasion when they were both guests at a house party at Blair Castle in Scotland. It was the ancient seat of the Duke of Atholl, and Mrs. Lehr thought Alva would be impressed, if not overawed by her surroundings. But even at Blair Castle Alva's passion for authenticity asserted itself. "It's not correct," she declared. "There are a lot of mistakes. My castle at Sandy Point is far more authentic."

Once she had built and rebuilt her three lavish American establishments, her restless energy was devoted to other projects. Socially spectacular marriages for her children, especially her daughter, were at the top of her agenda. "It was perhaps then," her daughter wryly noted, "that plans for my future were born."

Evidently it was of small concern to Alva that her own marriage was heading for the shoals. The source of all those millions she had spent on advancing the Vanderbilt banner, her husband, was no happier than his children under Alva's heavy-handed rule. He was the amiable clubman type, easygoing and tolerant; Alva's opposite, much as Tessie was Herman Oelrichs'. "Wholly unsuited to each other," was their daughter's verdict. "His gentle nature hated strife. . . . Why my parents ever married remains a mystery to me. . . . He was so invariably kind, so gentle and sweet to me, with a fund of humorous tales and jokes that as a child were my joy. But, alas, he played only a small part in our lives; it seemed to us he was always shunted or sidetracked from our occupations. . . . With children's clairvoyance we knew that she would prove adamant to any appeal our father made on our behalf and we never asked him to interfere. . . ."

There were rumors that Willie K., having absorbed the continental male's attitude toward marital fidelity, was chasing other women. But when he inherited half the Commodore's fortune and built the 1,400-ton yacht, which required a crew of fifty-three to sail, he named it the *Alva*, a mark of high and courtly favor among sportsmen. And Alva was allowed to decorate the boat in a dazzling and money-consuming style: It featured a library paneled in French walnut and furnished with a skylight.

From then on, Willie K. neglected the affairs of the New York Central, the keystone of the Vanderbilt fortune, and devoted himself to various amusements. Alva and their children shared in, at least, the cruises of the *Alva*. On a trip through the Mediterranean, the Vanderbilts and their guests learned just how impressive their yacht was from the seaward view. They were cruising into the Dardanelles when a Turkish warship, believing the *Alva* was a foreign navy's cruiser making an unauthorized invasion of the straits, fired two shots across her bow.

It was on a cruise to India, aboard another Vanderbilt yacht (the *Alva* having sunk, perhaps symbolically, after a collision at sea), that the marriage began to disintegrate rapidly. Consuelo recalled the "continual disagreements" between her parents, which were not muted for the sake of their children or the guests on that cruise. Divorce was still a shocking thing in the nineties, but it seemed inevitable. There were "constant scenes that so deeply wounded my father and harried my mother beyond control—scenes that embittered the sensitive years of my girlhood and made of marriage a horrible mockery. It was in such an atmosphere of dread and uncertainty that our last and longest yachting expedition was undertaken in my seventeenth year."

The cruise ended in a final flareup at Bombay, and Mrs. Vanderbilt took her children back to New York, via England, while her husband sojourned in Paris and allegedly was involved with a beautiful Parisian. Back in New York, Alva had decided on a divorce, and damn the social consequences. She filed suit in the autumn of 1894, not at all dissuaded by pleas from her in-laws or the fact that the only grounds for divorce in New York state were adultery. There was a futile attempt to ostracize Alva, but she was too well established as a member of the Great Triumvirate to be affected by any such maneuvers. Instead, characteristically, she took the counteroffensive and blacklisted anyone suspected of siding with Willie K. and his clan. "During the following months," Consuelo recalled, "I was to suffer a perpetual denial of friendships and pleasures, since my mother resented my seeing anyone whose loyalties were not completely hers."

On March 5, 1895, Alva became the first notable American society woman to divorce her husband, and that summer in Newport issued what was called the "Vanderbilt Declaration of War." Alva declared war on the premise that any divorced woman must be cast out of respectable society, no matter what the reason for the divorce.

She issued invitations, which amounted to summonses, for a ball at the Marble House, which anyone who valued his or her standing with the Great Triumvirate felt compelled to attend. Another coup that enhanced her position was the marriage she arranged for her daughter Consuelo to the Duke of Marlborough. Her position consolidated, she further demonstrated the following year that she made her own rules and society would have to accept them.

If divorce was shocking, remarriage, especially one taking place so soon after the decree had been granted, was earthshaking. Ever since the celebrated Vanderbilt cruises on the *Alva*, there had been speculation about the warmth of Alva's feelings about Oliver Hazard Perry Belmont, who invariably accompanied the family in its wanderings. Belmont was said to be Willie K.'s best friend, but according to the gossip he found equal or greater favor in Alva's eyes. The New York society columnists kept mentioning rumors that she would marry Belmont, but she kept denying the reports.

Less than a year after she divorced Vanderbilt, on January 11, 1896, Alva and Belmont were married in her new town house on East Seventy-second Street. The reason for the secrecy of their planning for that event then became apparent. For weeks they had been quietly trying to find a Protestant clergyman, of any sect, who would be willing to conduct the ceremony. Great though the temptation to share in the effulgence of a Belmont wedding may have been to some of the pastors, none would officiate at the wedding of a divorced woman. They finally had to turn to Mayor William L. Strong, and settled for a civil ceremony. Alva's two sons—but not Consuelo—were present. No other Vanderbilts, and none of the Belmont family, attended.

From then on the Vanderbilt family refused to acknowledge her existence, though she had a considerable claim on its gratitude. Until she took charge of its social advancement, as a New York newspaper pointed out, "the Vanderbilt family was unheard of in New York society, except occasionally when it was abused for watering railroad stock or damning the public."

Next season in Newport, Alva in her apotheosis as Mrs. O. H. P. Belmont was back on the throne she shared with Mamie and Tessie. Instead of hanging her head or pleading for understanding, she flaunted the fact that she was "the first woman in society to divorce her husband." It seemed to a Newport historian that any less forceful woman would have been proscribed by society, and even she suffered a temporary eclipse. Her bold personality, coupled perhaps with the secret yearning of many of her peers for a similar solution to their marital problems, allowed her to emerge unscathed by disapproval. She and her second husband were one of the more striking couples on the Newport scene during the 1890's and early 1900's. "Every year," it was noted, "the checks in Belmont's Poole suit seemed to grow bigger, Mrs. Belmont's curls to burn brighter. Eventually her hair ceased to be red, turning gradually to the color of faded American Beauty roses and finally to a rich purple."

There were occasional embarrassments, but they often stemmed from the lower orders. Once a week a charabanc loaded with tourists would make its appearance at Belcourt. One day the rubberneck bus showed up with the driver bellowing through a megaphone his highly original description of the Belmont life-style. Suddenly inspired, Alva rose from the head of the table and clapped her hands for attention.

"Oh, there's that dreadful man with the megaphone," she told her luncheon guests. "Do listen to what he says; it really is too funny for words."

She and her friends trouped out to the entry hall of Belcourt, the first floor of which was still stabling Oliver Belmont's much-loved horseflesh. They heard the tourist guide shouting:

"Here you see the home of a lady who has been much in the public eye. A society lady who has just been through the divorce courts. She used to dwell in marble halls with Mr. Vanderbilt. Now she lives over the stables with Mr. Belmont."

Not at all amused, she shooed her guests back up to the dining room.

Alva was forty-three when she married the second time and was becoming more concerned with the world outside the great houses. It was said her interest began veering from the social to the sociological when her first husband married the former Anne Harriman Sands, a lady renowned for her philanthropies and social crusading.

Whatever the motive, Alva soon became one of the more energetic and determined promoters of women's suffrage. Greatly though she had profited from her own two marriages, without which she might have wound up the wife of one of those languid ex-planters described in the works of the Southern Gothic school, she was convinced that her sex was downtrodden. She dominated Oliver Belmont as she had William K. Vanderbilt, so it could be said that her feelings on the subject of sexual oppression were altruistic rather than personal.

One of her first victories on behalf of her sex concerned the will of James B. Haggin, an elderly but dapper widower who had recently married again. He arrived at one of Alva's Newport receptions apologizing for his lateness and explaining that he had been detained at his lawyer's office, where he had been drawing up his will.

Generally speaking a person's last testament was regarded as a very private matter, especially among the rich, but Alva did not hesitate to tread on sacred ground.

"I hope," she said in her authoritative voice, "you are leaving a nice fortune to that sweet wife of yours."

"No," Haggin replied, startled at the suggestion. "Why should I? She is no relative. She is only my second wife. As a matter of fact I have left her practically nothing. I am leaving all my money to my own relations, my children by my former marriage. They have the first claim, after all."

In that moment Alva looked like one of her Confederate kinsmen raising his saber to lead his horsemen up the slope at Gettysburg.

"What?" she almost shouted. "You mean to tell me you are going to disinherit Pearl after she has been such a wonderful wife and put up with all your moods and your bad temper? I have never heard of such a disgraceful thing! Now listen to me: I won't allow you to do such a disgraceful injustice. You can't die with it on your conscience. Unless you change that will right away I'm going to tell everyone I know about it, and they will all take Pearl's part. You won't have a friend left. Now just think it over and have your lawyer make a new will."

Alva's habit of command was so compelling that a chastened Haggin not only revised his will the next day in the manner Alva advocated, but he sent her a basket of fruit and spray of orchids with a note reading, "Thank you for opening my eyes."

Eye opening would continue to be her preoccupation long after the Great Triumvirate ceased to rule in Newport.

12.

THE GREAT TRIUMVIRATE (II)

MRS. STUYVESANT FISH, Mamie to a select few, was the third and more complex, often self-contradictory member of the Great Triumvirate. As in a Russian troika, she was first among equals, even Alva Belmont deferring to her and Tessie Oelrichs conceding to her the sharper wit. If one person dominated the golden quarter-century of Newport, it was Mrs. Fish, the grandest (and often the least reverent) of the *grandes dames* of Bellevue Avenue. She had less money behind her than either of the other two triumvirs; she lacked Tessie's swanlike, if corset-bound elegance, and she was certainly no haughtier or more imperious than Alva, but neither could match her waspish intelligence. She seemed to be ruled by two conflicting desires: to uplift society and, conversely, to ridicule and satirize it.

Her ripostes were so devastating that they gained national currency, though she often claimed to regret that her fame outside the social world was based on her barbed remarks. Mrs. Fish, in fact, was downright rude, even to guests in her own home. People who arrived at Crossways, which she pointedly described as a "plain white house," though it was fronted by four large Corinthian columns, often were made to feel they were intruders. "Howdy-do, howdy-do," she would shrill. "Make yourselves at home." And sotto voce she would add, "And believe me, there is no one who wishes you were there more than I do." She greeted one guest at her reception with a blank gaze, then said, "Oh, I'd quite forgotten I asked you."

Even her dearest friends weren't spared the sharper edge of her tongue. One morning Alva Belmont angrily approached her at the Casino. "Is it true," she demanded, "that you said at Tessie's last night that I reminded you of a frog?"

Mrs. Fish rocked back on her heels and clutched at her bosom as though overcome by the thought of such malicious talebearing.

"No, no," she said on recovering from her mock seizure, "not a frog. A toad, my pet, a toad!"

That edged weapon, Mamie's tongue, on at least one occasion seriously damaged her husband's career. It was one of those instances of a wifely feud—and there must have been more of them than were ever recorded by financial or social historians— making shock waves that extended from Bellevue Avenue to Wall Street or, in this case, Chicago's LaSalle Street. A snub could be more costly to the snubber than the snubbed, but that consideration would not inhibit Mrs. Fish.

Mamie's mouth embroiled Stuyvesant Fish with E. H. Harriman, then reaching the height of his power as the chief mogul of the American railroads. Harriman controlled the Union Pacific, Southern Pacific, and other lines. Fish was merely president of the Illinois Central, which made him, on the corporate scale of values, a sprat to Harriman's barracuda. On the other hand, the Fishes were firmly entrenched in the aristocratic sense, one of the Old Families, while Harriman's father had been a Long Island clergyman and Harriman himself had worked his way up from officeboy in a brokerage firm. The disparity, obviously, could have been bridged without hostilities, but that wasn't the way the social game was played in Newport.

Mrs. Fish examined Mary Harriman's credentials when she presented herself for a summer in Newport, and found them wanting. Not only were the Harrimans unaristocratic, that would be forgivable under the less rigorous rule of the Great Triumvirate, but they were dullards, merely ambitious for social recognition (for Mrs. Harriman at least) to match Harriman's standing in the financial community. She passed over Mrs. Harriman when she gave a ladies' tea at Crossways. That was infuriating enough, but word also reached Mrs. Harriman that

Mrs. Fish had made disparaging remarks about her at the tea.

Mrs. Harriman immediately complained to Mr. Harriman, a meek-looking little man with a Milquetoast mustache, whose mild appearance concealed a wrathy disposition.

"I'll make those people suffer," Harriman vowed.

Corporate skulduggery was a Harriman specialty and he proceeded to infiltrate Fish's Illinois Central. His chosen instrument was a man named Harahan, who had risen from switch tender to company officer and member of the board of directors under Fish's patronage. Harriman's man organized an anti-Fish faction among the directors. At the next Illinois Central board meeting Harahan challenged Fish's authority, denounced his methods of management and called for his replacement. Fish's response lacked something in business etiquette but indicated the depth of his feelings. His only reply to Harahan was a blow that knocked the other man down. Fish then stalked out of the meeting and was removed from the presidency.

All that, because Mary Harriman hadn't been invited to Mamie Fish's tea party. And there was a sequel, according to Elizabeth Drexel Lehr, who recorded that the Fishes' daughter Marion on the morning after her father was deposed received a call from "one of New York's most eligible bachelors. He was waiting for her in the library. He explained that he had come to ask her to marry him. She stared at him in astonishment. 'But you were one of the people who voted against Father yesterday,' she exclaimed. 'They told me you had hurried back from Europe specially to record your vote. Can you possibly believe that I should marry you after that?' It was quite useless for him to explain that he had not expected that she would regard his hostility to her father from a personal angle. She asked him to leave the house and refused even to see him again."

That sort of disaster, which happened in 1906, would have wrecked many New York/Newport marriages, but the Fishes had been long and amiably married. Her husband was one of the few people in the world—perhaps the only one—who was spared the sharp edge of her tongue. On his part, there was a mountainous tolerance for, and glacial indifference to, Mamie's career as a Great Hostess.

Perhaps some of the durability of the Fish marriage was based on the fact they had been childhood sweethearts and had no unpleasant surprises for each other. Mrs. Fish was born Mary Ann Anthon (but always called Mamie by those who knew her well enough) in 1853, the same year as Alva Smith Vanderbilt Belmont. She was a New Yorker whose family lived only three blocks from the Stuyvesant Fish, Sr.'s, but when her father died, when she was twelve, the family had to move to humbler quarters in Astoria.

Aside from a pair of striking jet-black eyes, a part of her French ancestry, Mamie was anything but beautiful, nor did a hoarse, macawlike laugh add to her attraction. Furthermore, in some unexplained way, she managed to avoid any contact with an education. She could not spell the simplest words, could read a newspaper only with difficulty and could not write a legible hand. Functionally no more than semiliterate, she still aimed for perfection; as she told a daughter-in-law, "It doesn't make any difference what you decide to do in life, but you must do it better than anyone else."

A good marriage was at the top of her list. Somehow she lured young Stuyvesant Fish back into her social orbit, though they were separated by the then-considerable distance between Astoria and Manhattan. So far as American aristocracy could be said to exist, he was the genuine article. The Fishes, it was said, were distinguished and well-bred back to Revolutionary times and at the same time kept a middle-class attitude toward morality. They valued simplicity, country living at Glenclyffe Farms up the Hudson, and had nothing to do with Manhattan society. Hamilton Fish had been Secretary of State in the second Grant administration but escaped its tarring of scandal and corruption completely. Years after his death historians determined that Secretary of State Fish had single-handedly saved the Grant administration from the sort of disastrous scandal that would befall President Harding.

Both Hamilton Fish and his son Stuyvesant were working for the banking house of Morton, Bliss & Company when the latter resumed his courtship of Mamie Anthon. The Fish reputation for probity endured on Wall Street during a period of speculative piracy and recurrent scandal just as it had survived the second Grant administration. Its durability was suggested by the fact that Fish Senior, presented with a check in settlement of the Alabama Claims, signed on behalf of the government and Fish Junior for the banking house.

"I see the Father and the Son," was the sardonic comment of another member of the Morton, Bliss firm when he examined the signatures, "but where is the Holy Ghost?"

"That, sir," Fish Junior starchily replied, "is the mutual trust and confidence that makes the whole transaction possible."

Fish's career with Morton, Bliss was short-lived after he married Mamie Anthon. She was outraged when the firm summoned him back to New York from their honeymoon and persuaded him to quit the banking house and join the Illinois Central, then known for obscure reasons as the "Society Railroad." Further inspired by his strong-willed wife, he became president of the Illinois Central in 1887.

As the wife of a railroad president—with Fish commuting to Chicago while she raised their three children in New York—Mamie began making her presence felt in Manhattan society. She early formed an alliance with Alva and Tessie, largely perhaps because they were all three women of lively intelligence, a quality by no means prevalent among other society women. From the beginning Mrs. Fish assumed an imperial attitude, not only toward other aspirants to the social throne but her own family. Of her husband, according to Mrs. Lehr, she would say with a Napoleonic gesture, "Where would he be without me? I made him. I put him on the throne." Sometimes she made that statement in his presence and "he never contradicted her. Whatever she chose to do or say was right."

One man she did not prevail over was Commodore Bennett, who regarded the society pages of his New York *Herald* as an American surrogate for the *Almanach de Gotha*. Bennett had not only appointed Nicholas Biddle as "social advisor extraordinary" to the *Herald* but engaged William Bininger, a society gentleman, as editor of his society section. Accidents could happen, despite the watchfulness of Messrs. Biddle and Bininger. One night a makeup man inadvertently added to the list of guests at a reception given by Mrs. Fish a half-column from the sports section listing the ringsiders at a prizefight that night. Mrs. Fish was not amused next morning over her breakfast tray to read that John L. Sullivan, One-Lung Curran and other denizens from Hell's Kitchen or the Five Points had toddled through her reception line. She upbraided Commodore Bennett and his editors so violently that Bennett ordered that her name was not to be mentioned on the society pages again. Mrs. Fish was reinstated only after making a trip to the *Herald* building and apologizing to the Commodore.

Two years after Fish became president of the Illinois Central, Mrs. Fish decided it was time they joined the Four Hundred's seasonal migration to Newport. Tessie and Alva were already established there and Mamie could hardly advance her career by rusticating every summer on the Fish farm up the Hudson. Fish agreed with great reluctance, as Mrs. Lehr made plain:

"In many respects he still retained the simplicity, the austerity of his ancestors. I think in his heart of hearts he preferred their standard of life to that of the social world in which he lived. He would never play cards on Sunday, he hated ostentation and loved Glenclyffe Farms far better than Crossways at Newport or his fine house in New York. He loved to take his guests up to the commodious, old-fashioned bedroom, without running water of course, which he and his brother had shared all through their boyhood. 'None of the maids will sleep in it, it is not good enough for them; yet I spent some of the happiest hours in my life there.'

"He never really cared for society, and only tolerated parties for the sake of his wife, who could not contemplate life without them. Sometimes he would come back tired out after a long journey over his railroad and find the house full of a noisy crowd of guests, occasionally even his razors and shaving brushes commandeered by those unexpectedly staying over night. But he would only shrug his shoulders good-naturedly. 'It seems I am giving a party. Well, I hope you are all enjoying yourselves.' A big, silent man who never wasted words, he was a great contrast to Mamie Fish who kept up a constant flow of chatter. . . .'"

Mrs. Fish's climb to preeminence in Newport was littered with the metaphorically broken bones of those she bludgeoned into subservience. Her manner was one of studied insolence. Her attitude was that of boredom verging on repugnance for those who were naïve enough to be impressed by the self-anointed elite, whose company, however, she herself could not do without. Her method of attaining supremacy was to pretend she didn't give a damn for such superficial matters. She was a mistress of what later would be called the putdown, which she employed on people who had the superior resources to live more ostentatiously than the style decreed at Crossways. One hostess proudly showed Mrs. Fish around her house and announced, "And this is my Louis Quinze salon." Mrs. Fish stared around the room, then glacially inquired, "What makes you think so?"

To the clear eye of a child, there was something a bit too strenuous about Mrs. Fish's social manner, increasingly so as it must have become apparent to her that one reception or ball or dinner was much like another, with the same faces present, and that playing the social game was not so much like mountain climbing, with a glorious summit to be attained and a subservient world laid out at your feet, but more like living on a treadmill. Blanche Oelrichs (Michael Strange), who knew her as a girl, observed that "The hoarse laughter of 'Mamie' Fish was never still. She had the elements of a true comedienne, but her harsh gaiety had the bitter overtone of a grotesque disillusionment with herself and everyone else. One knew as one looked at and listened to her, that she sensed well the triviality in which she drowned her time, and that her brash mirth concealed an ever more exasperated cry at the impotence of the kind of life that went on around her."

Perhaps it was her inheritance of hardheaded sense, as well as an antic humor, that prevented Mamie Fish from ending her life as tragically as some of her peers. She would not become addled in old age like Caroline Astor and Tessie Oelrichs and many others who succumbed to various forms of insanity. She kept a grip on herself, retained her husband's devotion—costly though it was to him—and provided a proper rearing for their children. To the observant Richmond Barrett the soundness of the Fish marriage was a thing of wonder, considering the stresses of their environment and Mamie's dedication to the principle of upward mobility. As Barrett viewed the Fish menage, the raw-boned, farmerish-looking Fish "seemed curiously out of place among the dapper cotillion leaders and the blaringly jewelled women who filed past him. He never once balked, however, never flinched in his duties as the husband of a restless celebrity in the very thick of the struggle."

It seemed paradoxical that in the midst of all the tension of presiding over a volatile caste in Newport "she managed somehow to be a devoted wife and mother. The married life of the Stuyvesant Fishes wasn't so very different fundamentally from that of the Hamilton Fishes. They respected and deferred to each other; and even *Town Topics*, sniffing for the carrion smell of scandal on every breeze, never caught the slightest whiff of it in the vicinity of Crossways." Fish's income was modest compared to that of the husband's of his wife's circle but she "performed social miracles on a budget far below that of most of her rivals." In deference to her husband's simpler tastes, Mrs. Fish set aside one night every week for dining informally, without the floral centerpiece and dozens of guests. On that night Fish was served corned beef and cabbage, his favorite, while down in the servants' hall a fancier menu obtained, the servants protesting at being served such tenement-district fare.

There was never any doubt of who was the most important person at any gathering attended, or sponsored by, Mrs. Fish. As Eleanor Robson Belmont observed, Mamie agreed with the principle that "Wherever MacDonald sits, there is the head of the table." Her sense of superiority prevailed even in the stateliest company and was an integral part of the manner with which she imposed her rule of the Newport summers. Nor could it be withered by any missteps which would have humbled a lesser woman. Any gaffes she committed were usually converted into witty little triumphs.

As an example of her unflappable nature, Mrs. Belmont cited the luncheon party she hastily arranged for Bishop Brent, who had just arrived in Newport in an aura of acclaim for the missionary and diplomatic efforts he had supervised in the Philippines, where the largely Catholic population had taken up arms against the American occupation. The other honored guest at her luncheon was the Russian Ambassador George Bakhmeteff, whose insistence on the finer points of protocol had stirred dust devils all over the diplomatic map. "He always liked a bottle of claret to himself so he would not have to wait for the butler to refill his glass," as Mrs. Belmont recalled. "Mrs. Belmont had provided him with her choicest wine, *but* she had placed Bishop Brent on her right side and the Ambassador of All the Russias on her left. Needless to say, the going during lunch was difficult; the fact of his displeasure was evident."

It was hardly a reason for Russia to break off diplomatic relations with Washington, but it was one of those miscalculations that figured so large in the hothouse atmosphere of Newport society.

When the guests rose from the table, Bakhmeteff stalked over to Mrs. Fish and, in the tones usually reserved for delivering a stiff protest to the State Department, demanded, "Mrs. Fish, please explain. I do not understand. Is it customary in America to put an ambassador on your left and a bishop on your right?"

Mrs. Fish swallowed hard, then recovered her famous aplomb. "Oh, no," she assured him. "It is not customary. It just depends on which you put first, God or the Czar."

A lexicographer could have compiled a dictionary of insults just by following Mrs. Fish around for a few seasons. Like confectioner's sugar sprinkled on a poisoned pastry, she always addressed her victims as "my sweet pet" or "my sweet lamb"— largely because she found it difficult to remember the names of any but members of her family and a few friends of long standing. A few of the darts she launched:

Mrs. Fish to a guest apologizing for leaving early: "No guest ever left too soon for me."

To a male admirer begging to share one more two-step with her on the ballroom floor: "There are just two steps more for you—one upstairs to get your coat and the other out to your carriage."

To one of her ladies' luncheon parties: "Here you all are, older faces and younger clothes."

To the English polo player Tom Shaw Safe who hyphenated his name to Shaw-Safe after marrying a wealthy Newporter: "Howdy-do, Mr. Safe. I'm so sorry to call you Mr. Safe but I've forgotten your combination."

To a guest who complained that towels were missing from his bathroom and he had had to dry himself on a bath mat: "Pet, you were lucky not to be offered the doormat."

To another guest who asked how large Crossways was: "I really can't tell you. It swells at night."

To someone who, unaware of her dislike for opera, asked her if she liked the one she had attended the night before: "I'm never sure that I have my face fixed right. Sometimes when it is just right for listening to The Cradle Song I find that I am listening to The Ride of the Valkyries."

To a friend, after sighting James Hazen Hyde, a particularly epicene playboy, dressed in a sport shirt: "Who is that young man in a negligee?"

On being asked to sign her byline to a ghostwritten article about the splendid work done by Bishop Brent in the Philippines: "I wouldn't hear of it. If the article was good enough to interest anybody, everybody would know I couldn't have written it. If it wasn't, I'd be mortified."

To a young man who had just married well and who brashly guessed that Mrs. Fish's favorite flower was the climbing rose: "And I know yours, pet. The marigold."

Aside from achieving dominance, Mrs. Fish's main purpose during her Newport summers seemed to be enlivening the place. With all the amusements and distractions at hand, Newporters were stultified by boredom, in her view, and needed nothing so much as livelier entertainment. And that could come only from the outside. Thus, she might snare Crown Prince William of Sweden for one of her soirées, but she also had the chorus of *The Merry Widow* kicking up its heels for her guests, John L. Sullivan displaying his muscles, Irene Castle demonstrating the new dance steps she and her husband had invented.

And there was a memorable appearance at Crossways by the hoydenish Marie Dressler, then a musical comedy actress and later a film star. What shocked Mrs. Fish's more staid friends was that she appeared to accept Miss Dressler as an equal, unlike a rival hostess who invited Fritz Kreisler to dinner and told him to be sure to bring his violin. "But why, Madame?" Kreisler blandly replied. "My violin, it does not eat."

The meeting between Marie Dressler and Mamie Fish came about when the former was appearing in a vaudeville act at Proctor's Fifty-eighth Street Theater. "In my act," as Miss Dressler recalled, "I carried a basket of onions. All at once it seemed to me an excellent idea to throw them playfully at the spectators. The biggest one of the lot landed squarely on Mrs. Fish's head. . . . Imagine my surprise when a few days later, I received a note from her secretary, asking me to appear as a paid performer at one of Mrs. Fish's famous parties."

The comedienne agreed to appear at the party at Crossways for a hundred-dollar fee, but that wasn't all she extracted from Mrs. Fish. She had been invited to come in after dinner, much in the style of a strolling player being summoned by a medieval lord, but she boldly informed her hostess she wanted to sit down at the table with the other guests "so I can tell my mother I had dinner with Mrs. Stuyvesant Fish."

"I shall be proud," Mrs. Fish gallantly replied, "to tell my children that Marie Dressler had dinner with me."

Her fellow guests were surprised, indeed, when a mere performer occupied the place of honor beside Mamie at her table. "In those days, 'professionals' were not asked to dine when they came to entertain," Miss Dressler explained. "Mrs. Fish and I became firm friends and our friendship lasted through the years until her death. When Mrs. Fish began her reign, actresses were not accepted in society. They were, in fact, considered fast. Especially if they had ever worn tights. But when Mrs. Fish took me driving through the park in her elegant victoria day after day, New York society conveniently forgot my social shortcomings, and I received more invitations than I could accept."

Still, it was a curious friendship, predicated as Miss Dressler believed on "my refusal to take her and her friends too seriously. . . . Mrs. Fish had humor, courage, naturalness, and honesty. These were the qualities she admired most in others. Above all, she liked courage, even ruthlessness of a sort. . . .

"Imperious, generous, brilliant herself, dullness was the one sin that she could not forgive. She demanded that those who sat about her dinner table should be funny, or handsome, scintillating, or like herself, superbly arrogant. It made no difference to her whether their families came over in the *Mayflower* or in the last boat to unload at Ellis Island."

Undoubtedly Miss Dressler was shown a facet of Mrs. Fish's character not invariably on display. Mamie did not abandon her pursuit of dominance, of outdoing rival hostesses, in her effort to broaden the social spectrum and prevent society from dying of boredom.

Witness her maneuvers in what became known as the Grand Duke War, with the enormously rich and coldly arrogant Mrs. Ogden Goelet as her opponent.

An almost permanent guest at Crossways had been the lean, handsome and dashing James de Wolfe Cutting, who, according to Elizabeth Drexel Lehr, had "just that dash of Jewish blood that enriches and makes beautiful a human being." The platonic bonds between Cutting and Mrs. Fish were regarded as unbreakable, but Mamie's tongue, of course, could have cut through the Atlantic cable. The *entente cordiale,* from which Cutting benefited by having a secure base in Newport and Mamie from always having an attractive extra man around the premises, was ended abruptly one day when Mrs. Fish was in a fretful mood.

She told Cutting she was utterly bored with Newport that season, same old faces at the same old parties.

Cutting suggested, "Why don't you take a moor over in Scotland and then we could all come over and shoot?"

"Why don't I?" Mrs. Fish shot back. "Because I would like to be a *guest* myself some time."

Cutting took about two minutes to brood over the implication that he was a freeloader, packed his bags and immediately moved over to Mrs. Goelet's Ochre Court, which was a lot grander than Crossways.

Cutting's defection embroiled Mrs. Fish and Mrs. Goelet in a sizzling feud. Everyone cleared out of their patch of the social jungle as small animals flee when two lionesses start clawing at each other. Even Harry Lehr, the supreme arbiter of such affairs at the time, calculated he would only get mangled if he tried to make peace; Mrs. Fish with the other two members of the Great Triumvirate were close to omnipotent but Mrs. Goelet was a much-respected independent power. "When the Queens start fighting among themselves," Lehr said, "I always make for the nearest fence and sit tight on it. Nothing tempts me off it until I feel that it is the psychological moment for a truce. Then I do what I can to pour oil on the waters."

That moment certainly hadn't arrived when Grand Duke Boris of Russia, who had married the sister of the Czarina, appeared in Newport with his suite. Everyone was eager to know if America's plushest resort could compare with the Crimean summer palaces. Grand Duke Boris professed himself to be stunned by Newport's ambiance. "I have never dreamt of such luxury as I have seen in Newport," he said. "We have nothing to equal it in Russia." No one thought to ask him if The Breakers or Ochre Court really outdid the Winter Palace in St. Petersburg for splendor.

Here, obviously, was a guest to be treasured—and Mrs. Ogden Goelet had won him, along with the ducal suite.

Mrs. Fish, of course, was crestfallen at Mrs. Goelet's coup. She accepted Mrs. Goelet's invitation, in which a gloating element could be detected, to meet Grand Duke Boris at a luncheon at Ochre Court.

Then Mamie took the offensive. She announced a dinner and ball "in honor of Grand Duke Boris and his suite."

Two hundred guests would be invited for dinner alone. Hundreds more were summoned to the ball following it, including the whole membership of the New York Yacht Club, which was in Newport for the races. Harry Lehr as her chamberlain was arranging a cotillion built around Russian music. Then she invited not only the Grand Duke but Mrs. Goelet—neglecting, with malice aforethought, to send along an invitation for Mr. Cutting.

Perhaps she had not reckoned on Mrs. Goelet's equally intransigent disposition. The latter's attitude became apparent a few days after the invitations went out and Mrs. Goelet paid an afternoon call at Crossways.

"Dear Mamie," said Mrs. Goelet with a poisonous smile, which her victims sometimes likened to a bonbon laced with prussic acid, "I was thinking about your lovely ball this morning when I realized that you had quite forgotten to send an invitation to Jimmy Cutting, and you know he is staying with me at Ochre Court."

Mrs. Fish's black eyes glittered. "Oh, no, my sweet, I didn't forget. I have no intention of having Jimmy at my party. He has been to my house too often already."

"But," Mrs. Goelet replied, "I'm afraid you don't realize, my dear, that I couldn't possibly come to the ball if a member of my house party is not included in the invitation." She paused, finding the moment delicious because Mamie knew the harpoon was coming. "What is more, neither the Grand Duke nor any other member of my house party will be there."

"In that case, sweet pet, we shall miss you so much."

Mrs. Goelet tried to conceal her dismay at Mamie's cool reception of the possibility of a ducal ball without a duke. "I hope you haven't forgotten," she said, "that you sent out invitations saying 'to meet the Grand Duke Boris'? What are you going to do about that? Besides, he has five gentlemen in his suite, which means you will be short *six* men at dinner. Very well, dear, you must make your choice. Have Jimmy Cutting at your party or sacrifice the Grand Duke."

"I will not have Jimmy," Mrs. Fish bitingly replied, "if I am reduced to the naval training station for men."

She referred to the stratagem of desperate hostesses relying on the Navy's installations for extra men at their parties. The commanding officer would be instructed to send over the desired number of presentable youths, in uniform, almost as though the Navy were an arm of Newport society instead of, as most taxpayers fancied, the federal government.

In her despair, she summoned Harry Lehr for advice. "Turn the whole thing into a joke," he told her. "Make people laugh so much they will not be quite sure what happened."

So Mrs. Fish went ahead with her preparations, necessarily altered though they were. She was undeterred when Mrs. Goelet announced that on the evening of Mrs. Fish's dinner and ball "in honor of Grand Duke Boris," he would actually be the guest of honor at a small dinner party at Ochre Court.

Naturally their followers were thrown into a most frightful confusion. Which dragon was to be appeased? Which invitation to accept? Most, however, had already sent acceptances to Mrs. Fish's invitations and it was too late to send their regrets, unless they could provide affidavits affirming that their grandmothers had died in a remote city. Mrs. Fish's hot temper was more to be feared than Mrs. Goelet's cold displeasure.

On the evening of her gala Mrs. Fish radiated triumph. Her drawing power was attested by the fact that all those she had invited were filing through the door, including Lord Charles Beresford, J. Pierpont Morgan and Senator Chauncey Depew. "There was a thrill of expectancy in the air," as one guest would recall, "as they waited for the royal party to arrive before going in to dinner. Five minutes passed . . . no Grand Duke. Was he not coming? Some of them remembered the strange invitation they had received from Mrs. Goelet a few days before. There were hastily smothered whispers."

To guests with the temerity to ask whether the Grand Duke

would really make an appearance, Mamie replied, "Royalty is better never than late."

With that unsatisfactory and enigmatic tidbit her guests had to content themselves as they milled around the hall of Crossways until shortly before eight o'clock.

Then Mrs. Fish commanded silence and announced: "I was unable to have the Grand Duke Boris as guest of honor tonight, my pets. But I have someone far more important." She raised her voice to a bassoonlike blare. "His Most Gracious and Imperial Majesty, the Czar of All the Russias!"

The door swung open and Mrs. Fish dipped low in the prescribed curtsey. The other ladies also curtseyed. The men bowed low. When they dared to peer up at the personage who had made his entrance, they saw a gorgeous figure in scarlet uniform, chest glittering with medals and striped with ribbons, and wearing Mrs. Fish's ermine-lined opera coat turned inside out. It was not Nicholas II posturing before them, but Harry Lehr in one of his famous impersonations. "The whole room rippled with merriment . . . Mrs. Fish's party was saved," a witness recalled. (Next day Grand Duke Boris approached Lehr at Bailey's Beach and told him, "I hear you represented the Emperor last night. In Russia, that would not have been a good idea, but I only wish I had been there to see it. *Our* party was poisonous.")

The Grand Duke War could serve as a diagram of Mrs. Fish's methods of dealing with adversaries. It was a form of psychological jujitsu, with ridicule as the fulcrum on which her opponents were thrown off balance.

On only one or two occasions was Mamie herself unhorsed in the social wars. Once it was by a mere male, and by a dear friend at that, James Van Alen, who objected to her cavalier manners during musicales, which she detested. She made it a habit, despite the distress of music lovers, to talk in her macawlike voice throughout a musical program.

Once during yacht-race week Van Alen decided to give a musicale in honor of J. Pierpont Morgan. He invited Mrs. Harry

Lehr and Stuyvesant Fish, but not Mrs. Fish and Mr. Lehr, who also misbehaved at musicales.

Mrs. Fish tracked Van Alen down at Bailey's Beach and demanded to know why she and Harry hadn't been invited.

Van Alen screwed in his monocle, surveyed her severely and explained, "Very sorry, my dear, but I can't have you and Harry Lehr at this party of mine. *You make too much noise.*"

"Oh, so that's it," Mrs. Fish screeched. "Well, let me tell you, sweet pet, that unless we are asked there won't be any party. Harry and I will tell everyone that your cook has developed smallpox, and we will give a rival musicale, and everyone will come to it."

A compromise was finally reached. Mamie and Harry were invited to dinner but had to stay out on the terrace during the musical part of the evening.

Mrs. Fish spent most of her adult life scrambling for, then fighting off challenges to, the heights of social dominance. The struggle suited her combative nature, for queening it over Newport was a self-appointed, not an elective position.

Yet there was an element of pathos in the verse her family selected to be inscribed on her tombstone:

> Her life was turning, turning,
> In mazes of heat and sound,
> But for peace her soul was yearning,
> And now peace laps her round.

13.

"LITTLE BROTHER OF THE RICH"

To THE unenchanted masculine eye, Harry Lehr looked like "a coy and roguish pig in men's clothes."

There was nothing the men who paid the bills in Newport (so many of whom worked themselves to mental breakdowns or death) detested more than the elegant idlers who amused their wives, helped plan their parties and lead their cotillions, and encouraged social aspirations, which, of course, ran up more bills and drove the husbands that much harder.

They were a class of professional charmers, both more and less than what a later generation would call gigolos or lounge lizards, not indigenous to but thickly swarming in summertime Newport. None more grandly filled the role than Harry Lehr, who throughout the golden age acted as prime minister successively to The Mrs. Astor (after Ward McAllister fell from favor and before Mrs. Astor lost her wits), and to the trio that formed the Great Triumvirate. So formidable was his charm—or so compelling his talent for sycophancy—that Mrs. Astor even forgave him for having a father who had been "in trade." So able was he at enlarging his role as grand vizier to the ladies of the Four Hundred, at publicizing himself as the person who could secure the patronage of the super-rich, that even before he contracted a profitable marriage to one of the Philadelphia Drexels, he lived without signing anyone's payroll, without bouncing checks and without having to apply to the Overseer of the Poor. Nimble-witted Harry was on the cuff everywhere. A New York tailor made his suits without submitting a bill. A jeweler lent him jewels. The Waldorf-Astoria provided free lodging, Delmonico's and Sherry's begged him to dine without charge. The wives of railroad magnates secured passes for him on their husbands' lines. Mrs. Clarence Mackay saw to it that he could send cables and telegrams without having to dip into his walkaround money. In Newport he was a permanent guest who drifted from one great house to another—flitted, a snide observer might have said.

Harry was blond and dapper, boyish-looking well into middle age, with bright blue eyes, a high-pitched voice and a delightful chortle. He loved women's clothes, doted on the newest fashions, and once told his wife, "Oh, if only I could wear ladies' clothes; all silks and dainty petticoats and laces. . . ." One of his youthful triumphs was appearing as Princess Genevieve in the Paint and Powder Club's production of a comic-opera version of *Joan of Arc* in Baltimore. The critics commented on "a faultless pair of shoulders and a throat that might be the envy of many women, and a natural aptitude for dancing and posing. . . . He wore white silk with low square corsage, puffed sleeves and white gloves, and bodice ornamented with open green iridescent work. . . ." Whatever the nature of his sexual drives, or lack of them, it was obvious that he posed no threat to a husband in that line. He was a lapdog, not a stud.

That was his first qualification. His second was that he knew how to take the curse off sycophancy by calculated impudence; that to people cushioned all their lives in the false respect of servants and the flattery of those who wanted to make use of them or their money, an insult delivered in the right tone was a welcome antidote to the subservience that surrounded them. A well-turned insult from Harry Lehr came to be treasured, it was like being made a Knight of the Garter, because Lehr sprinkled them sparingly and only on those of great social stature.

Impudence, in fact, provided his first boost into the top echelon. During his first season in Newport, merely one of a small horde of extra men, he attended a ball at which The Mrs. Astor was a guest. Mrs. Astor was wearing a white gown festooned with her hoard of diamonds. As she passed by him, Lehr took a bunch of roses from a bowl and handed them to her, saying, "Here, you look like a walking chandelier. Put these on.

You need color." On a later occasion, when the Stuyvesant Fishes got up to leave a party, he snapped at them, "Sit down, Fishes. You're not rich enough to leave first." One day O. H. P. Belmont was showing off his stained-glass windows, which featured a concoction the Belmonts claimed was their coat of arms and included the quartering of Dunois, the Bastard of Orleans. "My dear Oliver," inquired Lehr in his loftiest tone, "why proclaim yourself illegitimate?"

Having early decided on the role he would play, he studied the careers of other cotillion leaders and the domestic structure of society—its overworked husbands and restless wives—and decided that he must always be a neutral in the war between the sexes. Absentee husbands would be pleased that their wives would be provided with counsel and companionship if he gave them no cause for jealousy. "That is the secret of my success," as he later told his wife. "Love affairs are fatal to ambition. I have seen the shore strewn with the wrecks of people who have given way to their passions, and I don't intend that mine shall be among them. If you have an affair with a single girl, you have to marry her whether it is a suitable marriage or not. If you are fool enough to go after a married woman, it always ends in disaster. Either she tires of you or you tire of her, and then what happens? At the best it means a rift in a friendship and someone's house closed to you; at worst you have a horrible scandal. I'm running no such risks. My position isn't stable enough for that."

Snubs and insults were the common currency of a society made insecure by so much infighting, by a competitiveness that was a mirror-image of the financial jungle from which the money came to support it. He knew how to defend himself in discomfiting situations: "There are three ways of taking an insult. You can resent it and walk out of the room, in which case you have committed yourself to a quarrel you may later regret; you can pretend not to hear, or you can laugh and turn it into a joke. I always choose the last, for I find it the most disarming. No one can quarrel with a man who laughs like an idiot."

During the early part of his tenure as Master of Revels for Mrs. Astor and her successors, Lehr often had to raise that defiant chortle of his in self-defense. Publicity feathered with darts that would have penetrated the self-esteem of a lesser man was shrugged off on the theory that malicious attention from the society editors was better than none. He merely smiled his buttercup smile over such items as:

"Harry Lehr, I hear, will spend most of the summer visiting friends at Newport, R.I. As bathing has become fashionable again among the swagger set there, Harry has provided himself with a particularly cute bathing suit of his own designing with which to ravish the eyes of the 400. The vest will be cut décolleté in order to expose the whiteness of his snowy neck, and the trunks abbreviated so as not to deprive his admirers of a full view of his shapely limbs, which will be modestly encased in silken hose. A chic sun-bonnet will protect his peach-blow complexion from the ardent rays of the fiery sun. . . ."

"Mr. Lehr holds rather a unique position in society, and he has an individuality not to be compared with that of anyone else. His family is not wealthy, he has no profession or business. . . . He is an expert with the needle and would be an invaluable addition to a swell millinery establishment, did he consider work compatible with his station in life. . . ."

". . . I ran across him at Worth's [the Paris fashion house] recently, where he had the whole establishment in commotion that was heard even out on the Rue de la Paix, while the presiding genius of the temple of clothes was literally tearing his hair out in handfuls in his atelier. The particular creation that was troubling Mr. Lehr's brain, the morning I saw him, was a combination of five colors which he insisted could be made into a unit. . . ."

Harry Lehr was not at all ashamed of such peacockery; it was one of the things that had raised him from the ruck of the middle class.

His background was respectable enough for anyone satisfied with staying among the bourgeoisie: father a German-American importer of tobacco and snuff, mother a pretty woman of Irish descent. Harry was born in 1869 in a comfortable red-brick section of Baltimore. His father, Robert Oliver Lehr, was a governor of the Maryland Club and a prosperous member of the community. His mother, the former Mary Moore, had social ambitions, which her third son (in a family of six) inherited in full measure. Harry's hopes of being hoisted into the fashionable world were dashed when he was seventeen and his father lost his money and died shortly thereafter.

Mrs. Lehr took the younger children to Europe, where her eldest daughter was married to a French wine merchant, and they finally settled in Cologne, the center of the Rhenish aristocracy, an ancient and architecturally elegant city. Harry never had the time or money to try his wings among rigidly classified gentry of the Rhineland. The Lehrs were living in furnished rooms in one of the poorer sections of Cologne, which he would always recall with a shudder. "We were all herded together. Such frightful furniture, cheap oleographs on the walls. What I felt coming home to it at night, that one shabby sitting-room with its smell of stale food, finding my sister Fanny doing all the housework, seeing Mother sitting by the window, crying quietly because she had no clothes to go out in, not even enough to eat."

Harry was forced to take a job clerking in a bank, where "one day passed just like the next behind the counter of the bank, getting spoken to like a dog, always counting out sums of money for other people to spend, money that would have lifted us out of all our worries, and then drawing one's own miserable pittance of a salary."

Young Harry was certain he was born for better things, but instead of absconding with whatever of the bank's funds he could lay hands on, he expressed his frustrations in a diary. "I must have beauty, light, music around me," he wrote. "I am like Ludwig of Bavaria. I cannot bear the cold greyness of everyday life. It withers my soul. Other clod-like people can stand it if they choose—I cannot!"

The Lehrs were rescued from exile in the Rhineland when Harry's eldest brother got a well-paying job and brought the family back to Baltimore. There they joined the shabbily genteel, and Harry was deeply offended when the family's old friends neglected to invite them to their homes. After brooding over his bruised feelings, he decided to "adapt," as he said, and "offer something in the place of money and position."

What he offered was clownishness. "I saw," he wrote in his diary, "that most human beings are fools, and that the best way to live harmoniously with them and make them like you is to pander to their stupidity. They want to be entertained, to be made to laugh. They will overlook almost anything so long as you amuse them. I did not mind cutting capers for them if I could gain what I wanted through it."

Harry pandered and capered his way into the top drawer of Baltimore society, trilling his ambitious heart out in the Paint and Powder Club theatricals, courting the dowagers, making himself agreeable and available at all times. He consciously chose his lily-of-the-field profession, confiding to his diary that "Other men have to sweat in offices. I made up my mind I never would." He soon became his native city's favorite jester. One night, while returning home from a party as escort of the current belle of Baltimore society, Miss Lulu Morris, he secured the kind of playful notoriety so valuable to his career. He and Miss Morris took off their shoes and danced in the fountain in Mount Vernon Place, and fortunately there were talkative witnesses. It made the papers. Fountain-wading became a society pastime—the fountain in front of the Plaza Hotel in New York was especially favored because it could provide a good-sized audience.

Lehr came to the kindly attention of the city's newspapers for the "adaptability" he had several years earlier decided was his proper attitude. "Harry Lehr is of all the young men in this city the one who does the most entertaining, not at his own home but at other people's. He is one of the few men of leisure in Baltimore, and has the one object of making himself agreeable. He is in frequent demand, and is constantly invited to houses where amusing people are desired. He is most versatile and had many accomplishments. Playing the piano, dancing the ballet, telling funny stories, pouring afternoon tea, designing his hostess's smartest costume, or speaking French with the foreign fellow guests are all matters of equal ease."

The beery heartiness of Baltimore's masculine world (the atmosphere of which was compellingly recalled by H. L. Mencken, also a Baltimore tobacco man's son) was not for Harry Lehr, who winced at the mere thought of saloons redolent of pig's knuckles, steam beer and cigar smoke, and opted for the salons of the city's more fashionable hostesses. In that feminine world he would conquer as a sexual neutral, he inevitably found his opportunity to step onto a wider and more expensively mounted stage. He met Mrs. Evelyn Townsend Burden and was invited— just as Newport's lushest era was beginning—to her Newport villa Fairlawn.

His first Newport season was a resounding success, especially after The Mrs. Astor became his sponsor. Ward McAllister had stumbled into the social shadows by then, talked and wrote himself into oblivion (or as Lehr put it, "Wardie was the voice crying in the wilderness who prepared the way for me"). Just then the dandified Elisha Dyer was serving in an interregnum capacity as the choreographer of Mrs. Astor's cotillions. Harry was appointed Dyer's coleader. They fell into tremendous tizzies, towering snits over the placement and execution of the quad-rilles, but always made up in time to preside over the cotillion. Lehr soon elbowed Dyer aside and became Mrs. Astor's unri-valed favorite. He would always be grateful to her for that leg up the ladder; "she has been kindness itself to me," he wrote in his diary.

That first season Lehr established himself as the prized ornament of any house party, dinner, picnic or ball. "Haven't you heard Harry Lehr's laugh?" a Newport society editor inquired. "That shows you haven't been within a hundred miles of Newport this season. Everybody within rifle-range of Newport has Harry's laugh down by heart. Not that it is stentorian, clangorous or of the ten-ton gun variety. Not at all. But its vibrations, once started, have an initial velocity of a mile a second, and by the end of the third peel, the very earth is undulating in unison, the church steeples begin to wag in perfect time, and the jaded souls seem acted upon by some new and potent stimulant. . . . Mr. Lehr is a Baltimorean. He has

money—a little, as Newport riches go; good looks, more, as
Newport beauty goes; but it was the laugh that made him king.
As Newport's court jester Harry is a wonder. He simply laughed
himself into the bosom of the ultra exclusives. He has held up the
town with his irresistible chuckle, and robbed it of invitations to
dinners, musicales, yacht cruises, barn dances, and heaven knows
what, at his piratical pleasure."

Michael Strange would always retain a sharply etched picture
of Harry crashing the Newport gates, or blowing them inward
with his caroling laughter—even those of her Aunt Tessie, the
formidable Mrs. Herman Oelrichs—with his "husky figure
gotten up in a white flannel suit, and a kind of comedy straw hat,
his mincing step, the timbre of his clown's laughter, the piggish
glint of his blond-lashed eyes, deprecation, hysterical nonsense,
and the deformity of a long sadness. Then he shifted Aunt
Tessie's poodles from one arm to the other, broke her up with his
buffoonery, and intrigued her with news of original figures for the
next cotillion. . . ."

With credentials like those his entry on the New York winter
season was assured of triumphant results. The ultimate sanction
was conferred when the bedazzled Mrs. Astor consented to dine
with him at Sherry's *on a Sunday evening*, not one of Mrs. Astor's
nights for dining out with anyone else. "Harry Lehr and his legs
and his witticisms," one society editor remarked, "have completely fascinated Mrs. Astor. To see that lady in a coquettish
raiment of white satin, with the tiniest hair dress, dos-à-dos
almost with Lillian Russell, I could hardly believe my eyes. And
she seemed to enjoy it, and nodded her head to the rag-time
tunes, and took the most gracious interest in everything. She
wore her famous pearls and was indeed a stunning sight."
Another paper, however, wondered whether Mrs. Astor wasn't
being a bit too democratic "breathing the same air as that of the
'middle classes,' though conceding that "Harry Lehr, dear child,
is irresistible."

Thereupon Lehr became a steerer for those establishments that
existed on upper-class patronage, and as his wife later wrote,
"suave maîtres d'hôtel smiled their delight when he ordered

meals that must have cost the management hundreds of dollars." George Kessler, the New York representative of a French champagne company, put him on the payroll, saying, "You and I can be useful to one another. I will give you six thousand dollars to sell my champagne." His name was acquiring such social magic that Diamond Jim Brady, who had begun aiming higher than the Broadway lobster palaces, paid a man-about-town several thousand dollars in hope the latter would arrange an introduction to Harry Lehr.

But Lehr wasn't taking on the likes of flashy Diamond Jim, that would have been asking too much, and the mind boggled at the thought of Brady capering in Mrs. Astor's drawing room. He did arrange the New York debut of the Pembroke Jones family when it came up from North Carolina with sizable social ambitions. "Feed New York well," was Harry's advice, "and it will eat out of your hand." So "their table groaned under the weight of rare Southern delicacies, rice birds and Indian corn brought up from their own estates, chicken and corn fritters, Sally Lunns and muffins cooked to perfection by their negro cook who had his special kitchen while their famous Russian chef, lured from the Czar's own household by a fabulous salary, prepared his elaborate menus in his own domain. The combined efforts of these two culinary artists were so successful that those who were inclined to raise disdainful eyebrows at Pembroke Jones' full-flavored jokes and noisy laugh dined with him and thereafter became his staunch champions."

And then Harry, from his standpoint, married wisely. It wouldn't do to take a great beauty as his wife, because that would discomfit the middle-aged and elderly women who were his patronesses. She must have an established position, and a sizable private income wouldn't hurt, since Harry had no intention of going to work and supporting a wife.

His choice fell upon Elizabeth Drexel Dahlgren, of the Main Line Drexels, who had been widowed after a brief marriage. She was rather plain, quiet, retiring, submissive; and there was money in the family. Mrs. George Gould, the daughter-in-law of Jay Gould, introduced him to her as "the most amusing man in

New York." And the young widow was charmed by his gaiety, his insight into the feminine psyche. "Conversation rippled around him," she recalled. "Impossible for anyone to be bored in his company. . . . All women were happy in his society. He liked and understood them. He had an almost feminine intuition. . . ."

When she asked Mrs. Gould for more information about Lehr, the former replied that it was "impossible to have a party without him. . . . The men don't like him very much. They call him one of the 'little brothers of the rich,' but that's because they are jealous of his popularity."

Lehr embarked on a vigorous courtship, but did not commit himself until she had been submitted to the approval of his leading patronesses. He gave a luncheon party at Sherry's—on the cuff, presumably—at which Elizabeth and Mrs. Astor, Mrs. Fish and Mrs. Oelrichs were Harry's only guests. At the end of it, in her best imperial manner, Tessie Oelrichs announced, "We four are going to take her up. We will make her the fashion." On the way home, Harry proposed.

She was "desperately lonely," and went to church to pray for guidance. She soon decided to accept his proposal after he told her, as she wrote in her diary, that "he was not 'animal' or 'emotional' (neither am I, but I thought all men were). He is the one glorious exception, the one pure and Godly man. . . ."

She was not deterred even when he told her that they would live on her income in the house she would buy for them on West Fifty-sixth Street. Wine merchant Kessler could no longer keep him on the payroll, Harry explained, and "I am afraid there is only one solution. You will have to realize that I am giving up a perfectly good livelihood because I love you far more than my career, and you will have to supply me with all that I am losing."

The effete aspects of his character did not dismay her. If he was a trifle epicene, well, no one had ever warned her against the dancing-man type. They were married at St. Patrick's Cathedral with the "whole of fashionable New York" in attendance, and she thought she detected a "spirit of mockery" in Harry's bright blue eyes during the ceremony.

Tragicomedy descended on their wedding night as their misapprehensions about each other were sorted out in a scene that might have resulted from a collaboration between Ibsen and a French farceur. Harry thought he had made it plain that he would be content with the title of husband. Elizabeth did not anticipate just how "pure" her bridegroom intended to be. In later years she recorded the events of her wedding night. They journeyed to a Baltimore hotel immediately after the wedding ceremony. In the dining room of their suite Elizabeth supervised the preparations for their wedding dinner. The room was crowded with crimson roses. Caviar, quails in aspic, Harry's favorite champagne (not the brand he had touted for Kessler) and a cabinet of Havana cigars she had bought for him were laid out in impeccable order. Beside his plate was the gold and enamel watch she had bought as his wedding present.

Elizabeth had just pinned a diamond brooch on her rose brocade gown when her maid appeared with a message from the bridegroom. Harry had decided to dine alone in his own room and suggested that Elizabeth do likewise.

A short time later Harry appeared, pale, expressionless, and announced that perhaps it was time to lay down the ground rules for their marriage. The matrimonial game as played by Harry Lehr was going to be a reflection of his social life—all gaiety on the outside, a somber practicality in private. He and Elizabeth, he told her, would lead separate lives except in public.

"In public," he informed her in a cool level tone, "I will be to you everything that a most devoted husband should be to his wife. You will never have to complain of my conduct in this respect. I will give you courtesy, respect and apparently devotion. But you must expect nothing more from me.

"When we are alone I do not intend to keep up the miserable pretense, the farce of love and sentiment. Our marriage will never be a marriage in anything but name. I do not love you, I can never love you. I can *school* myself to be polite to you, but that is all. The less we see of one another except in the presence of others the better."

Elizabeth was so stunned by that sadistic little speech she

could only whisper, "But why did you marry me?" Though a more spirited female would have at least broken that cabinet of cigars over his head.

"Dear lady," he replied in his world-weary voice, "do you really know so little of the world that you have never heard of people being married for their money, or do you imagine that your charms placed you above such a fate? Since you force me to do so, I must tell you the unflattering truth that your money is your only asset in my eyes. I married you because the only person on earth I love is my mother. I wanted above everything to keep her in comfort. Your father's fortune will enable me to do so. But there is a limit to sacrifice. I cannot condemn myself to the misery of playing the role of adoring lover for the rest of my life."

Here, surely, was her cue to hurl the quail in aspic at his sleekly barbered head, but Elizabeth listened meekly to the rest of his pronunciamento. She really had nothing to complain of, he explained, because he had been "honest" with her. He added:

"You will have a wonderful position in society. As my wife all doors will open to you. Perhaps you will remember that luncheon to which I invited you to meet my best friends? That was because I wanted to be sure that they would approve of my choice. Much as I wanted to marry you, nothing would induce me to forfeit my position in society to do so. But when I heard their decision to take you up I knew that you were going to be invited to all the most important houses in New York, and therefore there could be nothing to fear. . . .

"I suppose I am what novelists call an adventurer. I am not ashamed of it. . . . I believe we shall get along quite well together. But for God's sake leave me alone. Do not come near me except when we are in public, or you will force me to repeat to you the brutal truth that you are actually repulsive to me."

Harry then left her in the room she had arranged to his taste and celebrated his wedding night in private.

Elizabeth Lehr was too conventional to write off the marriage-in-name-only. A Victorian wife accepted her situation; this one was just a little odder than most. At that she fared better than Mrs. George Gould's sister-in-law, Anna Gould, who married the doll-like, golden-haired Count Boni de Castellane, who promptly ripped off more than his share of the Gould fortune.

Her memoir is laced with sardonic memories of her marriage to Harry Lehr. Mrs. Astor's motherly smile when Harry hastened to fetch Elizabeth's wrap when they strolled in a Newport garden because "she's so precious," and Mrs. Astor's unperceptive remark that it was "nice to see young people so much in love." Harry revealing his character had been shaped, or irreparably damaged, by snubs his family received after his father went bankrupt. Harry gurgling with delight when she allowed him to choose her gowns and almost had to be restrained from trying them on himself. Harry insisting time after time, quite unnecessarily, that "love of women is a sealed book to me." Peeking into Harry's diary and noting an entry made after Harry, as was his custom when they weren't going to a party, dined with his best friend Tom Wanamaker: "As always his company was like a draught of wine to me. How different from the chatter of women." Harry attending the notorious James Hazen Hyde dinner—which was said to have cost $200,000 and featured the importation of the great French actress Réjane to recite briefly from Racine—and spurning the caviar and terrapin in favor of hard-boiled eggs and a glass of milk, whimsically explaining, "I always love to do it at a party of this sort." Attending high mass at St. Patrick's every Sunday, and while he fingered his exquisite jade rosary, his lips moving in the responses, hearing him hiss at her, "What a perfect fright you are! Why on earth did you put on *those* shoes?"

Safely and prosperously married, Harry Lehr was free to pursue what he was pleased to call his career, aiding and abetting the amusement of the very rich. He would preside along with the dominant dowagers over a turn-of-the-century society in a state of disarray, largely because of a series of near-incestuous marriages, divorces and remarriages. Everyone seemed to be a blood relative, in-law or ex-mate of the whole Social Register and Newport swarmed with kissing cousins of every variety. Both upper and lower branches of family trees were becoming intertwined. The Vanderbilts were intermingled with the Wilsons and Goelets. O. H. P. Belmont, the grandson of the naval Perry brothers, had married both a Whiting and a Vanderbilt, though not simultaneously. Ward McAllister's Newport branch, the Wards, had married into the Astors and Chanlers. Even the old Knickerbocker families had ventured into marriages with the more recent entries into the Four Hundred.

It was one of the chief problems of Harry Lehr and his patronesses, as one social historian put it, to "keep the big unwieldy clan from settling again into a self-important stodginess. They were far more catholic in their tastes, more reckless in their experiments than McAllister. The 'new' people they were after must be dynamic, amusing, original, as well as outrageously rich; if they happened to be rather shocking, too, that didn't deter Harry and Mamie and Tessie and Alva from hauling them up over the side of the social band-wagon. They were impudently cynical about established conventions; dullness in their eyes was the one and only mortal sin. Here again, as in the case of their frequent loud laughs at the expense of the social order, they injured themselves and their cause more than they would have wished."

A free and easy sort of morality, largely based on the cautionary "don't get caught," sprang up in Newport. If Harry and his triumvirate didn't encourage that sort of thing, they did admit people to whom adultery was not the worst of sins. Transgressors whom Mrs. Astor would have blackballed were not even tut-tutted by her successors. A number of women, no longer satisfied by the purely verbal attentions of lissome young men and elderly dandies, took lovers on a Monday to Friday basis. Worst of all, the Newport amorality was being well publicized, not only by *Town Topics* but newspapers in general, just at the time the nation was trying to recover from the depression that had begun in 1893. Instead of being admired from afar by the rest of the nation, Newport was being denounced from pulpits, editorial pages and soapboxes.

Harry Lehr was not concerned with Newport's public-relations problems. The rest of the country might be decrying

Newport as a suburb of Venusberg, but he was obsessed with handing out advice on social acceptability. With a growing avuncularity, he delighted in pontifically enlightening newcomers with his maxims:

"Avoid Newport like the plague until you are certain that you will be acceptable there. If you don't, it will be your waterloo. Above all, don't take a house there and launch out giving parties. Try to get invited for a week or two on someone's yacht as an experiment to see whether you are a success or not. In that way you will leave your retreat open to you, and you can always pretend that the climate does not suit you and go back to New York without anyone witnessing your defeat. . . .

"Even after the first season or two, the battle isn't won yet. You have still got to be careful. Obey my three golden rules.

"First, be modest. Go quietly at the start; don't try to be original in your entertaining or your equipages. Follow the lead of others instead of striking out on your own.

"Second, never try to take any other woman's man, whether husband, lover or well-wisher.

"Third, never try to out-dress or out-jewel the other women."

The fate of those who disregarded Harry's advice, as his wife pointed out, was to consign themselves to the plebian masses thronging Narragansett Pier—only a few miles across the water, perhaps, but a galaxy away in spirit from the fashionable world. The losers, she said, "could only sit in the palatial villa they had so rashly acquired and accept their defeat with what grace they could. They seldom had the temerity to last out the season. A month of ostracism usually would send them over to the less aristocratic but more hospitable pastures of Narragansett, where they would try to console themselves with the big summer hotels on the water front. . . ."

During the first four years of their marriage, Elizabeth tried to live on Harry's terms, to accept the ego-crushing equation that she provided the money while he supplied the charm that made them so sought-after, so gilded with social success. She gave dinners for 150 people. She endured his tantrums, in which he would rage at her, "Isn't it enough that I have to endure your presence here? I hate the sight of you—you are hideous to me. The only thing you can do is provide me with money which I at least have the taste to spend properly."

Then, by her own account, Elizabeth fell in love with a man, ironically one whom Harry introduced to her, who was a paragon of looks, distinction and noble disposition. The "smouldering flame of rebellion in my heart," as she related in her Ouida-like style, "had almost died when I met X."

She would have left Harry for Mr. X in a flash, as she told it, except for one reason, her mother, "to whom divorce was an unbearable disgrace, who would not even allow it mentioned in her presence."

The resultant triangle was something like a magazine serial of the time. Harry pretended not to know that she had strayed. Elizabeth and Mr. X conducted themselves with a propriety later generations would find patently ridiculous if not incredible. "My whole heart went out to him in longing," she would write. She endured her loveless marriage only by assuring herself that after her mother died she would be free to marry the man she loved.

Meanwhile she put up with the emptiness of her society marriage and pitied Harry because "social ambition was the breath of life to him; he gloried in it, laughed when the journalists nicknamed him The King of Snobs." She accepted with sardonic amusement his first long-delayed compliment, "You see my work is bearing fruit. You are becoming a smart woman, Bessie." And she hugged to herself the occasional comeuppances Harry received from people who detected traces of the snuff-merchant's son in him. Once he invited the elegant James de Wolfe Cutting to dinner and listed all the other socially prominent people who would attend, adding, "I want you to appreciate that this is one of our representative parties." "Representative of what?" Cutting asked. "Embonpoint, I should think, judging from your list."

Though his own father had dealt in tobacco products, Lehr was one of those Newporters who were affronted when Frederick P. Garrettson, a graduate of St. Paul's and otherwise socially acceptable, decided to open a quality grocery. To drive home the point that going into trade was not regarded as soigné, Harry leaned across the table at a formal banquet and loudly told him, "Oh, I say, Garrettson, I am giving a dinner next week. Will you send me down a case of champagne?"

"Certainly," Garrettson retorted. "The usual cheap brand, I suppose?"

For the most part Elizabeth tried to live up to the image Harry had created for her and to content herself with joining in the laughter over his "drolleries," with interesting herself in his activities as a social arbiter, with treasuring such tributes to his talents for creating amusement as a letter from Mrs. Belmont: "Do, do exert yourself and let us all make the most of the hour with us. . . . Come to Brookholt. You will whitewash the black clouds hanging over you and grow warm in the reflected light, and I, in an endeavour to cheer you shall know the comfort I may give even if I fail to know it myself and thus your presence will bring its own blessing."

In his middle years Harry began to doubt that his strenuous fluttering as the most colorful of social butterflies had been worthwhile. Growing more portly every year, his face pinker and plumper, he had come to resemble more than ever an intelligent and well-bred porker, one covered with blue ribbons, but with a melancholy look coming into his eyes in unguarded moments.

He and Elizabeth began touring Europe almost annually as a distraction. In 1906 they appeared in Berlin for the autumn season. German prestige had risen amazingly in the world and Unter den Linden was filled with Americans who recognized that Berlin, like London and Paris, had become one of the social capitals. With a stirring of the Teutonic half of his ancestry, Harry was determined that he would be presented at Kaiser Wilhelm's court. A Berlin newspaper boasted that the "Berlin Court now has a greater attraction for the millionaires of the New World than the Court of King Edward. More and more 'Dollar Princesses' flying to Berlin, after having previously purchased their dresses in the Rue de la Paix in Paris."

When Harry did make his bow at the Wilhelmine court, he

was reported in a Berlin newspaper to have come a cropper. Under the headline CONTRETEMPS AT A COURT BALL, the journal not only summarized his career in unflattering terms ("despite his humble origin—and probably on account of the nobility of his good looks—he obtained the hand and the weighty millions of Miss Drexel and immediately afterwards made himself talked about in New York society through his eccentric behaviour") but claimed he appeared at the Kaiser's court as the "perfect exponent of the 'Gentleman-Cowboy' type—the latest achievement of American culture." The newspaper's account continued:

"Mr. Lehr followed the trail of his compatriots to the East and eventually arrived in Berlin accompanied by his wife. Through the influence of the American ambassador he managed to obtain an entry into Court circles. His debut took the form of appearing before the Grand Mistress of the Court in a check grey suit, coloured shirt, brown boots and a bowler hat, for he has the idea that, like the Prince of Wales, he is perfectly capable of starting a new fashion. . . .

"His attitude at the Court Ball caused a certain amount of half-amused annoyance. He decided that this was a suitable occasion to introduce another new fashion and appeared in baggy breeches, terminating a good four inches above the ankle, white silk stockings and patent leather shoes with diamond buckles.

"When the time came for the ladies' défilé, his wife, not having yet been presented at Court, had to take her place behind the other ladies of the Embassy. This seems to have provoked the anger of Mr. Lehr who appears to be filled with a sense of his own importance. Evidently under impression that he was directing a free fight with whisky bottles in a New York bar, he became rowdy and announced that the combined price of all the trash worn by all the other ladies in the room would not pay for his wife's jewels and that he could not allow her to stand so far behind. In order to avoid a worse scandal he was given into and his wife moved forward.

"This is anyway the story as it circulates in American circles in Berlin, who appear to be well informed regarding the adventures of their remarkable countryman. At any rate he can now boast in New York that thanks to his American 'spunk' he was able to upset the precedence at a Berlin Court Ball."

Harry indignantly protested the inaccuracy of that account, but the story was picked up and republished in the American press, with one newspaper inveighing against Lehr's "lowering American prestige by clowning at foreign courts." Certainly it was hard for his friends to imagine how, even through German eyes, Lehr could be seen as a "gentleman-cowboy" type; no one had ever detected the slightest Rough Rider tendency in his makeup, and there were many of the manlier types who thought Harry should have been flattered by the description.

All during their subsequent journeyings in Germany, Elizabeth wrote, they heard "echoes of that wretched article." They showed up in Dresden and announced their desire to be presented to the King of Saxony. St. John Gaffney, the U.S. consul-general in Dresden, refused to accede to their wishes and had to be bullied by Ambassador Charlemagne Tower in Berlin before he would see to it that Mr. and Mrs. Harry Lehr were presented to August IV of Saxony.

Before they left Germany, however, they got another chance to play the Berlin palace. This time their appearance was more successful, though Harry again insisted on wearing knee breeches and silk stockings because, as someone observed on that occasion, "he has the finest pair of legs in the room." The ladies' legs were, of course, covered by trains sweeping the floor, or the competition might have been greater.

This time, too, the Kaiser insisted that Harry be presented to him informally by Ambassador Tower. From all accounts Wilhelm had introduced a certain amount of levity to his court, not to mention a raucous informality in the conduct of foreign affairs, so it was not surprising he told Harry:

"I am curious to meet you, because I am told that you are the man who makes America laugh. I think we need someone like you in Europe."

Elizabeth continued to endure her loveless marriage year after year, Newport season after season, even when one of Harry's dearest friends, Mrs. Belmont, "fixing me with her gimlet eyes," one day told her, "You are not happy with Harry Lehr. You ought to leave him. I'll help you." When Elizabeth demurred, Mrs. Belmont replied, "You are an old-fashioned woman, Bessie. I am the woman of the future."

Her real loyalty, however, was not to her husband, who did not deserve it, but to her mother, who could not abide divorce. Within weeks after her mother died, Elizabeth consulted a Paris lawyer about getting a divorce and was told that "With the evidence I have here, there can be no possibility of your losing your case." Then she would be free to marry Mr. X, who had sent her a letter just after her mother's death and asked to see her as soon as possible.

A bathetic scene with Harry followed immediately after her visit to the lawyer's office. He somehow got wind of her plans and bought a diamond and ruby cross as a token of his sudden esteem—and no doubt his sudden terror at the possibility of being deprived of his only visible means of support.

When Elizabeth announced that she intended to leave him, he turned chalk white and looked as though he might swoon. "Bessie," he pleaded, "you would not leave me? I know you have been miserable. I have not been fair to you. But I am not like other men. I told you long ago that I cannot love any woman. All women are repulsive to me, from a physical point of view. I have hated you, hated the scent of your hair, the sound of your voice, because you represent womanhood to me, and so I have tried to make you suffer. Don't you understand? Won't you understand?"

Elizabeth did understand, to an extent that few women of her time would have, but she was determined to find a little middle-aged happiness on her own.

The denouement was the sort of plot twist that Edith Wharton, in her most dramatic mood, would have eschewed. A few weeks after Harry made his plea, Elizabeth instructed her lawyer to proceed with the divorce. Next morning Harry brought in the Paris *Herald*, their friend Commodore Bennett's newspaper, and told her, "There's something here you might be interested to read, Bessie."

"Just leave them there," she coldly replied, pointing to the bottom of the bed. She was determined not to give Harry any reason to believe he might be reprieved.

Waiting until she heard his footsteps retreating downstairs, she finally reached down to pick up the *Herald*, one of the top heads of which was DEATH OF FAMOUS AMERICAN.

Below Harry had marked the front-page story in blue pencil. It told of the death of her Mr. X.

There seemed to be no point in obtaining a divorce, and she stayed on as Mrs. Harry Lehr, his no longer quite so submissive partner, until his death twenty-eight years after that ruinous wedding night.

Part Four

THE GLITTER OF DECAY

14.

THE DOGS' DINNER
AND OTHER TRANSGRESSIONS

THE LONGER Mamie and Tessie and Alva stayed in power, the more they were influenced by the elfin humors of Harry Lehr, and the more society slipped from Victorian restrictions toward Edwardian sensuality and idiosyncracy, the summer gaiety in Newport turned increasingly frenetic in its pleasure seeking. Cotillions were going out, their quaint and formal patterns giving way to the turkey trot, the bunny hug, the kangaroo dip and other ballroom fads that indicated the nation was on the brink of mass zoophilia. Whatever restraint the super-rich had managed in the past was being flung overboard. A veritable mania for the overly sumptuous seized the resort. Newport parties at the feverish crest of the golden quarter-century seemed to have been staged by a pioneer film producer who had been told to forget about the budget and produce one spectacular after another.

Sheer display, on which it could be proved that vast amounts of money had been spent, was now the prescribed form, with quiet good taste deprecated as dowdiness or penny-pinching. There were floods of new money in the social game with the recovery from the depression of the mid-nineties and the demonetization of silver, which fattened the purses of "gold bug" Eastern bankers and capitalists.

Even with the solid old gold-standard dollar of the turn of the century, the sums spent on entertainment were impressive. Some of the wealthier hostesses spent up to half a million on entertaining themselves and their friends during the two-month summer season, and Mrs. Elizabeth Drexel Lehr was accurate in forecasting that such opulence would never be seen again. Into those July and August weeks were crowded balls, dinners, picnics and parties of every description, each designed to make the most striking impression. "Colossal sums were spent in the prevailing spirit of rivalry," wrote Mrs. Lehr. "I remember Mrs. Pembroke Jones [whose social ascendancy had been sponsored by Harry Lehr] telling me that she always set aside $300,000 at the beginning of every Newport season for entertainment. Some hostesses must have spent even more. A single ball could cost $100,000, even $200,000. No one considered money except for what it could buy."

The balls were so sumptuously mounted that they might have been produced and directed by David Belasco, the lavishness of whose productions had become a Broadway legend. Newport was, in fact, becoming more and more influenced by Broadway and sheer theatricality, as was demonstrated by Grace Vanderbilt's Fête des Roses gala at her Beaulieu estate. Social historian Wayne Andrews considered it "the great party of our century." It was so expensive and multifaceted an extravaganza, mock-modestly styled an "at home" by the hostess, that one of the guests, Grand Duke Boris of Russia gasped, "Is this really America or have I landed on some enchanted isle? Such an outpouring of riches! It is like walking on gold."

The occasion was so splendiferous that the New York newspapers, having dispatched an amphibious force of reporters and photographers, devoted only one column to President Roosevelt's political tour (he was merely running for reelection that summer) and four and a half columns to Grace Vanderbilt's hoedown. On that August evening in 1902, her son would recall, Mrs. Vanderbilt stood on the lawn, greeting her guests, "standing in a little green circle of light, looking like a portrait by Gainsborough in her *mousseline de soie* pale-green and white gown and huge plumed black picture hat. With the costume she wore her cabochon emeralds and diamond stomacher. Directly behind her on the lawn of Beaulieu stretched a midway some 275 feet long, enclosed in turkey-red calico and blazing with red calcium lights looking, as one guest observed, 'like a tunnel of fire.' At the entrance to the midway stood a large jar of orchids and a Persian rug." The estate was aglow with fairy lamps, and huge baskets of red roses were hanging everywhere to carry out the motif. A fireworks display of gold and silver cascades formed the backdrop against the moonlit waters of the bay.

The first part of the entertainment was the midway and its games of chance, with tents and booths in which the prizes were gold cigarette cases for the men and enamel vanity boxes for the women. Then everyone moved to the wooden theater built on the lawn by a hundred carpenters and other craftsmen and including a stage with professional lighting. The whole company of the Broadway success, *Red Rose Inn,* starring Irene Bentley and Eddie Foy, along with their scenery, props, baggage and stage crew, had been transported from Broadway. The Manhattan theater in which *Red Rose Inn* had been playing had to be closed down for two nights, and it was estimated that the total cost of Grace Vanderbilt's production would have supplied the necessary backing for any three of David Belasco's presentations. "How much money is there in the house?" comedian Foy, peering through the peephole in the curtain, inquired. "About 'steen billions," replied a fellow actor.

After the performance, which had been cut from three hours to one on Mrs. Vanderbilt's orders because she feared her friends would grow restless if subjected like lesser folk to the full-length version, supper was served inside the house and on the piazza. The showfolk, of course, were segregated; it would have been too daring to allow actors (and worse yet, actresses) to sit at the same table with the gentility. The cast was fed under a tent set up at the end of the midway, where it was felt they would be more comfortable. "Naturally enough," as a theatrical magazine remarked, "these supper tables became known as Bohemia, and the guests strolled into this ever-fascinating atmosphere and mingled there with the prima donnas, the comedians, and the chorus. Under the combined fire of experienced chorus eyes, Mr. Vanderbilt fled precipitately behind a Japanese vase."

During the supper, an army of workmen swarmed back into the estate and transformed the one-night-stand theater into a

ballroom. Two orchestras provided the music for a hundred
couples (Mrs. Vanderbilt had limited her guest list to two
hundred, causing one disgruntled, and noninvited, Newporter to
remark, "The Vanderbilt guest list is a victory in vacuums.
Nobody is there who ought not to be"). The dancers whirled over
rose petals strewn on the ballroom floor.

Mrs. Vanderbilt's "at home" ended with a sunrise breakfast,
and inevitably was the subject of moralizing editorials in the
more serious newspapers, which speculated on how many
starving slum children could have been fed with the money spent
on entertaining Mrs. Vanderbilt's guests for six or seven hours.

Newport, happily unaware that it was supposed to have a
collective social conscience, called for more wine and madder
music.

More or less imaginative motifs became the rage, and nothing
was spared to enhance them. The Newport estates were transformed into stage sets larger than even the Hippodrome could
have accommodated, and their hostesses anticipated C. B. De
Mille in the authentic detail of their productions.

There was Tessie Oelrichs' White Ball, which glittered for a
long time in Newporters' memories. Her forty-room chateau,
Rosecliff, which was designed by Stanford White several years
before the architect was murdered and which had been adapted
from Marie Antoinette's Court of Love at the Grand Trianon in
Versailles, included the largest ballroom in the United States. In
the forecourt and gardens were groupings of statuary on tall
pedestals which, critics said, gave them a World's Fair look.

For the White Ball Mrs. Oelrichs' Court of Love was
decorated entirely in white and guests were commanded to wear
all-white costumes. The crowning touch was a small navy, which
never set sail. Rosecliff overlooked the sea but not the harbor
with its sailing yachts. Tessie, however, decided that white sails
and masts must form the backdrop glimpsed through the tall
windows of her ballroom. She ordered a dozen full-scale ships
with white hulls and sails, in mock-up form, built for one night's
display. Placed in front of her white marble balustrade and

brilliantly lighted, they looked like a white fleet about to sail into the ballroom.

Newport's summer extravaganzas may have been the outgrowth of rivalry and crass social competition, but their artistic merits were, if a little on the florid side, undeniable. Mrs. Oliver Harriman wrote in a magazine article: "I have been present at famous receptions and parties in London and Paris and elsewhere in Europe. And I say to you, after most carefully weighing my words, that the balls in Newport are absolutely unparalleled for beauty and authentic magnificence. I go to a ball at Newport as I would go to the performance of the Russian ballet. Sometimes I find myself in some fabulous vineyard, where from the branches of the great tree hang thousands and thousands of bunches of huge green and purple and crimson grapes. Another evening I drift through a gorgeous Venetian pageant, some dense velvety painting of Titian's or Veronese's suddenly sprung to life at a magic touch. Or again it's a *fête champêtre,* all charm and airy sophistication. Or tonight's ball may be a visualization of all the dreams we have had while we listened to a Hungarian rhapsody, hundreds of gypsies wandering over a lawn, grouped around their camp-fires, singing their melodramatic hearts out. . . ."

The stress of all those occasions, the "terrifying sums" spent on them (as Elizabeth Drexel Lehr put it), "the libations poured out on the altar of snobbishness," must have contributed greatly to the incidence of mental breakdowns among Newport's great hostesses. So little humor leavened the intense solemnity, the desperate urge to outdisplay, in what was after all supposedly a process of enjoyment. You were only as good as your last party, to adapt a Hollywood truism. There were only a few flashes of wit playing over the scene, and they usually came, with a bitter or wounding effect, from Mrs. Stuyvesant Fish. The heartaches of the losers did not disturb her sleep. A young socialite named Bobby Van Cortlandt, annoyed at not having been invited to a recent Fish gala, languidly remarked, "I never can remember the name of your house, Mrs. Fish. Is it Crossways or Cross Patch?" "Well," she retorted, "anyhow it's a patch you'll never cross, young man."

To Richmond Barrett, surveying the increasingly costly magnificence of a Newport party among the top-drawer hostesses, it
seemed that only Mrs. Fish with the other two members of the
Great Triumvirate saved what was becoming a national institution—each affair reported in the newspapers the morning after
with as much detail as the latest political scandal—from sinking
beneath the weight of its scenery, props and wardrobe department. Mamie and Tessie and Alva, with Harry capering in the
background, "kept the tempo lively . . . saved the show from
bogging down . . . they had spontaneity and extraordinary
gusto; and their team-work was excellent."

But they did not always work at play in perfect harmony.
There were times when the temptation to outdo each other, as
well as the unaffiliated hostesses, was irresistible and they
succumbed to a form of what might be called up-womanship.

One time the dirty-trick department came into play was the
occasion of Mrs. Stuyvesant's grandest effort, her Mother Goose
Ball of August 1, 1913. The 200 guests invited to the ball were
commanded to wear costumes based on Mother Goose characters, and her ballroom was decorated in a fairyland fashion that
seriously depleted the Fish exchequer.

It was to be Mamie's last hurrah. She was getting old, and
Stuyvesant wasn't getting any richer, and she wanted to give
Newport something to remember her by.

Yet it was her dearest friend, Tessie Oelrichs, who maliciously
ruined the occasion, turned it into anticlimax.

Mamie was invited to be guest of honor at a dinner at Tessie's
Rosecliff just before the Mother Goose Ball—then she and the
others would drive in their carriages and limousines over to
Crossways for an all-night session of playing Little Jack Horner,
Little Miss Muffet and the others.

Tessie, however, made her "simple little dinner" such an
extravagant, sumptuous, many-coursed affair glittering with gold
plate and awash in champagne, that the Mother Goose Ball
seemed a drab little exercise by comparison. Her guests observed
that as Mrs. Fish stood at the head of the reception line her eyes
were red from weeping, and later she was seen snuffling into her

little lace handkerchief. How insufferable of Tessie to make her ball look like a barn dance out in the backwoods.

She stopped the music around midnight to read a poem composed (by someone else, she said, but evidently with her collaboration on its stinging theme) in honor of "Mary Goose, wife of Isaac Goose," the inspiration for her ball. Some of the lines must have pierced the self-complacency of more than one little Bo Peep or Miss Muffet, comparing the old lady in the Granary Burying-Ground at Boston to their frivolous activities. It read:

> In quaint old Granary she lies;
>   And all around her beats
> The pulse life that Boston pours
>   Through narrow, crowded streets.
>
> America's first woman poet;
>   Pause, ye blue-stockinged dame,
> And you in auto, or on wheel,
>   And read her simple name.
>
> That yet shall live when on your steps
>   Oblivion follows after;
> Enduring as a mother's love,
>   Fresh as a baby's laughter.
>
> And yet she was not learned or great;
>   No prophet of her times,
> This grandam by a cradle small
>   Crooning her ageless rhymes.
>
> She never tried to mold her world;
>   (That problem Superhuman!)
> She never had a higher aim
>   Than to be just a woman.
>
> Yet o'er what "modern woman's" work
>   Such consecration lingers?
> Her words are lisped by baby lips
>   And traced by babies' fingers.

So let her praise be sung—
More precious than all other;
Oh listen! down the centuries
The children call her "Mother."

If anything more was needed to put a damper on the ball, so tacky by comparison with Tessie Oelrichs' feast, that poem did it. Not even the most self-sufficient society lady wanted to be reminded how much she neglected her maternal duties in favor of her social life; to hear the lisping of baby lips or feel the tracing of baby fingers, when those caresses were largely reserved for nannies and governesses.

The Mother Goose Ball was supposed to last all night, but at two o'clock Mrs. Fish ordered the orchestra to play "Home Sweet Home" over and over until the last shepherdess and Tommy Tucker took the hint and left Crossways to its temporarily shattered mistress.

She could hardly have felt more favorably disposed toward Tessie Oelrichs after reading the *Town and Country* magazine's account, which slyly, between the lines, revealed just how she had been done in by her old friend's mining-camp humor:

"Mrs. Herman Oelrichs in the role of Mother Goose cooperated with Mrs. Stuyvesant Fish, the Fairy God-mother, in the most enthusiastic way by giving her dinner for 200 people preceding the Mother Goose and Nursery Rhyme Ball. . . . Can anyone imagine Mrs. Oelrichs as Mother Goose? Let no one try. Think rather of Marie Antoinette in Watteau dress playing at the simple life at the Trianon. . . .

"Everybody felt kindly towards Mrs. Fish's entertainment; the cleverness that took the place of ostentation appealed to people of all classes. . . . There were no exciting tales throughout Newport of a hilarious ending to the ball. During the last hour, the orchestra played 'Home Sweet Home.' The young people danced to the strains of the melody, singing as they circled the ballroom; the admirals, the dowagers, and all the elder people joined in the chorus. At three o'clock Fairy God-mother brought the ball to a close. But from her house about sixty young people went to Mr. Lanier's residence and danced until the clear light of day."

Next morning the word flashed around Newport that Mrs. Fish had announced her decision not to speak to Mrs. Oelrichs again. It took Harry Lehr, as the Metternich of Newport, most of the winter to patch up their friendship.

The rest of Newport chose not to be satirized out of its obsession with enjoying itself only through the expenditure of large amounts of money and thousands of man-hours work by the local artisans and their corps of servants. Throughout the resort's golden age there was a Louis XVI atmosphere of florid decoration, an overstuffing of stomachs with roasted gamebirds, a staging of theatrical spectaculars, a torrent of vintage champagne that brought a sclerotic flush to the face of Newport society. Too-muchness was to be noted even at what were proclaimed as simple little affairs for a few hundred intimate friends. Grace Vanderbilt's "at home" early in the 1902 season, which D. W. Griffith could have filmed for one of his death-of-a-civilization epics, was a sample of how the top dogs amused themselves.

One of the simpler affairs at the Marble House, merely a dance rather than a ball, called for the services of "many house servants and Berger's army of waiters dressed in Louis XIV style," according to the local society page. "There were nine French chefs in the kitchen; one course alone consisted of 400 mixed birds. Three orchestras played. . . . There was a remarkable floral feature near the grand staircase, a large bronze drinking fountain, surmounted by an immense plate-glass mirror. The basin was filled with tall lotus, water hyacinths, and tiny fairy lamps, while all around flocked a swarm of live hummingbirds. Hovering around the open flowers were also brilliant butterflies and bees, which Mrs. Hodgson, who had charge of the decorations, had imported for the occasion."

When the inveterate Anglophile James J. Van Alen gave a ball for his daughter May, the grand staircase was "festooned from floor to dome with garlands of thousands of American Beauty roses caught up with silk ribbons. In the drawing room, orchids were massed. The terrace was covered with an Egyptian tent, made of rich Egyptian tapestries. The floral decorations here were wild grasses, tall papyrus, lotus flowers and night-blooming water lilies."

And it took weeks for Mr. and Mrs. Pembroke Jones' artisans and decorators to convert their estate into a simple woodsy scene in which the local dryads and centaurs could frolic. "The supper tent was decorated to represent a woodland scene, the sides entirely enclosed and the ceiling hung thickly with the beautiful southern bamboo vine, brought especially from the South for the occasion. The temporary ballroom and theater combined was eighty-five feet long and forty wide; it was made of substantial material and entirely enclosed so as to be serviceable in any kind of weather. The decorative scheme was white and pale green in tone, lavishly emphasized by the use of 10,000 water lilies arranged in streamers on the ceiling and walls where they showed to the best advantage near the score of large plate-glass mirrors that lined the walls from floor to ceiling."

New money brought in by people with names no one would have recognized early in the nineties was responsible for much of the wave of extravagance. One batch of gaudy newcomers was headed by United States Senator Thomas F. Walsh, who had hacked a fortune in silver out of the Leadville, Colorado, mines and rented Mrs. O. H. P. Belmont's Beaulieu one season to make a sizable splash. His daughter Evalyn married John McLean, whose father published the Washington *Post*. Their married life was so hectic and later so publicized it really didn't need any embellishment such as the purchase of the doom-haunted Hope diamond.* When Mrs. McLean went in swimming off Bailey's Beach, she was always guarded by two detectives. "My God," she explained, "I've *got* to be watched," even though she didn't generally go swimming with her fabulous diamond on.

Perhaps it was the appearance of massive new fortunes, which

---

* The McLeans bought the diamond from Cartier's of Paris. It was said to have been worn, variously, by Marie Antoinette, a favorite of a Turkish sultan who was stabbed to death, and other ill-fated ladies. It was a huge blue stone originally said to have weighed 44¼ carats. One tale had it that the diamond came from India and had been owned by a maharaja before Marie Antoinette acquired it. It disappeared during the French Revolution and then popped up several decades later in England.

she could match not with her husband's money but her own sharp wits, that impelled Mrs. Stuyvesant Fish to parody the Newport Extravaganza. Either that or a sort of self-disgust, reflected by the poem she read at her Mother Goose Ball, over people laboring so hard to enjoy themselves and make that enjoyment highly visible. That there was something paradoxical, not to say heavily ironic, about a Great Hostess who could weep when her ball was overshadowed by her friend's dinner, and also satirize such affairs, seemed to have escaped her.

The dichotomy that occasionally afflicted Mrs. Fish was shown in the "Dogs' Dinner," which achieved nationwide publicity at a time when the country was floundering in the mid-nineties depression. She was cohostess with Mrs. Elizabeth Drexel Lehr at the latter's house, Arleigh, but the idea was Harry Lehr's. A hundred dogs, along with their owners, were invited; naturally it was their owners' pedigrees that were the more important.

The canine feast took place on the veranda, with many of the pets in fancy dress. They were placed around a low table formed by the leaves from dinner tables laid over a foot-high trestle. Din-din consisted of three courses served by Mrs. Lehr's servants, stewed liver and rice, fricassee of bones, and broken-up dog biscuits. "It must have been appreciated," Mrs. Lehr remembered, "because Elisha Dyer's dachsund so overtaxed its capacities that it fell unconscious by its plate and had to be carried home."

Unfortunately there was an uninvited guest. Lehr spotted a young man with a poodle wearing a paper ruffle around its neck lurking in the garden. Lehr showed him the gate. The gate-crasher turned out to be a newspaper reporter. Next morning there was his story in a New York newspaper telling how the bon ton of Newport's bow-wows was feasting on roast chicken and paté de foie gras. Preachers and editorial writers were provided with material for fulminations against rich idlers who, in the words of one of them, "wasted food on dogs that would have fed hundreds of starving people."

Still, the idea of giving parties that mocked the efforts of the more ambitious hostesses caught on for a while. Perhaps it was the perverse attraction of self-parody; a flashback to Marie Antoinette and the ladies of her court disporting themselves as milkmaids, or less distant in time, the Poverty Dinner given some years before in New York at which guests dressed like tramps, ate off shingles and drank out of tin cans.

Henry Clews, Jr., the heir of the New York stockbroker, issued invitations to a Servants' Ball, not for servants but for their employers. Each guest was commanded to appear as a maid, butler, valet, cook, chauffeur or whatever backstairs type he fancied. On the night of the ball, "no one had the courage to face their servants," as one participant recalled, "dressed in what appeared to be clothes purloined from their own wardrobes, with the result that Freedbody Park [in the center of Newport, where the servants often promenaded when off duty] was thronged with maids and menservants who had been given an unexpected evening off so that they should not witness their masters' and mistresses' departures for the ball."

Everyone agreed it was hilarious when young Clews, holding a duster in one hand and a pail in the other, greeted them at the door disguised as his own valet. Behind him in the entry hall Tessie Oelrichs was mopping the floor and O. H. P. Belmont was presiding as cloakroom attendant. Harry Lehr was impersonating the butler. Later the guests adjourned to the kitchen and prepared a curious menu of scrambled eggs, lobster Americaine, and spaghetti, which served as dinner. It was agreed that the spectacle of representatives of the greatest fortunes in America actually doing housework, taking off their own coats and hats and cooking their own food was excruciatingly funny, though the humor might have escaped many of those who read about the affair in their newspapers the next day.

The trend toward imitating the proles in their pawky pursuits, or "pigging it" as the English would say, continued with the William B. Leeds' "simplicity party." Mrs. Leeds' idea of the simple life was to take all the guests she could convey on their yacht *Noma* over to Rocky Point. There they had taken over the whole amusement park, throwing out genuine plebians from their playground, and shrieked with joy over riding the roller coaster and the water chutes.

No one seriously objected to such frivolities, but the so-called Monkey Dinner sponsored by Mrs. Fish and Harry Lehr was deeply frowned upon. It was their sardonic little joke, their comment on the snobbishness of resort society, a quality they themselves shared. Jokes that turn in on themselves sometimes do have a disastrous effect, as two such sophisticated persons should have known.

It was such a delicious joke that Mrs. Fish and her confederate planned that even Mrs. Lehr wasn't let in on the secret, though her home was to be the scene of the japery, as in the case of the "dogs' dinner." Mrs. Fish apparently preferred other people's houses for her practical jokes and reserved her own for statelier occasions.

Mrs. Lehr returned from a carriage drive to be informed that there would be an extra guest at their dinner the following evening. The visiting Chicago merchant prince Joseph Leiter, Lehr told her, had telephoned that he had a guest aboard his yacht whom he wanted everyone to meet.

Mrs. Lehr asked who the guest was. Prince del Drago of the Corsican nobility, she was told.

"Joe says he's a charming fellow," Lehr casually added. "I asked him whether he was any relation of the del Dragos we met in Rome, and he said that he certainly was. They all belong to the same family, only the Prince's is a distant branch. Joe thinks we'll like him immensely, but he warned me that he is a little inclined to be wild. He doesn't want us to give him too much to drink because he's not used to it. Anything goes to his head, and then apparently he is apt to behave rather badly."

Mrs. Lehr said she'd be delighted to have Prince del Drago at her table. Next day she was besieged with requests to meet the Prince and she was forced to lengthen her table and arrange new place settings.

That evening there was an assemblage of gilded names eager to be presented to the noble Corsican. At eight o'clock, with a blare of invisible trumpets and a flinging open of doors, in walked Joe Leiter and his companion. Surprise! Prince del Drago was a monkey in full evening dress. Everyone, Mrs. Lehr affirmed, was enchanted—so amusing to dine with a dinner-jacketed monkey. "He was given the seat on my right with Mrs. Fish who, like Harry Lehr, had been in on the secret all the time, on his other side," Mrs. Lehr wrote. "Throughout dinner he behaved admirably. I hardly like to write that his manners compared favorably with those of some princes I have met, but it would be no less than the truth."

Later in the evening as the wine flowed and the playful mood increased, someone recklessly slipped the guest of honor several glasses of champagne. Prince del Drago then betrayed his noble house by clambering up a chandelier and pelting the other guests with light bulbs, and had to be hauled back to the Leiter yacht.

It seemed an innocent prank until the more conservative element in Newport—including the elders rocking in their chairs on the porch of the Reading Room—read about it in the newspapers. One headline blared LEHR AND MRS. FISH HOLD UP AMERICAN SOCIETY TO RIDICULE. In cold print the joke did assume a sinister cast. At the very least it seemed a symptom of decadence; there was a phosphorescent glow of decay over gussying up a monkey and seating him among the social leadership of the nation; that was the kind of thing that brought down empires and fueled revolutions.

One newspaper editorial fulminated that "It is simply appalling to think of Mrs. Stuyvesant Fish becoming the leader of our society. In that case social life would be a long succession of monkey parties and equally undignified entertainments. I suppose our balls would all be more or less Indian war dances! It is dreadful to think of distinguished foreigners coming over here and judging us by Mrs. Stuyvesant Fish's entertainments, arranged with the assistance of Mr. Harry Lehr. New York society represents America in the eyes of the foreign world, and we should behave with a becoming sense of dignity."

The Monkey Dinner, it developed, was damaging to the impression Newport gave the rest of the country. Extravagance was one thing, silliness another; and people expected a certain measure of dignity in the people they were told to look up to. It served as a metaphor of high society going to any extreme in its boredom. In time, too, it acquired "all sorts of fantastic embellishments," as one Newport historian noted, "till in the end those two words 'Monkey Dinner' came to symbolize everything that was reprehensible in fashionable life. The well-bred little Prince del Drago had multiplied to a whole zoo of chattering bandar-logs. Mrs. Lehr's dinner had degenerated into a jungle orgy, with monkeys racing up and down the table, climbing all over the tipsy guests and hanging from the chandelier. If the public had been told that the mischievous creatures had shied coconuts at the company and cracked a few distinguished skulls, the story would in all probability have been accepted without a moment's hesitation." Mrs. Fish's social epitaph would not be her imaginative Mother Goose Ball but the Monkey Dinner.

None of that incessant entertaining, party giving, feasting and feting would have been possible, of course, without a large and industrious servant corps. It's a pity but the recorded history of Newport contains little information on the backstage crew that supported the efforts of all the social stars on the brightly lighted stage. A scholarly monograph could be written on the suave butlers and majordomos, the long-schooled chefs who made many of the more dazzling social careers possible; the nannies who relieved society ladies of their maternal duties and often their responsibilities; the social secretaries who tactfully saved their employers from error; the professional sailors who prevented the yachtsmen from going aground.

The backstairs world was as rigidly compartmented, as snobbishly systematized as the structure of the society they served. Between the butler and the most junior of the upstairs maids, between the chief cook and an apprentice gardener, there was a social and professional gulf as wide as that between Mamie Fish and the latest mining-camp hoyden coming to try her luck at crashing the Four Hundred. The servants were a mirror image of their masters. Each knew his place, each guarded the area of his responsibilities. No butler would think of soiling his gloves on emptying an ashtray, and no ladies' personal maid would consider making a bed or dusting the furniture. Often the lower members of the servants' caste were more respectful of the butler than of their employer.

One young Vanderbilt observed the pecking order of the servants' hall with a knowing eye. Stanley Hudson had been the Cornelius Vanderbilts' butler for more than twenty years, and next to Grace Wilson Vanderbilt was the most awesome personage in the household at Beaulieu. He changed his costume three times daily until at dinner only his black vest distinguished it from Cornelius Vanderbilt's. "Our butler never opened the front door or answered the telephone, relegating such tasks to the footmen. However, he did greet guests in the foyer, always speaking in the third person, such as 'If Madame will please be seated, I shall see if Madame is in.' He supervised the six footmen, clad in maroon breeches, white stockings, and buckled shoes, who set the table for luncheon and dinner, served meals, poured wine, and later washed the dishes. . . . After a dinner party, the chef left for his home as soon as the guests rose from the table, leaving in the butler's pantry trays of sandwiches to be served at the close of the evening."

Keeping those great houses on Cliff Walk and Bellevue Avenue in operating condition called for the services of hundreds of well-drilled servitors. Preparing and serving dinner for a hundred guests, invited on the spur of the moment by a feather-brained hostess incapable of boiling an egg, necessitated a heroic effort backstairs, but the lady of the house took the bows and was credited with being a magnificent household manager. The servant corps remained a faceless underground known by their Christian names, unchronicled and largely unsung. Mostly they were grossly underpaid, a circumstance noted by their employers only when they found that Herbert, the butler, and Maggie, the cook, were getting a rakeoff from the provisioners, or Aggie, the upstairs maid, was on the payroll of Colonel Mann's *Town Topics*, the ungrateful bitch. One of the few great ladies of Newport who recognized the help as fellow human beings was

Evalyn Walsh McLean, who had thirty people working to maintain Black Point Farm as a social center. The total payroll was $1800 a month, which didn't include their keep. Years later she was able to recall the first and last names of every one of the thirty servants, but she was an exception.

A few of the servants, thanks mostly to their masters' indulgence, became characters in their own right, picturesque personalities one catered to if one wished to stay in their employers' good graces.

One establishment pet was Azar, O. H. P. Belmont's man. Until Belmont married Alva Vanderbilt, Azar was his valet. Dressed in a Zouave jacket and wearing a red fez, he always stood behind Belmont's huge thronelike armchair when guests were welcomed to the hall of Belcourt. After his marriage Belmont promoted Azar to majordomo. "In a costume glittering with gold and eclipsing in grandeur any of his previous ones," one Belmont guest would write, "he would stand in the entrance between two English footmen in their court liveries and powdered hair and welcome the guests with all the pomp and ceremony of a Grand Vizier. His air of conscious superiority was unrivalled. He rose to every occasion with superb complacency."

Once, however, he was thrown desperately off-balance. His employers were about to board a train when Mrs. Belmont asked him to take custody of her large slavering French bulldog.

"Madame," he protested, with tears in his eyes, "do not ask such a thing of me. Sooner I would leave my master's service for ever. Never in my life has such an insult been put upon me. In my own land, Madame, I was a chief of camel drivers. I would rather die than lead a dog on a string."

Mr. Belmont, never having been a chief camel driver, had to take charge of the bulldog.

Another commanding personality was Mrs. Fish's butler for many years. Morton was English and possibly even a little haughtier than Mrs. Fish in her grander moods. "Everyone acquainted with the Fish household (including his employers) was more or less in awe of his superb impassivity," one of her intimates wrote. "He could wither the most brazen offenders with one glance of superiority. He had served in English ducal families, a fact which he never failed to impress on all with whom he came in contact."

Morton had one little failing, attested by the network of blown capillaries on his bladelike nose and cheekbones. He did like a touch of the sauce now and then, or as he put it, "I have a fine taste in wines through much service with the aristocracy." His tastes also ran to whiskey, brandy, gin and rum. And when he had overserved himself, he was inclined to grow testy of temper.

One day, severely hung over, he was outraged because Mrs. Fish had invited an unusual number of guests for lunch. Just after the last guest arrived, he confronted his employer and loudly informed her, "I suppose that because you happen to be Mrs. Stuyvesant Fish you think you can drive up and down the Avenue inviting whoever you like to the house. Well, let me tell you you can't. Sixteen is *my* limit for lunch. If you ask more, they go hungry."

Mrs. Fish discharged him, unfortunately, on the eve of one of her larger dinner parties. Next chapter: The Butler's Revenge. Morton dismantled every piece of her gold dinner service, unscrewing the various parts and leaving the floor littered with 300 bits of metal that looked like a jigsaw puzzle devised for King Midas. A wire had to be sent to Tiffany's, which dispatched two experts to reassemble the service just in time for the dinner.

Mrs. Fish was a martinet whose demanding temper was notorious at the employment agencies. She rarely managed to keep a servant for more than a year. One of her household rules was that even after the largest balls held at Crossways the ballroom and everything else had to be cleaned up before nine o'clock in the morning so she wouldn't have to face the disarray left by her guests. One servant who stayed with her for years was her personal maid, a Frenchwoman named Rose, who was given the dispensation of talking back to her employer.

After the reign of the bibulous but otherwise impeccable Morton, Mrs. Fish managed to keep one of his successors through the Newport season, but in her view the supply of domestic help was inexhaustible and their faces interchangeable. The butler had presided so efficiently over a Fish dinner party that Mrs. William B. Leeds complimented Mamie on having so admirable a chief assistant. "What I wouldn't give to have that butler of yours," Mrs. Leeds sighed.

Mrs. Fish rang the bell, and when the butler appeared, she told Mrs. Leeds: "Take him."

In a highly independent class by themselves were the Casino's ball boys, "shackers" as they were called, an obnoxious but necessary element in the tennis matches unless the players wanted to shag their own balls. Somebody had neglected to instruct them on their station in life or they had an ingrained disinclination toward behaving respectfully to the local lords and ladies; they also partook of the "townies' " resentment of the beauty and chivalry that descended on their birthplace every July and August and acted as though they owned the place.

The ball boys had to be recommended by their priest before the Casino management would hire them, but with few exceptions they "acted like hoodlums on the Casino turf," as one observer stated, and wore a sort of Hell's Kitchen uniform of red sweaters, caps with broken visors and well-patched trousers. There was no alternative to hiring local talent for ball-chasing duties, because the boys had established the rule that none but Irish Catholic ball boys be hired. "All attempts to improve their appearance and manners proved futile. Woe betide the stingy tipper on the Casino courts; he might be a power on Wall Street but the shackers could soon bring him to heel. They were slick little politicians, those boys, and for all their brass and impertinence, they knew how to hold onto their jobs."

None of those impudent young Celts disgraced himself so completely as the nameless footman who announced the guests at a costume ball. He was taken aback, naturally enough, when Mr. and Mrs. Henry Carter of Philadelphia approached. The diminutive Mr. Carter was impersonating Henry IV, which was easy enough to proclaim when Mr. Carter whispered his secret to the footman. But Mrs. Carter was the size of a Yale fullback and her assumed identity confused the footman, though she told him distinctly enough, "A Norman peasant."

"Henry the Fourth," bawled the footman to their fellow guests, "and an enormous pheasant!"

15.

BAILEY'S BEFORE THE BIKINI

IF THERE was one sector of summertime Newport where decorum was rigidly imposed, it was at Bailey's Beach. You might swing from the chandelier at one of Mrs. Fish's soirées and get away with it (if Mrs. Fish was amused), but if you appeared at the private beach showing one square inch more of your epidermis than necessary, you were blackballed from polite society. Fashion dictated that you be covered from wishbone to ankle. If you were female, in those decades before sun worship and a charcoal-brown skin were cultivated, you knew that only farmgirls risked the absolute pallor regarded as essential for beauty. Fashion and morality, for once, coincided; bathing at Bailey's—and everywhere else in the civilized world—was undertaken in full dress.

And if Newport's summer colony could be said to have the structure of a Chinese nest of boxes, each smaller and more exclusive than the other, then Bailey's Beach was the smallest and the hardest to penetrate. It was the "holy of holies of American society," as one resort historian put it. Membership in the Spouting Rock Beach Association, which owned and operated the beach, was strictly controlled, not only because of the determination to keep out undesirable or unclubbable elements but because of the limited facilities available. No American nabob, his wife and family could feel that he had made it socially until he had obtained membership and the cabana that went with it. "Bailey's Beach or Bust" was the unuttered slogan of all who came to Newport seeking acceptance.

Not that the beach was anything special as a beach. It was a small cove at the end of Cliff Walk, rather cramped and uncomfortable for anyone who really liked to swim rather than merely exhibit himself. Worse, there was a heavy growth of seaweed floating just offshore through which a marine biologist's dream of aquatic specimens scooted and darted. Swimming off Bailey's, in fact, could have been compared at times with being trapped in the Sargasso Sea.

The excluded townspeople found better accommodations at the mile-long public beach, which was roomier and cleaner and unclogged by seaweed, but which unfortunately lacked the cachet of sharing the sun, sand and sea with the Vanderbilts and Belmonts. At Bailey's, before it was rebuilt following the hurricane of 1938, the accommodations were rather spartan, more in the style of the vanished Boston Brahmins than of the lords of the Gilded Age. There was a wooden bathing pavilion no more salubrious in decor or comfort than those down on the plebian Jersey coast. The shelters each family used for undressing and dressing were merely wooden cubicles, with a pail of cold salt water for washing away the sand. The luxurious cabana, as developed by more epicene types down in Florida, was still far in the offing. A multimillionaire with the proper qualifications would rent four or five of the shelters for his family, but that was the only means of ostentation. Just being allowed past the gate conferred an immense feeling of privilege. One member of the club wrote:

"Only the elite could bathe at Bailey's Beach. It was Newport's most exclusive club. The watchman in his gold-laced uniform protected its sanctity from all interlopers. He knew every carriage on sight, fixed newcomers with an eagle eye, swooped down upon them and demanded their names. Unless they were accompanied by one of the members, or bore an introduction from an unimpeachable hostess, no power on earth could gain them admission. If they wanted to bathe, they could only go to Easton's Beach—'The Common Beach' as the habitués were wont to call it. There they would have the indignity of sharing the sea with the Newport townspeople, referred to by Harry

Lehr, who was fond of quoting the sayings of Louis XIV, as 'Our Footstools.' "

Bailey's, it is evident, was the place where the mighty could disport themselves in a full flowering of eccentricity without any outsiders to comment on their temporary lack of dignity. (An even more unbuttoned state prevailed at the Gooseberry Island Fishing Club, which was composed of Bailey's Beach's male inner sanctum. Its membership was limited to fourteen. On the islet just off Cherry Neck on the Ocean Drive, nude swimming was the main attraction, as well it might have been at a time when a bathing costume weighed almost as much as an Arctic explorer's. After swimming, the members dressed and repaired to their small green clubhouse, where a "select company" of ladies was entertained at lunch. The club was swept away by the 1938 hurricane and never reestablished.)

Bailey's at eleven in the morning was a spectacle of Victorian fun-making in all its cautious exuberance, as endearing and picturesque in hindsight as the gazebo, the pony cart, the bustle, and other artifacts of the period. Safe in their enclave from prying eyes and the even more intrusive camera lens—no photographer was ever permitted inside Bailey's until 1947, and then the honor went to the *National Geographic* magazine—the members could enjoy themselves as they pleased. Dowagers frolicked like porpoises, magnates whose frown could send a tremor through the New York Stock Exchange gamboled like spring lambs. The ladies wore full-skirted costumes and long black stockings—it was a historic occasion, and a shocking one, when Mrs. Herbert Parsons appeared without stockings one day just before the First World War, the first lady to display such temerity. Mrs. Parsons, the former Elsie Clews, was virtually placed in Coventry for her daring display of naked calves.

Mrs. August Belmont, Jr., the former Eleanor Robson and a celebrated actress, found that Newport was still trembling from the shock of Elsie's misconduct when she took over as chatelaine of the Belmont summer house By-the-Sea. "That first year—unfamiliar with the ancient or modern feuds of Newport—my mistakes were many and varied. One couple, who hadn't been invited to By-the-Sea for years by the senior Mrs. Belmont, accepted my invitation with alacrity. I placed the lovely, modern-minded Elsie Clews next to the formal, old-school chairman of Bailey's Beach, not knowing that he had refused to speak to her after she went in bathing there without stockings, in spite of the committee ruling in the summer of 1910 that long stockings were required articles for ladies at the beach.

"This was typical of the times. They assure me that the wording which was tacked on the wall of each of the ladies' bathinghouses at Northeast Harbor [the resort on Mount Desert Island near Bar Harbor] when the swimming pool was opened in 1918 was: 'Ladies in bathing suits are required not to lounge in the sun, as it may cause just criticism.' After that dinner Newport buzzed with gossip for days. . . ."

Provided the swimmer was properly covered from ankles to neck, however, he or she was permitted almost any sort of eccentricity. At times Bailey's Beach must have resembled a Mack Sennett comedy troupe on location.

James Van Alen, whose elegance was otherwise unchallenged in the summer colony, always went to sea, as one admirer recalled, "in the full glory of a monocle and white straw hat, thus proclaiming his whereabouts." He also puffed on a large Havana as he drifted about.

Mrs. O. H. P. Belmont, the formidable Alva, invariably made her appearance under a green parasol and "carried it belligerently into the water" as though to ward off any marine monsters she might encounter in the seaweed offshore.

Mrs. James Kernochan was one of the belles of the resort, yet when she showed up on the beach, she was an apparition to frighten off any cruising sharks. To protect her porcelainlike complexion, she armored herself in cumbersome black bathing shoes, a black blouse fastened with pearl buttons, a pair of bulky black pantaloons under a full black skirt, black jacket with billowing sleeves tied at the wrists, and thick ribbed black stockings. All this was topped off by a large black Mother Hubbard bonnet fastened under her chin. It was estimated that, dripping wet, Mrs. Kernochan must have weighed about 200 pounds.

None, however, took to the water with greater panache than Hermann Oelrichs, Tessie's absentee husband, who spent more time at Bailey's Beach than he did at Rosecliff on those rare occasions when he tore himself away from San Francisco. Oelrichs, a short fat man with the contours of a walrus, always appeared at the beach as though settling down for the rest of the summer; he carried a large lunch pail, a sizable flask of whiskey, several books and a waterproof cigar case. He would drift for hours offshore, a bulbous shape on the horizon, eating, quaffing, smoking and reading undisturbed by other swimmers. Sometimes he would drift a mile out from shore and be swept back to the beach by an incoming tide; frequently he had to be rescued by the Coast Guard before he could drift halfway to Nova Scotia on the Gulf Stream. Oelrichs did not like his maritime habits questioned and was outraged when he heard that some jester at the Naval War College had suggested that he was a menace to navigation and should be equipped with a buoy to warn off the coastal shipping.

All those amiable eccentricities would vanish in time, along with the proscription against showing more than a few inches of bare human skin.

Its exclusivity, however, would be maintained even after the rebuilding necessitated by the 1938 hurricane. There was a social grading process ordained as precise as the candling of eggs. The "A" memberships include eighty-one outside cabanas, each with two small dressing rooms; the "B" grouping consists of two hundred inside cabanas, and finally there is a locker room for those waiting to move up to the "B" and "A" grades. Despite the rebuilding caused by the hurricane, Bailey's would become no more prepossessing simply as a beach; it was and is the social cachet conferred by a membership that is more important than such amenities as a wide white strand.

Then and later the membership of Bailey's would take a certain perverse pride in their tiny enclave on the Atlantic shore. Some years ago, according to a resort historian, Mrs. George

Henry Warren appeared at a costume ball disguised as "Miss Bailey's Beach," her costume including a dress apparently made of seaweed festooned with orange rinds, banana peels, clamshells and other bits of debris. "But Bailey's protocol," he added, "permits no one to swim anywhere else. A British visitor who, a few summers ago, insisted on going down and taking a dip from the smooth rocks at the end of the beach was criticized as severely as an American might be for making his own rules at the Court of St. James."

Fortunately all the old lionesses of the Great Triumvirate period were long gone when the first bikinis made their appearance at Bailey's Beach.

16.

THE MARRIAGE MARKET

AMERICANS have always boasted that their matrimonial institution is based on love, and love alone, in contrast to the mercenary and other practical considerations of European marriages in the past. No *dot*, no dowry, no marriage brokers, no haggling over the joining of landowners' estates. The bartered bride was a tradition *not* brought over from the Europe of most of our ancestors.

In Newport the tradition of marriages based on romantic love was rooted in barren soil. Great fortunes and hoped-for dynasties could be disastrously weakened through mésalliance; the history of Jay Gould's heirs proved that. Heiresses had to be matched with heirs who would enhance the family's fortunes, either by marrying into an equally rich family, or one with higher social qualifications, or best of all into the English and European aristocracies.

The sons of such families were allowed considerable leeway in seeking wives, though they were discouraged from serious approaches to upstairs maids or ladies of the *Mam'zelle Champagne* chorus. They bore the family name, inherited its business or financial position, and would carry on somehow.

The girls, however, were regarded in many cases as chattels on the marriage market. They made their formal debut in New York coming-out parties and balls, but Newport was the display case for them. Summer was naturally the time for negotiating marriages. Newport and the several other fashionable resorts were thronged with eligible males, many of them fortune hunters, remittance men, cads, bounders, and muckers of all kinds. An anxious mother had to sort out the candidates and steer her daughter, forcibly if need be, toward a "suitable" marriage. If the family already had more money than it could spend in a century, what better way to add to its glory than acquiring an English lord or a French duke as a son-in-law? There was not only the glamour of the title, and the envy of rival matrons, but the entrée into international society afforded by a connection with the nobility abroad. Often, too, there was nothing a daughter wanted more than an aristocratic husband, even if his family's estates were entailed and its treasury urgently needed replenishing with American dollars.

More than anything else in the way of scandal and tales of extravagant spending, the Newport marriages outraged the rest of the country. Just before and after the turn of the century the newspapers broadcast lengthy accounts of various daughters of the Four Hundred being treated like chattels, of impoverished Old Families "selling" their daughters to the newly rich but socially underqualified or the wealthy upstarts "buying" an aristocratic European son-in-law. Novels dwelling sentimentally on this theme flooded the bookstores and spilled over into magazine serials. Newspaper cartoonists became downright savage in depicting a poor little millionaire's daughter, in chains, being shipped off to Europe to marry some la-di-da sprig of the decadent nobility. Soapbox orators used the forced-marriage theme to illustrate their contention that American capitalism was a brutal institution in all its aspects. The Newport villa had replaced Uncle Tom's cabin as the symbol of a new American slavery.

The tragedy of a number of Newport marriages may have been melodramatically enlarged upon in the popular prints and on the stage, but there was a gritty foundation of truth to the belief that a debutante was a pawn in the social game. Most girls were inculcated from puberty with the idea that their first duty, on being "finished" at school, outfitted by the best couturieres and proclaimed nubile at their debuts, was to contract a suitable marriage. The search among girls of families with depleted fortunes for the "right" husband often turned into tragicomedy.

Blanche Oelrichs, later the poet Michael Strange and the wife of John Barrymore (which proved a nonsocial marriage could also be disastrous), was a member of a wealthy family, but her father had consistently met with reverses in Wall Street. Abroad with her family, she was introduced to the wealthy and elegant Frederick Prince, who "spoke to me of his polo ponies at Myopia, his hunters at Pau, his apartments in London and Paris. . . . I began to wonder what it would be like to be an old man's darling." Daydreaming on that subject ended with the "appearance of a wife whom he had never mentioned." But there was still hope in the Prince family. "Almost immediately Mr. Prince, the conjurer, did pass up an extremely handsome son, with the jauntiest blond mustache, such gay good looks and laughing poise, and we fell in love over the first bouquet he handed me." It seemed certain to Blanche they would be engaged, until one day she returned home and found a farewell letter from her suitor. "Apparently Fred's father was sending him indefinitely out of Paris to conclude his studies at an obscure German university. . . . Of course it was the 'penniless Blanche Oelrichs' over again, and the theory of 'To whom that hath shall be given.' "

In vivid contrast were the experiences of May Goelet, certainly no prettier or more charming than Blanche Oelrichs, but a whole lot richer. Miss Goelet was twenty-four years old in 1902 and had made her debut a half-dozen seasons before. To be unmarried at her age was a cause for comment. That summer in Newport she had not attracted any eligible suitors so she headed abroad, heavily chaperoned, for the London season.

In London, it seems, her charms were magnified to an astounding degree, a process cynics might have attributed to the glamour of the American dollar. The clique of Anglo-American matchmakers, seemingly intent on wholesale transfusions of Yankee blood into brittle British aristocratic veins, took up her case. It was a good one; she was not only the daughter of one of New York's old-guard families but was related to, and entitled to a share of, the Vanderbilt and Astor fortunes.

A letter to her aunt, Grace Vanderbilt, made it seem that suitors were lurking behind every lamppost in Belgravia. First, Lord Shaftesbury "popped," as she put it, after knowing her for only three weeks. Despite that proposal, "the Duke of Roxborough is the man everyone says I am engaged to. . . . Mrs. Benson is crazy to make a match between Captain Holford and myself! And Lord Grey who married Captain Holford's other sister is very anxious to arrange it too. . . . Well, the next offer was from George Cornwallis-West, Princess Pless' brother. . . ." And so on. A prosperous American in-law obviously was prized equally with kind hearts and coronets.

By 1909 it was estimated that more than 500 American women had married titled foreigners, and the money that went with them in marriage settlements must have come close to unbalancing the American economy. It was further estimated that $220,000,000 went overseas as dowries.

On the evidence of her lively memoir, *Tragic Mansions*, the most perceptive observer of Marriage Newport Style was Mrs. Philip Lydig, the former Mrs. W. E. D. Stokes and before that Señorita Rita de Acosta. The Spanish-born Mrs. Lydig was not only a keen-eyed witness but a dashing adventuress on the Newport scene. Her dark hair and exotic features made her a favorite subject of painters. "That feverish small face," as Richmond Barrett described it, "with its opaque velvet skin under masses of black hair, was really almost a caricature. Her black eyes were extravagantly big; they looked like the half-blind headlights of some nocturnal moth that has blundered into sunshine." Adding to her golliwog look was a turned-up nose, almost startling in its impudence. Occasionally she turned out to play a few languid sets of tennis, on which occasions she always wore heavy gloves and a veil so thick it must almost have choked her. Only her huge black eyes were visible. Her gardenialike Castilian complexion was more important than appearing at the Casino in the correct costume. " 'Rita just hangs the veil on the peg of her nose,' a woman remarked one day; and it really was true. There was something comic but altogether beguiling about the perky tilt of that veil over that adorable little upturned snout."

Newport was as fascinated by Rita Lydig as young Richmond Barrett, largely because of her talent for self-dramatization. She was constantly reported at death's door, being rushed by private car to the Mayo Clinic, only to return as gay and talkative as ever. Despite the "gallant unobtrusive backing of one of the great American fortunes," she was so spendthrift that she was often tumbled into bankruptcy. Looking, as one Newporter said, like one of those whirling demimondaines captured by Toulouse-Lautrec, she was also the center of social, romantic or fiscal excitement during a Newport season.

Aside from the various crises she apparently generated for the purpose of keeping herself in center stage, she was married to an absentee husband whose activities were constantly the subject of gossip. Mrs. Lydig bore such humiliations with impeccable dignity. Once it was reported that his mistress in Paris was a ballerina who dressed in spectacularly bad taste. "I can't have you going around with a creature who looks like that," Mrs. Lydig informed her husband. She sent her husband's mistress to her own dressmaker to be properly outfitted.

Her own affairs, evidently, were conducted with élan, and a Latin taste for the melodramatic. One weekend she drove her electric car to the ferry landing to meet a former admirer, who immediately told her that he had rushed all the way back from Egypt to see her. Unless she took him more seriously, he had decided, life wasn't worth living. "Very well," Mrs. Lydig replied, "we'll die together." She then revved up her car as fast as it would go and crashed into a telegraph pole. Her car was wrecked, her admirer had to be removed to the hospital, but Mrs. Lydig walked away unhurt.

Newport would remember her not only for the daring with which she dressed herself—she always showed more of her bosom than was contemporarily respectable—and the dramas she created for herself, but her sole literary effort. Late in middle age, with her lively matrimonial and social careers behind her, she settled down and wrote with considerable candor about all she had observed on the Newport and Fifth Avenue scenes. In *Tragic Mansions* the actress gave way to the playwright; her subject was the unfortunate marriages arranged, mostly, by ambitious Newport mothers. "Some years ago," she observed, "it was more the fashion than it is now [she was writing in 1927] for rich American girls to marry foreign titles, but there are still a number of such marriages solemnized in fashionable churches every year, in spite of the fact that they have been notoriously disastrous in the past. They are frankly marriages of ambition, marriages without love, and they are instructive examples of how criminal such marriages can be."

In her Newport heyday, she saw a whole procession of Balzacian rogues from overseas descend on Newport to pick over the latest crop of heiresses. "They are a marvelous band of dissolute and dangerous men and women—Russian dukes, German princelings, Italian counts, Greek and Austrian and Roumanian noblemen, English gentlemen with suave manners and no means, women of title who make a living as go-betweens —all united in a smiling conspiracy to entrap the ignorant outsiders and to pluck them to their last cent."

The American female, in her belief, was not equipped to cope with the aristocratic-vulture type. She had been reared in the lingering American tradition formed by a chivalrous frontier attitude toward women. She had early been taught that her place was on a pedestal, from which she would be removed only to be elevated to the higher pedestal afforded by an advantageous marriage.

Naturally the American girl, no matter how sophisticated in the social sense, couldn't comprehend the venality, the depthless cynicism of the heiress hunters. "Love-making," she explained, "is at once a sport and profession for them. They do it with devotion and with skill. They enjoy it and they make their living by it. They pursue only rich women, of course, and if they bag a victim, they boast about it as proudly as any other sportsmen; and they even lie about it, if the bird gets away. No American girl is able to cope with them. She is accustomed to men who have some chivalrous feeling toward a woman—men who, at their worst, have a little pity for her as a fellow human being, and cannot carry on a liaison without feeling. These adventurers have no more affection, no more chivalry, no more pity than a wolf."

As an example of the tragedy that could result from one of those transatlantic matches based on the girl's money and the man's mercenary instincts, she cited the marriage of a girl she called "Virginia Cort," which became "the scandal of the fashionable world on two continents."

Her heroine's father had inherited a fortune and was a decent enough fellow, but her mother "married him ambitiously and led him such a miserable hen-pecked existence that he ran away with an openly immoral woman to force his wife to divorce him." Her mother got custody of Virginia, who was unimpressed by her mother's social ambitions. Her mother forced her into an engagement with an English peer who would enhance the mother's position, despite her father's efforts to prevent a loveless marriage. As Mrs. Lydig told the story:

"She was married with great pomp to the dissolute young lord, and her mother, like a simpleton, gave him independent control of Virginia's marriage *dot*. He continued to live the life to which he had been accustomed before his marriage, and it soon became evident that Virginia was trying to get her revenge by imitating him, but with no finesse whatever, with such outrageous simplicity that it was scandalous. She was credited with having as many lovers as Messalina. All England was shocked, and there was not a word offered in her defense when he put her out of his house one night, in the country, a cold winter night, and she had to walk half a mile in her night-dress to seek shelter in the gate-keeper's lodge.

"Having disgraced her, he divorced her, and no one blamed him. I saw her at an opening of the Royal Academy in London absolutely snubbed and ignored by everybody; and knowing what a dear, sweet girl she really was, it seemed to me heart-breaking. She retired to Paris and there she married a young French painter and lived, as I was told, in comparative poverty and complete obscurity. . . ."

Virginia's life had a happy ending, no thanks to her mother or the social system which bred her. Mrs. Lydig came across her in Paris years later and found that Virginia was still happily married to the unsuccessful painter. "When I saw how much happier she was than her old fashionable friends, and how much wiser in her way of life than they, I realized that instead of being wrecked by scandal, she had been saved by it."

So many of those girls offered on the international marriage market came from luxurious but loveless homes that they had little chance of happiness in any case, Mrs. Lydig believed. Often their parents had married under duress from their own families. To outsiders it might seem that a child reared behind the marble walls of a Newport "cottage," with his pony cart and governess and tutor, had a tremendous head start in life. But to Mrs. Lydig the child's "instinct of affection is confused and thwarted, 'badly conditioned' as the psychologists say, or unconsciously trained to respond to a 'servile image.' That may be why the rich girl so often elopes with a chauffeur and why the millionaire's son so often marries a chorus girl. It certainly seems to me to explain why the sons and daughters of the fashionable rich are so much less likely to be monogamous than the young men and women who have grown up in the common American home."

Typical of the loveless marriages in which the Newport set specialized was a beautiful girl "practically sold by an ambitious mother to one of the richest and most dissolute men in New York," and her son, who was "brought up wholly by servants." The young mother hated her husband so much that she couldn't stand the sight of her son, and left him in his father's custody when she obtained a divorce.

The boy, at fifteen, having taken his father as a model, was "coolly immoral and irresponsible, convinced that he could do anything he pleased because of his wealth . . . he seduced coldbloodedly the young daughter of one of my servants, and when her father appealed to me for help, the boy just eyed me cynically, as unabashed as some little animal without remorse and without imagination." The only question the boy had was, "How much does she want?" His father settled the matter with a $10,000 check.

As he grew into manhood, he gave every promise of being a perfectly amoral specimen, felt no responsibility for anyone but himself. Worse yet, he seemed to Mrs. Lydig not an exceptional case but just another link in an endless chain of biological misadventure, one monster begetting another. "Although he succeeded to a large estate on his father's death, he has no friends and no intimate connections except garage mechanics who perhaps admire him for his expert knowledge of explosion [sic] engines. He has recently become engaged to a very sweet and simple girl who has persuaded herself that he is a misunderstood and ill-treated character.

"He will undoubtedly ruin her life with cruelty. He is as dangerous to society as a maniac, being wholly without imagination for the sufferings of others, devoid of any generous or sympathetic emotion, and as powerful through his wealth as if he owned a magic ring and a genie to do his bidding. He is, as I see him, entirely the product of a loveless marriage and a home in which there was no affection. . . ."

When she inveighed against the kind of marriage in which an American fortune was bartered for a European title, Mrs. Lydig undoubtedly had uppermost in her mind the dictated marriage of Consuelo Vanderbilt to the ninth Duke of Marlborough. It was a textbook case that started, as Cleveland Amory remarked, a "veritable tidal wave of titled foreigners sweeping over American heiresses." Not long afterward Mrs. Ogden Goelet's daughter May was married off to the Duke of Roxborough. After that came royal carpetbaggers from every house that had once laid claim to a throne; the Russian province of Georgia would supply enough princely husbands for every social colony from Bar Harbor to Beverly Hills.

Consuelo Vanderbilt was eighteen, early in 1895, when she became an integral part of her mother's calculations. Alva Vanderbilt had just decided to divorce William K. and probably had decided to marry O. H. P. Belmont. A spectacular marriage—her daughter's, that is—would distract people from her own domestic plans. That spring Mrs. Vanderbilt trotted her daughter around Paris for the inspection of eligible young men. The market was brisk, and "I had five proposals of marriage. When I say I had, I mean that my mother informed me that five

men had asked her for my hand." All had been refused as
lacking the requisite pedigree, with only one, the German Prince
Francis Joseph Battenberg (of the house that married into the
British royal family and during World War I changed its name
to Mountbatten) received serious consideration.

Alva refused to listen to Consuelo's pleas that she wanted to
pick her own husband, that she was in love with Winthrop
Rutherford (a well-born young man, but American and therefore
lacking the patent of nobility) and wanted to marry him.
Rutherford had accompanied the Vanderbilts on the yachting
trip to India. By her daughter's account Alva proceeded to
eliminate Rutherford from the running with a coldly brutal
determination:

"Later I learned that he had followed us to Paris but had been
refused admittance when he called. His letters had been
confiscated; my own, though they were few, no doubt suffered the
same fate. . . . I knew that my mother resented my evident
misery, and her complaints about what she satirically termed my
'martyrdom' did not improve our relations. Like an automaton I
tried on the clothes she ordered for me. Visits to museums and
churches were varied by concerts and lectures. I went to a few of
those deadly debutante balls which I no longer cared for and
danced with men who had no interest for me. . . ."

The spring crop of marriageable noblemen being in short
supply, Mrs. Vanderbilt left Paris for London, with her rebellious
daughter still in tow. There, the advice of Lady Paget (the
former Minnie Stevens of New York) and Lady Randolph
Churchill (the former Jennie Jerome), a member of the American element of the hard-living "Prince of Wales set," was sought.
To young Consuelo Lady Paget seemed "Becky Sharp incar-
nate," a brittle, worldly-wise woman, who received the Vanderbilts with the "condescension that seemed to infect the habitués
of the inner circles of London society." Lady Paget surveyed
Consuelo through a pair of hard green eyes and announced that
if she was going to be sponsored by her ladyship, "she must be
able to compete at least as far as clothes are concerned with far

better-looking girls. Tulle must give way to satin, the baby *décolletage* to a more generous display of neck and arms. . . ."

The chosen candidate, it soon developed, was Charles Richard John Spencer-Churchill, ninth Duke of Marlborough and master of Blenheim Castle at the age of twenty-four. Consuelo was introduced to him at a dinner party in Belgravia and was placed next to him at the table, "a rather unnecessary public avowal of her [the hostess's] intentions." The thing she particularly noticed about him at that first meeting was that he "seemed inordinately proud" of his well-shaped hands.

The candidature of the Duke was in abeyance for the time being, and she received, through her mother, several proposals "evidently dictated by a desire for my dowry." The Vanderbilts returned to America, where Consuelo had a secret meeting with Winthrop Rutherford on a bicycle path on Riverside Drive, at which they decided to be secretly engaged and to elope if her mother wouldn't consent to their marriage. Then Consuelo was hauled back to England; apparently her mother had received word from the Lady Paget circle that the Duke of Marlborough was now willing to entertain the possibility of marriage, terms to be arranged, accommodation of the ducal life-style to be considered in deciding on the amount of the dowry.

Stately old Blenheim, the tremendous cost of its upkeep, made the Duke as much a victim of the matchmakers as Consuelo Vanderbilt. Later he would tell Consuelo that he himself gave up the person he loved, "for to live at Blenheim in the pomp and circumstance he considered essential needed money, and a sense of duty to his family and to his traditions indicated the sacrifice of personal desires."

Consuelo rather liked the Duke but returned to America with her mother firmly set against the idea of marrying him. The Duke had been invited to join them at Newport in September and she had only six weeks in which to thwart the plan. Her problem was how to get in touch with Rutherford, "my Rosencavalier" as she thought of him, and be rescued from her mother's clutches. In 1895, it was still possible for a young woman to literally be held captive, and that was Consuelo's fate.

The marble palace in Newport had become her prison, with her mother and governess as the warders. "I was never out of their sight. Friends called but were told I was not at home. Locked behind those high walls—the porter had orders not to let me out unaccompanied—I had no chance of getting any word to my fiancé. . . ."

Finally Consuelo had it out with her mother, told her she had no intention of marrying the Duke of Marlborough or any other man of her mother's choice. Alva, though already planning to secure her own happiness through remarriage, a project that would be made socially smoother by Consuelo's marrying a nobleman, flew into a violent rage at her daughter's show of independence. "I suffered every searing reproach, heard every possible invective hurled at the man I loved. I was informed of his numerous flirtations, of his well-known love for a married woman, of his desire to marry an heiress. My mother even declared that he would have no children and that there was madness in his family. . . . In a final appeal to my feelings she argued that her decision to select a husband for me was founded on considerations I was too young and inexperienced to appreci-ate."

Alva wound up by threatening to shoot any man who married Consuelo in defiance of the maternal will. At the end of their night-long session of recrimination, Consuelo felt "as if all my youth had been drained away." Later that day Alva sent a friend to tell Consuelo that her naughty desire to marry the man of her own choice had caused Alva to have a heart attack. Not quite believing that fib, she asked to see her mother for a final appeal. "Your mother will never relent," she was told, "and I warn you there will be a catastrophe if you persist. The doctor has said that another scene might easily bring on another heart attack and he will not be responsible for the result."

Under that threat—a false one as indicated by the long and strenuous life ahead of Alva—Consuelo yielded and said she would march to the altar under her mother's orders.

With that, Alva sprang out of her supposed deathbed and the

atmosphere of the Marble House changed from that of a prison to a center of frenetic social activity. The place fibrillated with preparations for what Alva proclaimed would be the most magnificent fete in Newport history, at which the Duke of Marlborough would be introduced to the elect of American society. Alva imported from Paris as favors for the cotillion an assortment of French etchings, fans, watchcases and mirrors, all of the Louis XIV period, each bearing a medallion with the imprint of the Marble House.

Certainly the ball was everything that money could buy. Alva and Consuelo received their guests in the Pink Room with its facings of Nubian marble, Consuelo in a white satin gown trimmed with lace that had belonged to her maternal grandmother. The whole ground floor of the Marble House had been transformed into an artificial garden, the bronze fountain in the great hall filled with hyacinths and lotus from the Nile as its centerpiece. White silk lanterns made in China were hung all over the house and its grounds.

Metaphorically enough, Richard T. Wilson, the hetman of the famous marrying Wilsons, led the cotillion with Consuelo on his arm. The Wilsons were another Confederate family, like Alva's, which had prospered through selling blankets—not of the finest quality, perhaps—to the Confederate army and running cotton to England through the Union blockade. After the war they migrated to New York, the eldest son marrying an Astor, their eldest daughter matched with Ogden Goelet, another daughter married to a promising British diplomat. Pale and slight, with a touching vulnerability, Consuelo looked more than ever like a Dresden figurine that night.

Everyone agreed that Alva had outdone herself but the expected climax, the announcement of Consuelo's engagement to the Duke, did not come off. Actually he had not yet formally proposed; perhaps there was a hitch, it was whispered, in the negotiations over the size of the dowry.

In those days anyone marrying into the Churchill family—as Jennie Jerome's father could have testified, his own fortune bled white before Jennie was acceptable as Lord Randolph Churchill's bride—was subjected to bargaining sessions as exhausting as those in a Levantine bazaar.

As late as September 19, Alva was somewhat testily denying to reporters that Consuelo and the Duke were engaged. Then one evening, the fiscal matters apparently settled by representatives of their families, the Duke proposed to Consuelo in the Gothic Room, which, Consuelo ironically remarked later, was "so propitious to sacrifice." At least there was no sentimental frippery about the proposal. "I was content with his pious hope that he would make me a good husband and ran up to my mother with word of our engagement. There was no time for thought or regrets. The next day the news was out, and a few days later Marlborough departed to see something of a country he even then announced he would never revisit. There was in his sarcastic comments on all things American an arrogance that inclined me to view his decision with approval. . . ."

Came the wedding day, November 6, 1895, by which time Consuelo had been advised of the cost of buying a husband for her. The dowry was, in fact, staggering. It came to two million pounds sterling—$10,000,000 at the then-current rate of exchange—not a bad price for a young man of no great beauty or promise, no attainments except the hauteur in which he had been schooled since birth.

The wedding took place at St. Thomas' Episcopal Church, which was festooned with flowers from the dome to the pews and resounded to music provided by Walter Damrosch and a sixty-piece orchestra. In that gorgeous setting, what matter the bride's feelings? ("I spent the morning of my wedding day in tears and alone. . . . I felt cold and numb. . . . My mother had decreed that my father should accompany me to the church to give me away. After that he was to disappear.") The vicinity of the church was thronged with people innocently envying an American princess marrying a genuine English duke. During the rendition of hymns celebrating the sacredness of love and marriage, she shyly glanced over to the Duke, perhaps in hopes of catching some trace of sentiment or affection on the cold

Churchillian features, but "I saw that his eyes were fixed in space."

Her last glimpse of her mother came when she and Marlborough were driving away from the Vanderbilt mansion on Fifth Avenue. Alva was hiding behind the draperies and peering out to watch the culmination of her aspirations, her daughter whisked away at the side of an aristocratic husband. Now, Consuelo thought, "she is free to let ambition give way to a gentler passion."

As an early example of Lend-Lease, Consuelo's marriage turned out as might be expected. The stately pace of life at Blenheim, the exhausting duties of a chatelaine almost daily called upon to settle disputes among the servants, the gloomy discomfort of living in dark high-ceilinged rooms not much more comfortable than the accommodations in the Tower of London, the stuffiness of Edwardian country life, all added up to a crashing bore; yet they stayed married for eleven years until "the nervous tension that tends to grow between people of different temperament condemned to live together had reached its highest pitch."

They separated in 1906 and were eventually divorced, but it wasn't until just after World War I, and Consuelo was the mother of grown sons, that she fell in love again. The man was a pioneer French aviator and World War I military pilot, Jacques Balsan, whose family was devoutly Catholic and would not receive Consuelo until the matter of her first marriage had been cleared up. Their only recourse was to apply to the Rota of the Roman Catholic Church, an ecclesiastical tribunal that alone can annul a marriage. The grounds for annulment were that Consuelo had been forced into her marriage to Marlborough, and by then her mother, now the widowed Mrs. Belmont, had mellowed sufficiently to testify before the Rota on her daughter's behalf. It was the first and last time Alva Smith Vanderbilt Belmont was known to have humbled herself. "I forced my daughter to marry the Duke," she confessed. "When I issued an order, nobody discussed it. I therefore did not beg, but ordered her to marry the Duke." The annulment was granted.

That was the long-deferred happy ending to one of those notorious Newport marriages.

There were many other marital horror tales, some of them detailed by the fascinating Mrs. Lydig, who compiled such a chronicle of matrimonial disasters it is incredible that any Newporter ever bothered with posting the banns, that Free Love did not sweep the place like a tropical fever.

One forced marriage related by Mrs. Lydig involved a beautiful woman who thereby was "launched into fashionable life with everything, apparently, to make her happy," including a Newport cottage, a Manhattan town house and a chateau in the south of France. Still, it was a loveless marriage she found barely endurable. One day, after about ten years of marriage, she invited Mrs. Lydig and other friends to a lunch at Sherry's, at the end of which, over coffee and cigarettes, she informed them that she had just learned that she would die of cancer in four months. Further, that she did not intend to see her husband or their two sons, or any of her friends, ever again. "I'm going to shut myself up on the top floor of my house, with two nurses I'm very fond of, and I ask you not to write or call or send flowers or books or anything. Just leave me as I am. You don't know what a feeling of peace I have. You don't know what a *release* it will be." And she added, "I've lived a silly life. I've had nothing—everything and nothing. If anyone were to tell me I'm not going to die, I couldn't bear it. My husband—oh, God, I'm so glad to be leaving him!"

The lady stuck to her plan and "died without another word to any of us."

Mrs. Lydig also recalled a girl she named "Betty Gower" who had inherited forty million dollars, met a Russian nobleman in Newport and was whisked off to Paris. After taking sizable chunks out of her fortune, he left her for another woman but not before passing her along to a "handsome Greek who could boast that he had once had a royal mistress and showed—to prove it—the dagger with which his princess had killed herself." The girl had become alcoholic under the Russian's tutelage, then was introduced to drugs by the Greek as a means of extracting money from her more readily. Not even her remaining millions could save "Betty Gower" from dying of addiction to cocaine and absinthe.

With the loosening of what surviving Victorians called moral standards in the Edwardian decade, Newport became a whirligig of marriage . . . divorce . . . remarriage. Resort society had attained such an urbanity, in contrast to earlier years when a divorced woman was cast out like the heroine of *East Lynne* (though not, of course, into a raging snowstorm), that no one blinked when at one wedding the bride was given away by her ex-husband.

Few Newport matings were, however, as hectic as that of Milton J. Budlong, an automobile manufacturer from Illinois, and his first wife. The lady sued him for divorce twenty-one times. Necessarily a state of siege obtained most of the time at their cottage, fittingly named The Reef. The servants were loyal to Mrs. Budlong, and when her husband was undergoing one of his frequent periods of banishment, he was forbidden to enter the house. Every morning during such periods, with the servants keeping a close watch on him, he was permitted to stand under Mrs. Budlong's bedroom window. After he made the penitential gestures she required, she would raise the window and throw him one clean shirt. Next morning the performance would be repeated. Finally he got tired of humbling himself and pleading for reconciliations, and married a less demanding woman.

In an atmosphere febrile with the tensions of marriages contracted for financial or dynastic reasons, it was little wonder that Newport ventured far ahead of the rest of the country in enjoying what certain prophets, largely based in Greenwich Village, were proclaiming as the New Freedom.

Just after the turn of the century it was generally known, even among the wives, that many husbands were keeping mistresses, and within a few years the wives would also be conducting extramarital affairs. Resident moralists blamed the tendency on the European influence, citing the fact that in Paris the practice was so systematized that when a man went out driving with his mistress, she always sat on his left side so his friends could tactfully glance the other way, while his wife or any respectable female companion always sat on his right side.

One prominent Newporter remarked of her husband, "Yes, I am his wife but I have an assistant down the street."

The ladies accepted the situation, generally, with grace, resignation, and an occasional barbed comment. As a boy, Cornelius Vanderbilt, Jr., remembered his mother and aunts "discussing the subject on the lawn of Ochre Court in their stiffly starched organdy gowns and plumed hats. As the late afternoon sunshine threw soft, shifting shadows over their tranquil figures, they looked like Raphael Madonnas sitting there. 'Of course he has a mistress,' Aunt Belle remarked as matter-of-factly as though she were speaking of some gentleman's valet. And Mother and Aunt May nodded calmly as though this were the most natural thing in the world."

It appeared to young Vanderbilt, however, that "illicit affairs were countenanced in Newport only if they were conducted discreetly among the very best people," that Newport was never in danger of aping Saratoga Springs "with its carriage-loads of women from the demimonde, blazing with diamonds and vivid with paint. . . ."

During the years just preceding the First World War, as Michael Strange would remember them, there was an increasing acceptance of infidelity as the normal concomitant of domestic life, and the "young married couples, who in my mother's and father's time had been exchanging a gallantry that was really chivalry and not likely to be dangerous to domestic happiness, were superseded by a set a good deal more in earnest over their forms of enjoyment. The *marriage à trois* began to be an accepted fact that every pretty woman had her beau—her serious beau—and defied the breath of scandal with amusing nonchalance, often leaving her electric brougham or runabout in the open road for all to see, near Paradise, or Hanging Rock, a specious chain of virgin woods designed by Providence to get lost in with the right person." By then, of course, the Grand Triumvirate and other matriarchs of the Victorian breed had either disappeared or lost their grip; it was all a far cry from the night when Mrs. Stuyvesant Fish discovered that a young female guest at one of her parties had slipped away and gone for a moonlight ride with an admirer, and banished her from her circle.

After the First World War, too, the younger generation of Newporters began to opt out of the elaborate prenuptial and wedding ceremonies because they seemed to put a curse on ordinary happiness. When Grace Vanderbilt, the daughter of Grace Wilson Vanderbilt, decided to get married in 1927 to mining engineer Henry Gassaway Davis, she invited only her brother Cornelius Vanderbilt, Jr., to the wedding. She and Davis were married at the Little Church Around the Corner, then left immediately for a British Columbia mining camp where Davis was employed. "For three months no word came to them from my family," her brother recalled. "Grace told newspaper reporters that she had eloped with Henry to avoid 'an English suitor' selected by Mother. She had chosen to settle down in a tiny backwoods shack, with no servants or comforts, to be with the man she loved."

No happy marriages in Newport except among the townspeople? There were, of course, but they were not the chosen subject of resort chroniclers, memoir writers and society editors. Unsung and unremarked, they were their own reward.

17.

THE LAST GOLDEN SUMMER

OLD NEWPORTERS would always consider the summer of 1914 the last of the golden age. Newport would continue to be a social capital for many years, its cottages staffed and maintained, a new generation filling the empty places at the Casino and the Reading Room and on Bailey's Beach; but something hard to define, something of the old grace and elegance, would never return. Nobody can say, even now, that Newport fell to the barbarians or has quite been trampled over like Bar Harbor, Cape Cod and its offshore islands. But it has never been quite so effulgent since the months just before Europe went to war.

Actually both the spirit and the physical beauty were damaged before the Austrian Archduke was killed at Sarajevo and international society, like the proletarian masses, was plunged into the first of the wars that struck far behind the battle lines with Zeppelin raids and Big Bertha barrages.

Two things, the combustion engine and the sinking of a transatlantic liner, contributed to the malaise that would cause Newport's decline. One detracted from its serenity, or to use an overworked and borrowed word, ambiance. The other destroyed its conviction, so essential to a social group afflicted by many neuroses and insecurities, that they were somehow the elect, invulnerable to fate, anointed with a special protection against mischance.

A terrible chill spread from the sinking of the *Titanic*. When that disaster occurred in the spring of 1912, the fashionable world on both sides of the Atlantic considered itself a special insulated part of humanity, with qualities most acutely and unsparingly described by the British novelist Vita Sackville-West as constituting "atrophy of the soul." Continuing her indictment in *The Edwardians*, she charged that "you would never forget your manners; but you would break a heart. . . . You would not defraud others; but you would defraud yourself. . . . You will never tell lies—avoidable lies—but you will always be afraid of the truth. . . ."

The *Titanic* was more than a great, luxurious ocean liner; it was a symbol of what that world could accomplish. It was described in God-defying terms as "unsinkable." When it sailed on its maiden voyage from Southampton, its first-class cabins were taken up by the rich and powerful on both sides of the Atlantic, eager to make the claim they had sailed on the first voyage of the mightiest ship ever built. It epitomized the impregnability of a Western civilization that had never seemed so united (barring occasional tantrums from the German emperor), so prosperous, so firmly set on the road to progress.

And then came the incredible bulletins from cable stations along the North Atlantic shore, the news that the *Titanic*'s hull had been ripped open by the invisible underwater spur of an iceberg, that the ship was sinking and passengers were taking to the lifeboats. One horror after another, people of great wealth or fame reported lost, the liner disappearing into the depths and resting on the bottom like a castle in the sea. Never mind that hundreds of immigrants in steerage were barred from the lifeboats and never had a chance to escape from the ship's slanting decks. What struck Newporters as ominous was that so many millionaires had failed to escape the disaster—an Astor, a Guggenheim, a Straus, two Wideners, a Ryerson, a Sutton . . . the list seemed as though death were raiding the Social Register and Dun & Bradstreet's Triple-A ratings. If Colonel John Jacob Astor with his fortune of $125,000,000 was not safe aboard the finest ship ever built, could anyone be considered impervious to the misfortunes that befell lesser people?

In Newport, Michael Strange wrote, the *Titanic* disaster "came as if some great stage manager planned that there would be a minor warning, a flash of horror" to warn of greater catastrophes just ahead. A certain cozy certainty evaporated from those long-protected lives.

Already, however, some of Newport's serenity had been destroyed by the stench and noise, not to mention more lethal possibilities, brought by the automobile. The quiet charm of carriages parading up and down Bellevue Avenue was replaced by the uproar of the combustion engine. "Instead of the smart precise rhythm of horses' hoofs, the muddle of motor machines and braying horns," one commentator wrote. "Not that Newport declined when the horse fell from his high estate; as a matter of fact, it reached the very height of its fame in the years immediately preceding the First World War. Still, it is undeniable that no summer resort has ever had quite the same old scintillant quality since 1900."

Even the dowagers were willing to adapt themselves to the automotive age and usually opted for an electric brougham, which, with its tiller instead of a steering wheel and its silent and stately progress, they could operate themselves. The electric cars looked like mobile telephone booths. Even Mrs. Stuyvesant Fish, who disliked all activities not likely to promote her social ascendancy, was tempted by the joys of motoring. A salesman brought out an electric brougham for her to try out in the driveway at Crossways. He assured her that anyone could operate an electric car; there was only one lever to worry about, you pushed it forward to go forward, back to reverse yourself, pulled it upright to stop. It seemed simple enough, but it soon became apparent that Mrs. Fish was not geared for the new age. First she ran straight into the front door of Crossways. Persuaded to try once more, she got safely out on Bellevue Avenue and knocked down a pedestrian. Thoroughly panicked, she pulled back on the lever and knocked down her victim a second time. (Because of the lightness of the vehicle he was not seriously damaged.) She pushed the lever forward and ran the pedestrian down a third time. The battered fellow got up again and ran for his life. Mrs. Fish had managed to halt the car in the middle of Bellevue Avenue, got out and refused ever to drive again.

At first the automobile was regarded as a sporting vehicle, and motoring as a harmless pastime. Yet as early as the summer of 1905 it was brought home to Newporters that the automobile, driven at speeds rarely over twenty-five or thirty miles an hour, could be turned into a deadly weapon.

The first intimation of its fatal possibilities came about four o'clock on the sunny afternoon of August 19, 1905. There had been a gay, vinous luncheon party at the Clambake Club given by Mrs. Clement Moore. Among the guests were Evalyn Walsh and her brother Vinson, daughter and son of the mining magnate Thomas F. Walsh, who had come to the club in their chauffeur-driven Mercedes limousine. Young Vinson Walsh, however, insisted on driving the car home with his sister, Mrs. James L. Kernochan, Herbert Pell, Jr., and Harry Oelrichs as his passengers. Walsh may have been a trifle overstimulated, but nobody worried about that because the automobile was a sort of grownup's toy, more or less foolproof, not like handling the reins on a brace of spirited horses.

"Vinson," his sister would alway painfully remember, "drove us swiftly past the other automobiles and turnouts. . . . We climbed the grade behind the beach, then started down Honeyman's Hill. We were going fast when I heard something like a pistol shot and the Mercedes began to sway and pitch. A rear tire had blown out. One of us screamed, and in that second we struck the flooring of a bridge that carried the road over a creek. I heard the chilling sound of splintering wood, and then our car bounced through the rail and threw me into dreadful darkness. My face was pressed into mud and water; I could, with tremendous effort, bend my neck. . . .

"Everything seemed to happen with incomprehensible slowness. I saw Alfred G. Vanderbilt bending over the creek bank. I called for Vinson and someone said he was hurt a little. Actually right then his mind was a blank and he was dying. Eloise Kernochan, one hand to disordered hair and with her summer frock all torn and stained with mud and blood, was being helped into a trap. . . . Then Fifi Potter Stillman leaned down, and I breathed her fragrance as she touched me softly on the face. I shivered, and she took off a lovely coat of Irish lace and placed it over me. . . ."

Harry Oelrichs' young sister Blanche learned of the accident in shocking fashion. "About this time," she would recall, "I had my first whiff of the coming racket; of what the machine could do with a little over-statement in festivity. For one afternoon in midsummer, as I stood on the porch waiting for my pony carriage, I saw a phaeton turn in our gate, driven by a lady in all her seasonal finery, with beside her a man covered with dirt and mud, his head thrown back on the seat, looking as though he were dead, and I realized with horror that it was my brother Harry. . . . Nor will I forget the stillness of my father, standing waiting on the porch for the phaeton to draw up, and the gentleness with which he lifted out my brother, to carry him in and lay him on his own bed, while all of us loitered about the darkened rooms until the doctor's visit told us that he was only stunned and suffering from a broken arm."

But Vinson Walsh had been killed, and his sister seriously injured in the accident. It gave Newporters pause, but not for long. The automobile was increasingly taking over the graceful sweep of carriage drives along the shore and turning them into roadways; carriage houses were being converted to garages with the stink of gas and oil; and one Augustus Jay was remembered by a disgusted chronicler as eternally "loose on the narrow lanes with an infernally pumping, stinking Mercedes."

And there were less mechanical matters than the automobile and a faultily designed English liner to disturb the tranquility of Newport during the several years preceding the First World War. The most pampered women in America—as the old gentlemen on the porch of the Reading Room never tired of telling each other, their wattles purpling with outrage—were not only joining in, but leading the campaign for women's rights. Not only that, but at least two members of the Great Triumvirate were also brandishing their assegais and stamping their feet in the suffragists' cause. The Marble House—and thank God old Oliver Belmont wasn't still alive to see the day—had become a powerhouse of feminist intrigue and agitation.

Newport's involvement with the crusade, and it was a dead-serious one, no matter that its participants had formerly been known for their obsession with the trivialities of a social career, was largely powered by Alva Smith Vanderbilt Belmont. What more, the reactionary old clubmen asked each other, could Alva want of men after having married her way into two great fortunes?

A lot, she could have told them. During the years following her second husband's death, she had been conferring and conspiring with Mrs. Emmaline Pankhurst, her daughter Christabel and other leaders of the English women's rights movement, and had even sheltered Mrs. Pankhurst in Paris when the latter was being sought by the police for the violence of her methods.

Her daughter Consuelo recalled that Mrs. Belmont shared with Mrs. Pankhurst "a common hatred for the genus man although they both delighted in men's company."

Alva's explanation for the paradox was contained in a letter to a friend: "My first experiences in life gave birth to my belief in militant woman suffrage. I found that even at the age of seven that boys looked down upon girls. I can almost feel my childish hot blood rise as it did then in rebellion at some such taunting remarks as: 'You can't run.' 'You can't climb trees.' 'You can't fight.' 'You are only a girl.' But no young would-be masculine bravado ever expressed twice such slurring belittlements of me."

She would brush aside any questioning of the depth of her belief in the integrity of her sex that recalled that not many years before, in negation of what surely must be one of the chief rights of the female as an individual, she had forced her daughter to marry a man she didn't love.

All that was in the past, she might have replied, the dark and inglorious past when a female was still chained to the social rules that the male sex had fashioned for her.

Soon, as her daughter observed, with what may have been mixed emotions, she was "sacrificing her time, her wealth, even her personal feelings" to the movement. At first she was mostly involved with the European sector, discussing the tactics and ideology of the movement with the Pankhursts, attending the

Biennial Convention of the Woman Suffrage Alliance in Budapest. The tactics of the suffragettes were becoming more violent that year, 1913; not only were women chaining themselves to the railings outside Parliament in London, but Emily Wilding Davidson, to dramatize their cause, threw herself under the hoofs of King George V's horse at the Derby at Epsom and was killed.

By then Alva had decided to turn her attention to the masculine resistance in her homeland. The men she knew in American society, above all her two easygoing husbands, had never been quite so overbearing as their brothers in England and on the Continent, but the laws they promulgated denied women the right to vote and made them legally the chattels of their husbands. Certainly few women in her set could be said to suffer much from male domination; it was the other way around, if anything, but she (and so many others with meek, wife-abiding husbands) resented the impression they had of masculine superiority.

She fired off a letter to New York's Committee on Criminal Courts when she learned it had taken up the question "What Shall We Do with the Young Prostitute?" Infuriated by the wording of the question, she wrote the committee:

"That the victims of men's recognized and accepted vices need protection none can deny; but why call upon the general public to furnish the necessary funds? Why collect money for the benefit of State and City and then divert it into channels for succoring human beings whose viciousness and undesirability were forced upon them by a class of self-indulgent criminals of the male population who have the power to vote against every decent measure brought before the electorate? . . . Arrest every man, rich or poor, young or old, who traffics in human bodies; fine him heavily according to his means, and the $700,000 necessary to provide an enlarged refuge for his victims will soon be raised. There is no difficulty in arresting the woman of the streets or the inmate of the house of ill repute; therefore the task of detecting men of the same caliber should not be among the impossibilities, and according to statistics, they outnumber women twenty to one. Find a means of hauling these men into court, see that the

man-ruled courts and man-made laws can bring them to
justice. . . ."

That was the opening shot in her campaign against the
American bastions of male supremacy. She sailed off to America
leaving her daughter Consuelo, now divorced from the man her
mother had forced her to marry, with wry reflections on feminist
zealotry: "When in the company of suffragettes a perverse desire
to condone all men's errors possessed me, for I found female
self-sufficiency somewhat ridiculous. To hear Christabel Pankhurst orate against the male sex, as if their presence in this world
were altogether superfluous, made one wonder how far prejudice
could contaminate a brilliant intellect."

Back in New York Alva began rallying her old friends in the
Four Hundred to lead their lower-class sisters in a huge display
of feminine solidarity, the Women's Vote Parade. Women from
all over the country came to New York to swell the marchers'
ranks to 50,000; even that aging sex symbol, Lillian Russell,
proclaimed herself a suffragette and promised to join the march
from Central Park down Fifth Avenue to Washington Square.

Alva would not listen to remonstrations from Mrs. Fish, who
told her, "My dear Alva, you'll never be able to do it. It must be
all of three miles and you've scarcely walked a step in your life."

"All the more reason why I should begin now," Mrs. Belmont
retorted. "After all, my dear, I must have something to interest
me in my old age. I've ordered a white pleated walking-skirt and
strong shoes. I shall walk every step of the way."

On the great day Mrs. Belmont placed herself at the head of
the throng of stenographers, sweatshop workers, shopgirls, nurses,
schoolteachers and housewives, and with banners flying behind
her—and Lillian Russell a mere extra in the pageant trudging
along under a huge plumed hat—marched down Fifth Avenue
past the great mansions in which she had won her social wars. It
was the start of a revolution and Mrs. Belmont undoubtedly saw
herself as its Joan of Arc.

Harry Lehr and his wife watched from a window in the newly
built St. Regis Hotel, with Harry observing that "The dear old
warrior has got something to fight for at last." Mrs. Belmont, his

wife recalled, "looked as serene and unself-conscious as though she had been in her own drawing-room when she stepped out proudly at the head of a long procession headed by brass bands and flanked by mounted police."

Mrs. Belmont's metamorphosis from social careerist to social crusader did not stop with the New York demonstration. That summer she gave the old gents on the Reading Room porch something to fume about when she announced that she was reopening the Marble House and turning it over to the Political Equality Association, of which she was a founder and leading agitator, for a convention. Battle-axes and she-dragons from all over the country, soapboxers and radical hellions of every stripe would be descending on Newport and ruining its serenity. This was going too damn far. Even their women folk agreed that Newport was no place for such serious business. Let Alva confine her rabble-rousing among the anarchists in Union Square down in New York.

"This was really carrying enthusiasm too far!" as Elizabeth Drexel Lehr summed up the attitude of the summer colony. "By all means walk in processions, or demonstrate your sympathies in any way that appealed to you, but why let loose a horde of fanatics on the stronghold of your friends, said everyone. The rumours of discontent reached Mrs. Belmont's ears, but she paid no attention to them, and the preparations went forward. An enormous tent was erected on the grounds, a platform was built for the speakers. . . ."

Men were invited to join in forwarding the cause, in learning just how they had oppressed their womenfolk for centuries. The membership of the Reading Room, of course, declined in a body. And many of Alva's old followers in the social whirl of seasons past just couldn't picture themselves joining her *new* friends in raising such an undignified clamor, or slyly told each other they already had the best of all possible worlds and couldn't be bothered with getting the vote and involving themselves with a lot of cigar-chewing politicians.

When the conclave opened under canvas previously used to shelter more frivolous gatherings in the garden of the Marble

House, Mrs. Belmont also met with resistance from two unexpected quarters. She had expected to enlist her younger son, Harold, to introduce the speakers, but he violently objected and was more successful than his sister in thwarting his mother's will. With some heat he told his mother he wouldn't have anything to do with a mob of suffragettes. Perhaps he was remembering the day he tried to persuade Consuelo to hold out against marrying the Duke of Marlborough because "he is only marrying you for your money," and how his sister wept when he told her that.

Governor Plothier of Rhode Island agreed to address the convention and asked what he should say in his speech. Mrs. Belmont's response was to write it for him; a fiery oration practically calling for the overthrow of existing institutions by militant womanhood. The Governor, however, scrapped it and substituted ten minutes of platitudes.

The horde of bluestocking types descended on the Marble House to hear such speakers as Rose Schneiderman, vice-president of the Women's Trade Union; Judge Mary M. Barthelme of the Chicago Juvenile Court; Mrs. Maud Booth of the Volunteers of America; Katherine B. Davis, New York's commissioner of correction; Julia C. Lathrop, the head of the Federal Children's Bureau; Mrs. Florence Kelly, secretary of the National Consumers League; Mrs. Helen King Robinson of the Colorado State Senate, and Kate M. Gordon, president of the Southern States Women's Suffrage Association. Not to mention an English suffragette who told the conclave, "They say in London that I've got the brains of a man. Well! I should like to see the man whose brains I have!"

Mrs. Lehr was present as a secretly amused observer and noted the visible distress of Azar, the Belmonts' longtime Egyptian majordomo, who looked like one of his ancient counterparts in fallen Rome putting up with a band of female Visigoths bivouacked on his master's estate. "Poor Azar's consternation was boundless as hundreds of women . . . swarmed into the house that had earned the reputation of being one of the most exclusive in Newport . . . women in shirtwaists, their jackets hanging over their arms, women carrying umbrellas and paper bags. Man-hating college women with screwed-back hair and thin-lipped, determined faces; old countrywomen red-cheeked and homely, giggling shopgirls. Azar had never seen such guests. What a contrast to the elegant garden parties of former years, the splendid entertainments that had been his greatest pride. It was too much for him!"

At the end of the convention there was a considerable brouhaha when Mrs. Belmont's personal banner, bearing the four white stars on a blue background that served as the battle flag of the suffrage movement, had disappeared. Naturally it was suspected that some male infiltrator had stolen the banner. But it showed up again several weeks later, long after the last militant had disappeared from the Marble House with her umbrella and reticule. There was a dinner party given by the Elisha Dyers, which was interrupted by the butler's announcing "Mrs. Carrie Chapman Catt," a hallowed name in the suffrage movement. In walked Harry Lehr in drag. He was wearing a gown of which Mrs. Belmont's banner formed the train. She was not amused.

Her ingathering of suffrage workers would always be remembered, not for any startling achievements, but for the chins-up advice she gave to a young suffragette who confessed that she was often depressed by the hopelessness of their cause:

"Brace up, my dear. Just pray to God. *She* will understand."

Once the glinting menace of the women's rights crusaders had vanished from the scene, Newport settled down for summer-as-usual. Why should anything change? And yet it already had, just before the owners of the great houses, their families and their corps of servants opened up their cottages for the season. Only the most acute could have sensed the upheaval that would extend like a burning fuse from an overseas dispatch, on the front pages but not played up, which began, "The Archduke Francis Ferdinand, heir to the throne of Austro-Hungary, and his morganatic wife, the Duchess of Hohenberg, were assassinated yesterday in the town of Sarajevo. . . ."

No one took that event very seriously, not even in Europe, and Newport's summer colonists gathered undismayed for another brilliant season.

The weather, as in western Europe, was perfect, the best anyone could remember. Long serene days filled with a golden haze. Summer had come early and would stay late, contributing to the cloudless tranquility of the weeks following that dispatch from Sarajevo and subterranean rumblings that a world so long at peace, generally speaking, might soon settle its grievances on the battlefields.

During those July days, only the alarmists sensed that something terrible was in the wind, that the cozily insulated world of the privileged might be endangered. Yet it was the last golden summer of Newport's quarter-century heyday. "Newport was brilliant that summer," Michael Strange would remember in her memoir. "I see it all through continuous sunlight and laughing gatherings of people at Bailey's Beach with its brown belt of seaweed that concentrated a veritable stench of the ocean. And on the Casino lawns dotted with hatbands of the most exclusive clubs, and ravishing *dames du monde,* with chiffon parasols, mushrooming over enormous hats and pompadours."

The Russian artist-Prince Troubetzkoy was painting a society lady's portrait, and the young Archduke Franz Josef, on the other side of the battle lines soon to be drawn, was going to be the guest of Mrs. Ogden Goelet, who was arranging a ball in his honor with what was now being called an "old-fashioned" cotillion. And despite the war fever coursing through imperial Vienna, the Archduke did appear—"young, pale and dark, with that fateful Hapsburg look"—and could be seen even by the commoners riding by in Mrs. Goelet's carriage.

And then came reports that the Grand Duke Alexander, brother-in-law of the Czar, would also be coming over for the season. He was the lordliest personage ever to condescend to inspect the American aristocracy in Newport. Even as the news from Europe became more ominous, the resort's hostesses were preoccupied with scrimmaging for the right to entertain either or both visiting royalties. They were "deliriously tossed between

Hell and Heaven at the advent of royalty. The scramble was cruel. Football was dainty in comparison." And one young matron who managed to be presented to the Grand Duke at a dinner party given by Mrs. Ava Astor would remember "all the ladies lined up directly afterwards in the ballroom for their introduction" to the Russian nobleman whose title three years hence would be as defunct as that of a Byzantine prince. There was a tumble of emotions in her republican breast and "I experienced a species of self-loathing for catching the mass nervousness before the Grand Duke entered."

None of the survivors of that climactic summer would forget Newport in its rose-gold perfection. Nostalgia may have colored their memories, but the resort had reached its apex as the epitome of all that was luxuriously cosseted in American life. The horseless carriage had not yet entirely displaced the horse-drawn carriage; there were still plenty of applicants to fill out the servant corps; the federal income tax was more of a sting than a bite; the airless grace of the old days still lingered like a scent of lavender. Mr. Ward McAllister and Mrs. Caroline Astor could have entered one of the great houses arm in arm and not been taken aback in ghostly surprise at any of the changes (though they would have been well-advised not to haunt Alva Belmont's convention of the women's rights crusaders). As Michael Strange would poetically recall, "The ballrooms had great cachet; and the gardens were wonderful with the moonlight picking out the marble steps, and richly dramatic planting, while a waltz played in the distance. That extraordinary pre-war gaiety of Newport! In retrospect it is really quite dramatic, for it seems to me that in those years, an age related in many ways to the ones preceding it—Victoria and Pontius Pilate surely ripened under tempos more similar to one another than ours to Victoria's—was wiped out, and superseded by what the Prophet in Revelation might well call 'A new Heaven and a new Earth.' "

As July came to a close, however, even the giddiest hostesses and the most determined pleasure seekers were made aware of the gigantic war machines moving toward a collision three thousand miles over the horizon from Bailey's Beach. More than the rest of isolated America, Newport, through its international marriages and its social connections, was concerned with what was happening in the European capitals; even those Newporters without such personal ties to England and the Continent were threatened by the prospect of being deprived of caviar, champagne, the more elegant motorcars and Parisian fashions, the rehabilitating stays at South German spas, the London season, spring in the Bois de Boulogne, the box in the State Opera of Vienna.

By the end of July the fateful declarations had been made and the armies set in motion. Newport was overcome by the "dreadful oppressive sense of what was going on over in Europe." There was a slow growth of pro-Allied, pro-Central Powers, pro-neutrality factions, but for the most part the more warlike Newporters were outraged that President Wilson was opting for caution; not so much the professionals at the Naval War College, the torpedo station and the other military installations but "particularly the civilians were dying to get our swaggering tall young Americans 'over there' to bayonet the Boche." The professionals could remember what war was like in the Philippines and Cuba.

Perhaps greater concern was felt for the many Newporters who had gone over to Britain and Europe that spring and had planned to return in time for the Newport season but were caught in the disruption caused by the outbreak of war, the cancelled sailings of the British liners, the railroads preempted by the military for troop movements. Cables crisscrossed the Atlantic detailing their plight, which was heightened for those "trapped" in London and Paris by the fears of bombing raids from the Kaiser's fleet of Zeppelins. In Paris, the aging Commodore Bennett, well-remembered by older members of the resort colony, was still publishing the Paris *Herald* and served as a rallying point for Newporters caught in the French capital. The Commodore, still a fire-eater, would not join them in the Stateside rush; he would stay in Paris even after the capital was evacuated as the German armies approached the crossings of the Marne.

In London, about two thousand Americans, including many of those who sojourned every summer in Newport, were "caught disastrously short by the ruinous complication of a simultaneous crisis and the Bank Holiday, and were both rich and stranded," as a Briton observed. "They plodded from hotel to hotel waving attested cheque-books and valid letters of credit . . . pleading poverty with their handbags full of diamonds."

Many of the refugees, as they had begun to think of themselves, washed up at the Ritz-Carlton in New York to recuperate before plunging into what was left of the Newport season. Among them were the William B. Leedses, who had taken a house in the English countryside just before Sarajevo. They regaled Newport dinner tables with their vicarious experiences of the war just starting, recalling with particular admiration their handsome young footman William, who came to Mrs. Leeds and announced his intention of enlisting in the army. Mrs. Leeds tried to dissuade him, but he stiffened his upper lip and replied, "My duty to England comes before anything else." She was so impressed by his ardent patriotism that she gave him a check for two years' wages and sent him "off to war" loaded down with hampers of food, pipes and tobacco, and everything a warrior might need in the trenches.

Around Newport the footman William became a sort of shining symbol of the valiant British confronting the Kaiser's legions. Mrs. Leeds' servants in her American establishment were similarly impressed and raised a fund to be sent to William for his widowed mother's upkeep. What a shock was in store for Mrs. Leeds when later that year she dined in the New York home of the Elbridge Gerrys. The handsome footman entering with the soup was William who, foreseeing conscription, had obtained the job with the Gerrys just before they left England for the United States.

The war was causing all sorts of embarrassments for Newport hostesses. Before it had been declared, Mrs. Cornelius Vanderbilt had announced a dinner in honor of Count Bernstorff, the German ambassador to Washington. The date was set for the second week in August, by which time the German armies were storming into France and Belgium.

As the time of Count Bernstorff's arrival neared, Mrs. Vanderbilt probably hoped that he would succumb to a diplomatic headache and stay in Washington. Yet she would not call off the dinner, despite her husband's opposition and the divided feelings in Newport. Grace Wilson Vanderbilt had "strong German sympathies," as her son noted. Back in 1902, when she was beginning to assert herself socially, Prince Henry, the brother of the Kaiser, who was visiting New York, had given her a leg up by visiting her box at the Metropolitan Opera. A year later Kaiser Wilhelm and members of his family had boarded the Vanderbilt yacht, the *North Star,* when it was anchored in the Bay of Naples, and were guests of honor at a Fourth of July banquet. Subsequently she had formed strong social connections with the German embassy group in Washington, particularly Count Bernstorff, a handsome and persuasive Prussian much sought after by New York hostesses.

Her husband, however, was anything but pro-German and announced that he would absent himself from any table graced by the Prussian diplomat. He had been commissioned as a lieutenant colonel in the New York National Guard and was certain the United States would soon enter the war against Germany. "He pointed out to Mother," his son recalled, "that she ought to be ashamed to be entertaining the German Ambassador when her many French and English friends were engaged in such a terrible war and her two English nephews were in front-line trenches."

Urbane as ever, Count Bernstorff appeared in Newport. Most of those invited to Mrs. Vanderbilt's dinner also showed up, having been urged by their hostess not to bring up the subject of the war at her table. As her son Cornelius, Jr., described the scene:

"The Count had the position of honor at Mother's right. As she sipped her *consommé double* Mother's practiced eye swept over her guests, the five immense gold bowls of American Beauty roses and Japanese iris, the footmen deftly pouring wine; without an

apparent break in her rapt interest in her handsome guest of
honor, she noted that an argument of some heat had broken out
between two guests down by the salt, that a male guest was
wearing a particularly handsome set of black pearl vest buttons,
and that Gerald, our immensely fat English butler, looked
slightly distrait.

"The footmen began removing the white Sevres soup plates
with their deep blue and gold borders. When they seemed
unusually slow about bringing the fish, Mother caught Gerald's
eye; he bowed and hurried noiselessly out into the butler's
pantry. He did not return. . . ."

Perhaps, then, Mrs. Vanderbilt began to feel a tremor of
alarm. She knew, but disregarded the fact, that most of her
servants were either French, English or Belgian. Their national
sympathies, or indeed any of their personal feelings, were hardly
any of their employer's concern. Surely the varlets wouldn't
dare . . .

"Mother missed the thread of what von Bernstorff was saying,"
her son continued. "She smiled radiantly, but one slender white
hand began tugging at the side of her flame-colored chiffon
gown—always a danger signal. As Mother's servants well knew,
an eight-course dinner must be served in an hour flat, even if
slow eaters dropped three courses behind. So forceful was the
effect of Mother's personality that the servants trembled to fulfill
her every whim; this was particularly remarkable because they
knew, however heinous the offense, she could seldom bear to fire
anybody."

Ten minutes passed without any sign of the next course.
Finally a little Irish kitchenmaid, being a neutral as far as the
war was concerned, came into the dining room with a note on a
silver salver. It was a message from the backstairs junta:

"We the undersigned regret to inform you, Madam, that we
cannot any longer serve the enemy of our respective countries.
We have thrown the rest of the dinner into the dustbin and we
have all left your service. There is nothing else to eat in the
house. We hope you all enjoyed the soup, for we took good care
to spit well into it, every one of us, before it went to the table."

Suppressing a strong urge to vomit, the guests rose from the table after Mrs. Vanderbilt read the bulletin aloud. They were about to disperse, wondering what the world was coming to, when "one of the guests suggested jokingly that the men serve dinner." Uncooked food was found in the pantry and was prepared for the table "amid much hilarity." Next day, despite their announcement that they had all quit her service, the servants returned to their duties; both they and their employer pretended nothing had happened, but it seemed likely that a plate of soup would never again look quite so appetizing to Mrs. Vanderbilt.

That summer Newport was also agog over the overseas adventures of Lily Oelrichs Martin, the older sister of Michael Strange. Her first marriage, to Peter Martin, was the culmination of a Newport romance. Martin, however, had suddenly gone raving mad in the midst of a dancing party in Paris two years before and subsequently died. The fragile Lily had fallen in love with Prince Borwein of Mecklenburg-Strelitz, whose social graces were said to be on a par with a Prussian grenadier kicking in the doors of a conquered village and whose habit it was to punch his orderly when displeased.

Despite his aggressive disposition, Prince Borwein begged Lily to smuggle him out of Europe because he didn't want to serve in the German army. "At her suggestion," as Mrs. Lehr gleefully recounted, "he had disguised himself in dingy threadbare clothes and got taken on in the stokehold of a liner on which she was a passenger. The plan worked so perfectly that no one had any inkling of his identity. She laughed very much as she described their stolen meetings on deck, she in her dainty evening gowns, he in his grimy stoker's overalls."

Restored to his former princely self, Prince Borwein was trotted around Newport for the approval of Lily's friends, which they coolly withheld. Nevertheless Lily married him and they went to San Francisco, a city that seemed to have a magnetizing attraction for some members of the Oelrichs clan, until Prince Borwein had a change of heart about his duties to the Kaiser. The Germans were winning on all fronts and the Prince yearned for his *Pickelhauben* and his sword belt. So Lily, "restless and unhappy now beyond words," as her sister observed, had to smuggle him back to Europe and back to the embrace of his regimental comrades.

The war years, particularly after the United States became involved overseas, turned Newport khaki-drab. Ladies rolled bandages, knit socks and addressed Liberty Bond rallies. Earnestness of any kind ill became the queen of resorts. The monotony was briefly relieved when Assistant Secretary of the Navy Franklin D. Roosevelt came sleuthing after some of the colony's homosexuals for preying on servicemen.

Only by hindsight would it be realized that some of the magic of illusion, of a sustained mood had been lost, the thread of continuity snapped, and Newport would never recover the exuberance of its pre-1914 years.

EPILOGUE

INDUBITABLY there was an afterglow of Newport's quarter-century of effulgence as the most elegant of American summer resorts. The twenties passed in its mellow light; a decade some believe was even more brilliant socially than the preceding ones, but they were mostly people who hadn't known the days of the Great Triumvirate. A gathering darkness fell with the closing of the decade and the 1929 stock-market crash. The thirties saw the depletion or disappearance of many of the fortunes that had fueled Newport's exuberance in its glory days, and during World War II the final blow fell. The servant class all but vanished, lured away by the war industries, and was never to return in numbers sufficient to maintain what Henry James had called a herd of white elephants.

All its foolish splendors as an American annex of Vanity Fair, all its witless rivalries, its tiny tragedies of social rejection, its flaunting of possessions, its vaunted exclusiveness became unwise in the public relations sense. A Rockefeller would much prefer being photographed eating a frankfurter on the lower East Side than pouring champagne at one of his estates. Modern wealth disguises itself under layers of social concern, proclaims itself obsessed by the underprivileged, seeks privacy for its revels and publicity for its campaigning for reform. It can't be accused of having failed to learn from the fate of aristocracies of the past.

So the Newport of the Gilded Age and the slightly more tawdry period that followed now quietly closed out its existence. No German U-boats had surfaced to pound the marble mansions along Cliff Walk to flinders, but the Newport of the twenties saw little or nothing of the imperious ladies who had reigned before the world war. Mrs. Fish, in fact, died before the war was over. Harried by the necessity of breaking in yet another butler and housekeeper in time for her birthday party, she suffered a stroke and died shortly thereafter in 1915. Tessie Oelrichs, too, had died. Alva Smith Vanderbilt Belmont lived on, one of those Southern-lady hummingbirds made of some indestructible alloy, but Newport never saw her again and the windows of Marble House stayed dark.

The indomitable Alva exerted herself in Europe throughout the twenties, always in counseling range of her much-managed daughter Consuelo, and bought a chateau near the one occupied by the latter and her husband at Saint Georges-Motel. Her vigor was unabated even into her seventies, also her tendency to change and rebuild her immediate environment. "She was forever critically surveying her demesne," her daughter recalled. "Walking in the garden with Jacques and me, she would suddenly stop us and, pointing to the river which flowed past the house, would say, 'This river is not wide enough; it should be twice as large,' and when next we came an army of workmen would have enlarged it. A great forecourt separated the village from the house. It was sanded instead of being paved. 'This is all wrong, it should be paved,' my mother commented severely; and the year of her death old paving stones brought from Versailles covered the court."

She also found the energy required for involving herself in various causes, busying herself with the affairs of an international organization concerned with women's rights and headquartered in Geneva. Women had won the vote in America and England, but Mrs. Belmont's feminism was kept blazing by fresh reports of female conditions in China, of harems in the Moslem world, of masculine repressions in still-British India, and she wouldn't have that sort of thing anywhere.

It came to her attention that the neighboring village of Augerville-la-Rivière possessed a beautiful church but no effigy of St. Joan of Arc, whom she regarded as a pioneer leader of the women's rights movement. She was a Protestant and therefore could not donate a statue of St. Joan to the church, so she chose Mrs. Harry Lehr, then living in Paris and on the verge of becoming an English baroness, as her Catholic intermediary. An elaborate ceremony was organized for the installation of St. Joan's statue, with the Archbishop of Orléans persuaded to preside but with Alva as mistress of ceremonies. It was sort of a medieval pageant, which started out from her chateau with Alva and the Archbishop leading the procession. "With St. Joan held aloft on a dais," her daughter wrote, "the Archbishop, surrounded by acolytes and priests, we marched in procession to the church, passing through a throng of kneeling villagers. Mrs. Lehr, as donor of the statue, had a prominent position behind the Saint, and her chatter, which she was unable to restrain, desecrated the solemn silence. My mother, who could always be relied upon to dominate a situation, furiously and loudly observed, 'Bessie, will you shut up!' Thankfully I observed that, obedient as we all were to such admonitions, Mrs. Lehr thereafter maintained the dignified deportment the occasion decreed." Later Consuelo had to explain to their French Catholic guests why her Protestant mother had installed the statue, that "it was Joan as a militant rather than Joan as a Saint that appealed to my mother."

Mrs. Belmont lived on to her eightieth year, died in Paris and was removed to St. Thomas' in New York for the funeral. The procession from the church included hundreds of her former comrades in the suffrage movement, as she had ordained in her will, but one last request—one of the few in a life that was one act of will after another—was denied her. St. Thomas' would not allow a woman to deliver the funeral oration.

The court comedian of the Great Triumvirate, Harry Lehr, ended up more tragically than any of the trio whom he devoted himself to entertaining and collaborating with on their social triumphs. He began showing symptoms of a mental breakdown, evidently a form of melancholia, just after the war broke out when he and his wife were living in Paris. "Gradually," Mrs. Lehr wrote, "he started to lose touch with the very things that had once held the essence of life for him."

Word of his mental or psychic decline reached New York and offered Mrs. Stuyvesant Fish, only a few months from her own death, the chance of yet another barbed witticism. She wrote him:

"They say, sweet lamb, that you have lost your mind. Come back to New York if you have. You know quite well that you won't need any mind to go with the people in our set."

During the war years in Paris, Mrs. Lehr observed, he "grew steadily worse. . . . As he felt life slipping from him he tried to recapture it in the only way he had understood it. He sought it in crowds, in laughter, in the company of people who were amusing themselves."

Just after the Armistice he was sent back to the States for treatment. On bidding him good-bye, Mrs. Lehr expressed hope that American neurologists could bring him around. He then spoke the last coherent words she would ever hear from him. "No, no, Bessie," he said, adding in Italian, "The comedy is finished."

In America, the doctors finally tried brain surgery as a last resort but his malaise could not be reached by the knife. He was returned to his wife in Paris virtually a human vegetable, "unable to speak except for a jumble of meaningless sounds." Three more years passed before death released him. After his funeral, which attracted little attention from the social world, Elizabeth Lehr found the diary he had kept for years. All she would say of it was that it demonstrated that Harry "had known love. . . . His diary was a love story." But she didn't specify what variety of "love" he had known, and left the world to guess.

The years just following the end of the war also saw the passing of two other men who, somewhat less comically, had loomed over the Newport summers.

James Gordon Bennett, who had contributed so much to the sporting aspect as well as memories of some hectic merrymaking, was still lording it over his newspaper empire when he died in 1919, still an expatriate in France. It had been years since he had last descended on Newport and deliciously terrified the statelier hostesses; the last years of his life were spent on the Riviera trying to recoup his fortunes, after a lifetime spent trying to dissipate them. His three newspapers were sold to satisfy the conditions of Bennett's will, which directed, in his sardonic style, that a home for indigent journalists was to be established in his name, but there was nothing left when his postmortem finances were sorted out.

Even Colonel William d'Alton Mann, the terror of Newport summers past, departed quietly enough, just about a year after Bennett. His power to terrify had greatly diminished since a Newport incident had led to the legal drawing of his fangs. He had established a magazine called *Smart Set*, which H. L. Mencken edited and which published some notable and respectable prose and poetry. *Town Topics* stayed afloat but took a more serious, and therefore less profitable, attitude toward the scene it had surveyed so minatorily. "Saunterings" became much less a gossip column and much more a platform for the Colonel's idiosyncratic opinions of contemporary life. Weekly he advised the Allies on the correct strategy for conducting their operations. He also decried the antipornography crusades of the "unspeakable" Anthony Comstock, supported the women's suffrage movement (making himself an unlikely ally of Mrs. Belmont), decried the Prohibition act as "the law to make this country safe for hypocrisy" (the epicurean Colonel tasting his first shot of bootleg whiskey must have been a study in culture shock), and virulently campaigned against President Wilson's second marriage.

Instead of the gunshot wound his enemies had predicted for him, pneumonia claimed his life in the spring of 1920 shortly after his warning that America would turn to isolationism and one result would be a second war against "naturally brutal" Germany. A major general and three colonels attended his funeral, the coffin bearing the saber he had flourished at Gettysburg but no sharpened quill to symbolize the longer and more notorious phase of his career.

For years the Colonel had been boasting that his safe was crammed with enough "dynamite" to blow New York society apart, a disaster avoided only by the kindness of his heart. When it was opened after his death, it was apparent that Mann had been running one of his many bluffs; it contained nothing but a brandy bottle and a few stale cigars.

Social historians and historians of society, not necessarily the same, have generally agreed that a Newport summer reached the height of its brilliance before World War I. To recapture some idea of its grace, Richmond Barrett said, it would have to be "bathed in the transparent atmosphere of those summers before the age of poisonous monoxide gas dawned." Later commentators, such as Cleveland Amory, held, however, that it was the much later death of Mrs. Hamilton McKown Twombley, the last grandchild of Commodore Cornelius Vanderbilt, in 1952, that "marked the end of Newport's era of elegance." Obviously there is roughly a four-decade gap between those end-of-an-era pronouncements. It can be bridged by grasping their differing vantage points. Mr. Barrett knew the resort in its golden age, while Mr. Amory came along much later and was not disturbed by personal acquaintance with the pre-automotive charm that had been destroyed.

Certainly Mrs. Twombley, in the last half-century of her ninety-eight years on earth, had conducted herself in the Vanderbilt *grande dame* style. Her annual invasions of Newport resembled a royal procession and included fifteen automobiles, all painted in her favorite shade of maroon, with her servants wearing uniforms of the same color. Her French chef was paid so handsomely that he was able to retire to a Newport cottage of his own.

Mrs. Twombley, too, had that high-handed sense of individualism that marked the other great ladies who ruled over Newport's uppermost echelon. In 1935, she decided to attend the California wedding of her grandson to the niece of Douglas Fairbanks, Sr. She did not trust the airplane, and even a Vanderbilt could no longer command a private railroad car. Driving out in one of her Rolls Royce limousines seemed the only way she could make the journey in the style to which she had long been accustomed. On the other hand, it was mid-Depression and desperate characters were known to be roving the land and might waylay such a luxurious conveyance. So on the journey out to California and on the journey back to the guarded enclave of Newport, where the Depression was remarked upon only when old friends suddenly lost the means of staying there, Mrs. Twombley disguised as her maid sat in the front seat of her Rolls beside the chauffeur. Her maid, impersonating Mrs. Twombley, rode haughtily in the back. If they had run into any desperadoes, of course, it would have been the maid who submitted to their exactions.

Before and after World War II, another female swashbuckler, one of those breezy Western ladies who, like Tessie Oelrichs, have occasionally let fresh air into the social vacuum, made a considerable impact on Newport. She was Mrs. Perle Mesta, the heiress to an Oklahoma oil fortune and the widow of a wealthy machinery tycoon. Mrs. Mesta invaded Newport with the brio to be expected of a lady who would become the heroine of a musical comedy, *Call Me Madame*, and be portrayed by Ethel Merman. Not for her the Ward McAllister dictum that a newcomer must spend her first several seasons in demure submission while the senior lionesses of the Newport pride inspected her credentials and tested her qualifications.

When she arrived at the resort in 1929, the Arthur Curtiss Jameses, of the Anaconda Copper fortune, still represented the old guard of the pre-World War I era. Their parties, she observed, were "on the conservative side . . . we once had to listen all evening to Mr. James play Bach on his pipe organ." The main attraction was the Swiss-farm setting the Jameses had created, complete with livestock, farmhands dressed in Alpine style, and a hundred men working around the place to maintain the illusion that their corner of Newport was a bit of old Switzerland.

That first summer Mrs. Mesta let it be known that her cottage, Mid-cliffe, was going to generate a centrifugal force. Her first move, which caused a swiveling of lorgnettes, was to invite Vice-President Charles Curtis, whom she had become friendly with during the 1928 political campaign. It was bad enough that

Curtis was merely the Vice President, but he was also part Kaw Indian and had begun his career as a jockey on the county-fair circuit of Kansas and Oklahoma.

"The announcement in the *Times*," she recalled, "caused no little stir in Newport, which was pretty snobbish in those days. In addition to the fact that Curtis had no social standing, a few of the hostesses pointed out that he was part Indian. Yet he *was* the Vice President of the United States, and no Vice President had ever before visited Newport while in office. The town announced a big celebration for him, and I soon had more requests for his presence at parties than could possibly have been filled during his stay. . . . He completely won over even the most snobbish of the Newports because he was so natural and had such charm."

Every year thereafter she corralled notables and celebrities to grace her dinner table. She obeyed most of the rules of formality which had long obtained in Newport; "there'll be no *dropping in* or any of that sort of thing here," she firmly announced. But her parties, like those she gave during the winter season in Washington, were designed to be entertaining as well as lavishly mounted.

They were planned, she said, to be "seventy percent talent and thirty percent audience." People could no longer be satisfied simply with admiring each other's elegance. In the old days it was considered pretty daring to have the violinist Albert Spalding drop by to entertain, she reflected, but "I've had everything from a roomful of gypsies to Ike Eisenhower singing 'Drink to Me Only with Thine Eyes.'" General Eisenhower's vocalizing, it should be added, was a feature of one of Mrs. Mesta's parties before he became President.

She was one of the last really exuberant presences on the Newport scene. The leveling process in American life has been revolutionary in its impact on Newport; the summer places, like those of fallen czars and dethroned kings in Europe, are no longer privately owned but have become museum pieces of one kind or another. Even rich people can't spare enough from the Internal Revenue Service's takings to pay for the upkeep, the property taxes and the wages demanded by the available servants. Living in the grand style, as some have discovered, isn't easy. The café singer Gertrude Niessen in 1941 bought Tessie Oelrichs' old estate Rosecliff for $21,000 though it had once been valued at $2,500,000. Weary of living in hotel rooms, she enjoyed Rosecliff's twenty-two bedrooms and twenty-two baths for a time. Several years later, however, she left the mansion without engaging a caretaker and forgot to turn off one of the taps in a bathroom. By midwinter there was a sheet of ice several inches thick over the carpets Tessie Oelrichs had chosen with such taste and expense; furthermore the water bill was so high that Miss Niessen decided to sell Rosecliff and cut her losses.

Henry James's white-elephant imagery turned out to be an accurate forecast of the fate of Newport's marble cottages. The depreciation in their value was startling, as indicated by the price Gertrude Niessen paid for Rosecliff. In 1925 the ten largest were assessed at $2,773,000 but a quarter-century later they were valued at only $823,150. One by one they were abandoned by the families whose antecedents had built them with high dynastic hopes. The Breakers was turned into a museum for tourists; the Goelets gave the hundred-room Ochre Court to the Catholic Church for a girls' college. Others, like Rosecliff, had been taken under the protection of the Preservation Society of Newport.

There are few left to mourn the passing of queenly Newport. None who could write so poignantly as Michael Strange of the pre-1914 Newport and what had happened to it, who remembered from her girlhood how "the laughing circle of 'intimates' swelled into the clamor of great crowds in white ballrooms, heavily filigreed with gold. . . . I saw the sentiments inspired by a little too much testing of fine wines exchanged for the raucousness and moroseness of liquor often bolted to give the skull a reprieve from deadly anxiety. . . ."

That the stately old homes of Cliff Walk and Bellevue Avenue were turned into tourist attractions was not the worst indignity imposed on the former queen of resorts. For eighteen years it was the site of the Newport Jazz Festival and during the sixties was stormed by mobs that prefigured the Woodstock ingathering and were accompanied by occasional outbreaks of violence and destruction. The youthful stampede to Newport during the week of the jazz festival often resembled a retake of that obligatory sequence in early Soviet films, the storming of the Winter Palace. But in 1972 the festival's promoters removed their enterprise to a likelier venue; it is still called the Newport Jazz Festival but is staged in seemlier surroundings at Hempstead, Long Island.

Now there is a statelier and more fitting celebration called the Newport Music Festival, a program of thirty concerts, ballet and opera productions, which deliberately summons back the days when the phaetons rolled down Bellevue Avenue and the nights when the marble palaces glowed on magnificently unthrifty occasions. During the summer of 1973, as though to wipe out the memory of the jazz festivals, the old Vanderbilt estate, The Breakers, was opened for the American premiere of the French comic opera *Les Visitandines*; and further to signalize the determination to recapture something of the older Newport, Arthur Curtiss James' Swiss farm, closed down since James' death in 1941, was reopened and guests were served an "Alpine" buffet of galantine of duck, lobster Bellevue, glazed trout, filet of beef and salmon Russian style, a menu to astound any genuine resident of the Alps.

And every fourth year something of the old excitement is revived by the America's Cup yacht races, which have not yet been overly democratized. The multicolored sails and the gonfalons of various yacht clubs testify that the seascape is still incomparable. Newport stays on the map of the American consciousness. It almost became the setting of the summer White House a decade ago. Just before his assassination, President John F. Kennedy, whose wife's mother and stepfather are commanding figures in the summer colony, planned to lease the Annandale Farm near Newport for that purpose. How well the liberal Mr. Kennedy would have been received by the more sclerotic conservatives is problematical, but Newport no longer has the capacity for arrogance that resulted in the snubbing of one of Kennedy's distant predecessors.

Cinematically, at least, Newport's great estates still represent the extravagance of the American past, preserved as they are in the amber of nostalgia. In the summer of 1973 the producers of

The Great Gatsby found that the genuine Long Island settings of Scott Fitzgerald's novel were no longer presentable on film. Only Newport could provide the haunting elegance of the exteriors they required, and so Mia Farrow as Daisy and Robert Redford as Gatsby played their love scenes among the towering statuary in the terraced gardens and forecourt of Rosecliff where Tessie Oelrichs once reigned. Antique Packards and Mercer runabouts were retrieved from old carriage houses, and there were enough gilded names still summering in Newport to flesh out the throng of dress extras with a Van Alen, a Rhinelander and a Pell, among others. If there was a sense of disorientation aroused by reflections that Newport had become just one more picturesque location for Hollywood producers, it became evident when some of the extras playing great ladies of the past had to be rebuked for ordering around other extras playing servants, but in that moment something of the hauteur of the old Newport stirred back to life.

One could imagine the shades of Tessie, Mamie and Alva smiling with sardonic approval from an upper window.

NOTES ON SOURCES

THE COMPLETE listing of most of the sources indicated below under the authors' surnames may be found in the Bibliography, which follows.

1. THE HAPPY FEW

A quick gleaning of Newport's historical background may be found in Elliott, *This Was My Newport*, VII–XXII; Wecter's *The Saga of American Society*, 455–56, and Amory's *The Last Resorts*, 179–80.

Nancy Randolph's melodramatic life has been partially recounted by William Cabell, *John Randolph of Roanoke*, and Gamaliel Bradford, *Damaged Souls, passim.*

The description of William Beach Lawrence is from Elliott, 237.

The Newport *Mercury* editorial deploring the advent of "summer business" is quoted by Sirkis, *Newport: Pleasures and Palaces*, 51. Miss Sirkis' volume is composed largely of photographs detailing the glories of Newport's past.

Robert Dunn's recollections of Newport in his boyhood were contained in his autobiography, *World Alive*, 24–25.

The summer resident quoted on the antipathy between year-round residents and the summer people was Mrs. Elizabeth Drexel Lehr, *King Lehr and the Gilded Age*, 139–40.

The quotation from Henry James, *The American Scene*, "The Sense of Newport."

Maud Howe Elliott's quick sketch of Robert Louis Stevenson in Newport is from *This Was My Newport*, 101.

Bret Harte's sojourn in Newport is described by O'Connor, *Bret Harte: A Biography*, 141, 148–50.

Mrs. Elliott on Edith Wharton as "Pussie Jones of Pen Craig Cottage," *op. cit.*, 99.

2. THE COMING OF THE WHITE ELEPHANTS

Henry James' reflections on what had happened to Newport under the impact of new money, *The American Scene*, "The Sense of Newport."

The foundation of many Civil War fortunes is traced by O'Connor, *Gould's Millions*, 39–40, and Myers, *History of the Great American Fortunes*, *passim*.

Mrs. John Francis' comments on August Belmont's life-style, Amory, *The Last Resorts*, 184–85.

Eleanor Robson Belmont's comment on the servants employed at By-the-Sea, her autobiography, *The Fabric of Memory*, 82.

Dixon Wecter's comment on August Belmont's conversion, *The Saga of American Society*, 341.

Emanie Sachs' recollection of the "Jewish Newport" on the Jersey coast is quoted by Birmingham, *Our Crowd*, 306.

Ward McAllister's background is outlined by Tharp, *Three Saints and a Sinner*, *passim*.

McAllister's San Francisco career is briefly recaptured in his memoir, *Society As I Have Found It*, 22.

McAllister's social maneuvering in Savannah, *ibid.*, 81–83.

The list of his Patriarch's committee, *ibid*,. 213.

His recollection of Isaac Brown, *ibid*,. 124.

The poem eulogizing Brown's services to New York society was quoted by Amory, *Who Killed Society?* 117.

McAllister's reflections on how he reorganized New York society and his division of its membership into "Nobs" and "Swells," *Society As I Have Found It*, 211–12.

His description of the Banner Ball, *ibid.*, 324–25, 330–31.

His remarks on the expensive aspects of the new society, *ibid.*, 349–51.

McAllister's methods of staging a *fête champêtre*, *ibid.*, 111–13.

Description of the coaching accident following one of McAllister's outings, *ibid.*, 197–98.

The disaster that befell a party given without consulting McAllister was gleefully detailed by him, *ibid.*, 200–3.

How McAllister arranged a picnic for President Arthur, *ibid.*, 259–63.

President Arthur's snubbing by the Casino servants was related by Amory, *Last Resorts*, 178, and Lehr, *op. cit.*, 142.

3. NEWPORT'S FIRST QUEEN

Senator Henry Cabot Lodge's remembrance of things past in Newport is from his *Early Memories*, 48.

Mrs. Astor's jewelry collection was itemized by Tharp, *op. cit.*, 64.

The Vanderbilt biographer quoted on Mrs. Astor's "hardening" of the social caste system is Hoyt, *The Vanderbilts and Their Fortunes*, 231.

Mrs. Astor's leniency in regard to Ellin Prince's marriage to James Speyer is related in Kavaller, *The Astors*, 114.

How Mrs. Astor was forced to learn to coexist with the Vanderbilts is outlined by Hoyt, 255–56.

McAllister's list of the "Four Hundred" was published by the New York *Tribune*, March 24, 1888.

Mrs. Astor's Newport cotillions, her ambiguous relations with her husband, and the latter's involvement in their daughter's marriages and extramarital affairs are reported by Kavaller, *op. cit.*, 125, 119–21, 131–32.

Ward McAllister's difficulties with the Chicago press and his consequent downgrading by society, Dedmon, *Fabulous Chicago*, 222–25.

The Astor family historian quoted on Mrs. Astor's mental condition during her last years, Kavaller, 140.

Her greeting of "imaginary guests long dead" was related by Morris, *Incredible New York*, 116.

4. THE COTTAGE INDUSTRY

Russell Lynes' remarks on "social competition among the rich" and its resultant spending sprees are from his *The Tastemakers*, 137.

Amory on the naming of the marble cottages, *Last Resorts*, 173.

Observations on the changes of costume ordained for the fashionable in Newport, Kavaller, *op. cit.*, 123.

Mrs. Philip Lydig's recollections of a French writer's reactions to Newport and the domestic tragedies he sensed behind the walls of its mansions were contained in her memoir, *Tragic Mansions*, 13–15.

Michael Strange's childhood memory of a couple who sacrificed everything to attain social status in Newport is from her compelling autobiography, *Who Tells Me True*, 46–47.

The background of Richard Morris Hunt is detailed by Lynes, *The Tastemakers*, 131–37.

Quotations from Hunt and from others on his work, *ibid.*, 131, 137–38, 141.

Consuelo Vanderbilt's memories of her childhood at the Marble House and its chilling effect on her, Balsan, *The Glitter and the Gold*, 24–25.

The Vanderbilt grandson quoted on his recollection of The Breakers is Cornelius Vanderbilt, Jr., *Queen of the Golden Age*, a biography of his mother, 5–6.

The overpowering omnipresence of the hydrangea, Newport's favorite bloom, is tellingly recaptured by Barrett, *Good Old Summer Days*, 81–82.

5. THE MASCULINE GENDER

Recollection of Ogden Goelet on his grape diet, Strange, *op. cit.*, 47.

The proclivities of the Reading Room's membership, their patronage of Blanche's parlor house, and their control of Newport's solid economic and social base, Barrett, *op. cit.*, 39, 125–26.

The New York *World*'s interview with James J. Van Alen was quoted by Amory, *The Last Resorts*, 196.

Van Alen's idiosyncrasies were described by Lehr, *op. cit.*, 124–25.

A description of Robert Garrett's "court" was provided in eccentric detail by Lehr, *ibid.*, 123–24.

Garrett's disastrous business career and his losing encounter with Thomas Scott of the Pennsylvania Railroad were recounted by Myers, *op. cit.*, 516.

6. THE WAYWARD COMMODORE

James Gordon Bennett's background and business career is abstracted from the author's *The Scandalous Mr. Bennett, passim.*

Mrs. Lehr's account of Bennett's disgrace, perhaps too favorable to her friend Bennett, *op. cit.*, 116.

The story on Bennett's horsewhipping by Fred May was published by the New York *Sun*, January 4, 1877.

The Newport newspaper defense of Bennett's conduct was reprinted by the Boston *Herald*, January 7, 1877.

The story about Bennett wearing a coat of mail when Fred May appeared in Paris was told by Camille Clermont, *Confessions of the Gentle Rebecca*, 188.

The "fiery" quality of Bennett's entertainments was portrayed by Elliott, *op. cit.*, 153.

How Bennett kidnapped three of his lady friends on his yacht was related by Balsan, *op. cit.*, 63.

The Newport historian quoted on Bennett's streak of deviltry was Barrett, *op. cit.*, 40.

Captain Candy's invasion of the Reading Room on horseback was recalled with relish by McAllister, *op. cit.*, 355–58.

Newport's pride in the Reading Room was recorded by Barrett, *op. cit.*, 41.

Harry Oelrichs' collapse on his return from a round-the-world trip with Bennett was recalled by his young niece (Blanche Oelrichs), Strange, *op. cit.*, 35.

The description of Bennett's Domino Ball and its unexpected climax was provided by McAllister, 357–58.

7. THE TERRIBLE COLONEL

The interview with Colonel Mann in which he boasted of his determination to uplift high society was published by the New York *Times*, July 7, 1905.

His influence on Newport and the fear with which each issue of *Town Topics* was awaited were described by Barrett, *op. cit.*, 120–21.

Colonel Mann's background is detailed in masterly fashion by his biographer, Andy Logan, *The Man Who Robbed the Robber Barons, passim,* and in O'Connor, *Courtroom Warrior*, a biography of his prosecutor, District Attorney William Travers Jerome, 158–60.

Mann's diatribe against the contemporary laxness of social standards was quoted by Amory, *Who Killed Society?* 25.

Mann's method of retailing gossip in the *Town Topics'* columns was analyzed by Logan, *op. cit.*, 138–39.

The stampede of late callers at the magazine's offices on press night, *ibid.*, 141–42.

Quotation from Mann on the subject of *Town Topics'* moral purity was included in the article by his former hireling, Robert Rowe, in *American Mercury*, July, 1926. The *Mercury* then was edited by H. L. Mencken, who was also a former employee of Colonel Mann's. Early in his career Mencken edited *Smart Set*, a Mann publication.

The Newport historian who remarked on the prevalence of guilty consciences among the wealthier Newporters was Barrett, *op. cit.*, 122.

The omnipresence of *Town Topics* spies in Newport and their gossip-gathering tactics, *ibid.*, 121.

Michael Strange's encounter with the magazine's chief Newport agent and its aftermath were recalled in her memoir, 67–69.

District Attorney Jerome's plot to trap Colonel Mann is outlined by O'Connor, *Courtroom Warrior*, 161–63.

Norman Hapgood's editorial condemning *Town Topics* was published by *Collier's Weekly*, November 5, 1904.

The account of the Mann and Hapgood trials is drawn from O'Connor, *Courtroom Warrior*, 161–63.

8. SCENES FROM SPORTING LIFE

Americans' adoption of the English attitude toward sports was noted by Mrs. J. Borden Harriman, *From Pinafores to Politics*, 40–41.

The activities of the gentlemen farmers were covered by Amory, *The Last Resorts*, 176–78.

Maud Elliott's description of a fox-hunting spectacle is from her memoir, *op. cit.*, 197.

Her recollection of the coaching parade, *ibid.*, 200.

The routine of leaving calling cards at each mansion was recalled by Vanderbilt, *op. cit.*, 185–86.

Recollections of the splendor of the equipages and horseflesh in the coaching parade were drawn from Barrett, *op. cit.*, 65.

Julia Ward Howe's letter lamenting Belmont's stabling of his horses on the first floor of his house, quoted by her daughter, Elliott, *op. cit.*, 203.

The social strata of the horse shows were explored by Barrett, *op. cit.*, 70–77.

The anecdote concerning yachtsman William Douglas was recounted by Harriman, *op. cit.*, 41.

The Kat-Bote Club's list and officers and its anthem were recalled by Elliott, *op. cit.*, 214–15.

Description of a Clambake Club outing was contained in a letter written by Charles Oelrichs, *ibid.*, 218.

The first tournament match held at the Casino was recalled by Mrs. Elliott, *ibid.*, 207.

Dickie Sears' obituary was quoted by Amory, *The Last Resorts*, 200.

Mrs. John Jacob Astor's tumble from the Casino grandstand, Barrett, *op. cit.*, 54–55.

The Casino's board of governors' difficulties with players during a rained-out tournament week were recapitulated by Barrett, *op. cit.*, 52–53.

The first automobile race at Belcourt was related by Amory, *The Last Resorts*, 203.

9. NAVAL NEWPORT

The social importance of Fort Adams was conveyed by Elliott, *op. cit.*, 234–35.

Alfred Thayer Mahan's connection with the Naval War College is related by Taylor, *The Life of Admiral Mahan*, *passim*.

Commodore Luce's attempted evasion of Newport's social lionesses, Elliott, *op. cit.*, 248–49.

The quotation from Mahan appeared in his article, "A Twentieth Century Outlook," *Harper's Magazine*, September, 1897.

Jonathan Daniel's recollection of pre-World War I Newport is taken from his memoir, *The End of Innocence*, 110.

The anecdote concerning the admirals' abstention during the Secretary of the Navy's visit to the Naval War College, *ibid.*, 112.

Newport during World War I and its patriotic fervor, Elliott, *op. cit.*, 255–56.

Franklin D. Roosevelt's investigation of vice conditions in Newport during World War I, Daniels, *op. cit.*, 231–32.

10. THE PERILS OF SOCIAL CLIMBING

The society reporter's remarks on the intensity of the Newport social struggle were cited by Vanderbilt, *op. cit.*, 169.

His recollections of his mother in action as a society leader, *ibid.*, 163–64.

Alice Roosevelt's pretending to be a "contrite puppy" when she fell in disfavor with Mrs. Vanderbilt, *ibid.*, 165.

The social historian who commented on how many dowagers lost their minds, Amory, *The Last Resorts*, 207.

The Oelrichs family's vicissitudes during a relatively impoverished period, Strange, *op. cit.*, 42–44.

The incidents involving the young woman rejected by Newport society until she married the "right" man and the matron ostracized because of the scandal attending her remarriage, Barrett, *op. cit.*, 48–51, 70–71.

The New York *Morning Telegraph*'s comment on the "dullness" of the Newport season was quoted by Lehr, *op. cit.*, 56.

The insipid quality of the table talk of Newport husbands, *ibid.*, 57–58.

Consuelo Vanderbilt's recollection of the constraints imposed on her in girlhood is from her memoir, Balsan, *op. cit.*, 26.

Lord Napier's caustic remark to Emily Shaunberg on her excessive use of makeup was recorded by Elliott, *op. cit.*, 206.

11. THE GREAT TRIUMVIRATE (I)

Mrs. J. Borden Harriman's remarks on the "grand duchesses" were made in her memoir, *op. cit.*, 51.

Mrs. James Keene's yearning for the simpler life in California was recalled by Elliott, *op. cit.*, 162.

Description of Mrs. Ogden Mills' hauteur, Harriman, *op. cit.*, 51.

The gentler qualities of Mrs. Paran Stevens, *ibid.*, 42–43.

Tessie Fair's family background was gleaned from Oscar Lewis' biography of the Comstock Lode developers, *Silver Kings*, *passim*.

Mining historian who marveled over the wonders of the Comstock discoveries was quoted by Lewis, *ibid.*, 141.

The differing characters of Tessie's parents were analyzed by Lewis, *ibid.*, 178.

Herman Oelrichs' family background was provided by his niece (Blanche Oelrichs), Michael Strange, *op. cit.*, 13.

Her description of Tessie's restlessness behind the glittering façade of social success, *ibid.*, 48–49.

Tessie Oelrichs' struggles to maintain an attractive figure were related by Barrett, *op. cit.*, 97.

The disheartening effects of the Oelrichs will on Tessie, and her eventual disintegration were described by her niece, Strange, *op. cit.*, 91, 124.

Alva Vanderbilt's description of herself as a trailblazer for society women was quoted by Lehr, *op. cit.*, 121.

Her fight for the Leeds' social cause, *ibid.*, 120–22.

Consuelo Vanderbilt's comment on her mother's "combative nature," Balsan, *op. cit.*, 6.

On her father's easygoing character, *ibid.*, 5, 11.

Alva as a patron of the fine arts, *ibid.*, 7.

On her career as a builder of great houses, Lehr, *op. cit.*, 175.

The details of Alva's divorce are contained in Hoyt, *op. cit.*, 290–92. The corespondent in the case was one Nellie Neustretter, originally of Eureka, Nevada, who was identified in Alva's suit as a "demi-mondaine" living in Paris. The trial of the divorce suit was held in a courtroom barred to the press.

The picture of Alva and her second husband as a "striking pair" on the Newport scene, Barrett, *op. cit.*, 87.

The newspaper comment on Alva's success in lifting the Vanderbilts to social eminence was quoted by Vanderbilt, *op. cit.*, 40.

The charabanc incident was related by Lehr, 146.

Alva's bullying of James B. Haggin over changing his will was witnessed by Lehr, *op. cit.*, 221–22.

12. THE GREAT TRIUMVIRATE (II)

The origins and outcome of the Fish-Harriman feud were explored by Lehr, *op. cit.*, 170–71; Logan, *op. cit.*, 193.

Mamie Fish's frequent claim that she was the making of her husband's career was reported by Lehr, *ibid.*, 169–70.

Mamie's difficulty with James Gordon Bennett over the transposition of guest lists, O'Connor, *The Scandalous Mr. Bennett*, 143.

Stuyvesant Fish's hatred of ostentation was noted by Lehr, *op. cit.*, 169.

Mamie's "brash mirth" and the suggestions of a "grotesque disillusionment" were recorded by Strange, *op. cit.*, 57–58.

Stuyvesant Fish "curiously out of place" on the Newport scene, Barrett, *op. cit.*, 105.

Mamie's dinner for the Russian ambassador and the bishop from the Philippines were described by Belmont, *op. cit.*, 83–84.

Mamie's relationship with Marie Dressler was recalled by Dressler in her memoir, *My Own Story*, 132–34.

Mamie's maneuvers in the "Grand Duke War" were observed by Lehr, *op. cit.*, 131–36.

Her banishment to the terrace during one of James Van Alen's musicales, *ibid.*, 125–26.

The verse on her tombstone was taken from Matthew Arnold's "Requiescat."

13. "LITTLE BROTHER OF THE RICH"

The description of Harry Lehr as a "coy and roguish pig" was by Barrett, *op. cit.*, 85.

Lehr quoted on his methods of self-advancement in society and on how to react to insults, Lehr, *op. cit.*, 58, 59–60.

The Lehr family's struggles during its sojourn in Germany, *ibid.*, 50–52.

The newspaper comment on Lehr's conquest of local society was published in the Baltimore *Sun*, May 2, 1890.

The newspaper stories about Lehr and Mrs. Astor dining out together were quoted by Barrett, *op. cit.*, 86–87.

George Kessler's offer to make Lehr a champagne salesman, Lehr, *op. cit.*, 41.

The bilking of Diamond Jim Brady in his campaign to acquire Lehr as his social sponsor is told by Burke, *Duet in Diamonds*, 153.

Lehr as sponsor of the Pembroke Jones' debut, Lehr, 67.

Mrs. Lehr described the tragicomedy of her wedding night in candid detail, *op. cit.*, 43–46.

The problems of Lehr and his dowagers in eliminating the "stodginess" from Newport society were conveyed by Barrett, *op. cit.*, 119.

Lehr's advice on how to win acceptance in Newport was quoted by his wife, Lehr, *op. cit.,* 112–14.

Elizabeth Lehr's affair with "Mr. X" was related in her memoir, *ibid., passim.*

The letter from Alva Belmont to Harry Lehr was quoted by his wife, *ibid.,* 173–74.

Berlin newspaper coverage of Lehr's appearance at Kaiser Wilhelm's court was quoted by Lehr, 205–07. Lehr had adopted the practice of wearing knee breeches from the presentations at Buckingham Palace. When Lehr was presented to August IV of Saxony during a later phase of his German tour, Mrs. Lehr recalled, the King of Saxony wore spurs at the court ball and ripped swatches of material from the hems of his dancing partners' gowns.

Mrs. Lehr's attempts to leave her husband, *ibid.,* 251–55.

14. THE DOGS' DINNER AND OTHER TRANSGRESSIONS

Mrs. Jones' habit of spending $300,000 on a Newport season was reported by Lehr, *op. cit.,* 138.

Mrs. Vanderbilt's "Fête des Roses" ball was described by her son, Cornelius Vanderbilt, Jr., *op. cit.,* 175–79.

The comment on the feeding arrangements for the actors was from *Theater Magazine,* September, 1902.

The Great Triumvirate's efforts to "keep the tempo lively" were observed by Barrett, *op. cit.,* 99.

Mamie Fish's Mother Goose poem was quoted by Amory (*Last Resorts*), 223.

Town and Country's report on the Mother Goose ball was quoted by Barrett, *op. cit.,* 100–1.

The Marble House dance, the Pembroke Jones' and James Van Alens' parties were covered by the Newport *Daily News,* August 28, 1895, July 27, 1899, and July 2, 1902.

Evalyn Walsh McLean's appearance on the Newport scene was recalled in her autobiography, *Father Struck It Rich,* 123, 125, 173–76.

The story of the "dogs' dinner" was told by Lehr, *op. cit.,* 226–27.

The Henry Clews' "servants ball," *ibid.,* 227–28.

Details of the "monkey dinner," *ibid.,* 150–52.

Newport historian's comment on how the monkey dinner became a symbol of Newport extravagance, Barrett, *op. cit.,* 102.

Characterization of Vanderbilts' butler, Vanderbilt, *op. cit.,* 285–86.

Mrs. McLean listed all thirty of her Newport servants in her autobiography, *op. cit.,* 204–5.

Majordomo Azar and his place in the Belmont household were described by Lehr, *op. cit.*, 146–47.

Mrs. Fish and her trials with Morton the butler, *ibid.*, 143–44.

The independence of the "shack boys" at the Casino was noted by Barrett, *op. cit.*, 46–47.

The footman who announced the "enormous pheasant" was cited by Amory, *The Last Resorts*, 176.

15. BAILEY'S BEFORE THE BIKINI

Bailey's Beach was characterized as the "holy of holies" by Barrett, *op. cit.*, 127.

Watchfulness of the beach's paid guardians was noted by Lehr, *op. cit.*, 139.

Eleanor Robson Belmont's recollection of the rigidity with which the long-stockings rule was enforced at Bailey's Beach from her memoir, *op. cit.*, 84–85.

The eccentricities of several notable bathers at the beach were detailed by Lehr, *op. cit.*, 139–40.

Mrs. George Henry Warren's appearance at a costume ball as "Miss Bailey's Beach" was recounted by Amory, *Last Resorts*, 251.

16. THE MARRIAGE MARKET

Michael Strange's misadventures in the marriage mart were recalled in her memoir, *op. cit.*, 103–4.

Not all intercontinental marriages were unhappy ones. Lord Curzon, the great proconsul of Britain during its imperial heyday, married Mary Leiter, the daughter of Levi Leiter, the Chicago real estate magnate, and it turned out happily enough.

Mrs. Philip Lydig's fascination was described by Barrett, *op. cit.*, 111–12.

Mrs. Lydig's treatment of an importunate admirer was recounted by Amory, *Last Resorts*, 202.

Mrs. Lydig's observations on the international fortune hunters are from her memoir, *op. cit.*, 78, 162–63.

Her story of the "Virginia Cort" marriages, *ibid.*, 78, 104.

May Goelet's letter about her numerous suitors quoted, Vanderbilt, *op. cit.*, 186–88.

The estimate on the amount of money settled on foreign bridegrooms is from Myers, *op. cit.*, 378.

Consuelo Vanderbilt's recollections of her mother's efforts to obtain a titled husband for her, Balsan, *op. cit.*, 34–35, 41–47.

Description of the ball honoring the Duke of Marlborough, Hoyt, *op. cit.*, 294–95.

The Duke of Marlborough's proposal was quoted by its recipient, Balsan, *op. cit.*, 51.

Details of the dowry are from Hoyt, *op. cit.*, 296. The couple also received a $100,000 annual allowance from the Vanderbilt family.

Mrs. Lydig's story of the society woman who preferred to die alone is from her memoir, *op. cit.*, 50–56.

Milton Budlong's state of marital siege was related by Amory, *The Last Resorts*, 238.

Michael Strange discussed the growing incidence of the *mariage à trois* in her memoir, *op. cit.*, 117.

Grace Vanderbilt's unstylish marriage was recounted by her brother, Vanderbilt, 283–84.

17. THE LAST GOLDEN SUMMER

The impact of the *Titanic* disaster on Newport was recalled by Strange, *op. cit.*, 110.

The commentator who deplored the coming of the automobile was Barrett, *op. cit.*, 133.

Vinson Walsh's fatal accident was recalled by his sister, McLean, *op. cit.*, 41–42; also Strange, *op. cit.*, 41–42.

Alva Belmont's involvement in the women's rights movement was recalled by her daughter, Balsan, *op. cit.*, 215–18.

Her letter to the New York criminal courts committee, quoted, *ibid.*, 216–17.

Her daughter's reflections on Mrs. Belmont's crusading with the suffragists, *ibid.*, 218.

Her participation in the New York Women's Vote Parade was described by Lehr, *op. cit.*, 222–23.

The women's rights convention held at the Marble House and its attendant confusions were recalled with malicious glee by Mrs. Lehr, *ibid.*, 222–26.

Michael Strange's remembrance of the brilliance of the 1914 season in Newport is from her memoir, *op. cit.*, 110–11.

The excitement caused by the appearance of the Russian Grand Duke and the Austrian Archduke, *ibid.*, 112–13.

The plight of the rich Americans "trapped" in London by the outbreak of war, Cameron, *1914*, 78–79.

Mrs. Leeds' embarrassment over her footman, Lehr, *op. cit.*, 269.

Mrs. Cornelius Vanderbilt's disastrous dinner party honoring Count Bernstorff was related by her son, Vanderbilt, 250–53; Lehr, *op. cit.*, 271.

Lily Oelrichs Martin's misadventures with Prince Borwein were told by her sister Blanche, Strange, *op. cit.*, *passim*, and Lehr, *op. cit.*, 267.

EPILOGUE

Consuelo Vanderbilt recalled the closing years of her mother's life, Balsan, *op. cit.*, 287.

Her description of the installation of a statue of Joan of Arc, *ibid.*, 288.

Harry Lehr's tragic end was told by his wife, Lehr, *op. cit.*, 284–88.

The story of Commodore Bennett's closing years, O'Connor, *The Scandalous Mr. Bennett*, *passim*.

Colonel Mann's death was recounted by his biographer, Logan, *op. cit.*, 244–49.

Mrs. Twombley's style of living is conveyed by Amory, *Last Resorts*, 239–40.

Perle Mesta's Newport triumphs are recounted in her memoir, *My Story*, 54–57.

Michael Strange's recollection of the "laughing circle of intimates" is from her memoir, *op. cit.*, 394.

BIBLIOGRAPHY

Aldrich, Lillian, *Crowding Memories,* Boston, 1920.
Amory, Cleveland, *The Last Resorts,* New York, 1952.
————, *Who Killed Society?,* New York, 1960.
Balsan, Consuelo Vanderbilt, *The Glitter and the Gold,* New York, 1952.
Barrett, Richmond, *Good Old Summer Days,* New York, 1941.
Belmont, Eleanor Robson, *The Fabric of Memory,* New York, 1957.
Birmingham, Stephen, *Our Crowd,* New York, 1967.
Burke, John, *Duet in Diamonds,* New York, 1972.
Cameron, James, *1914,* New York, 1959.
Clermont, Camille, *Confessions of the Gentle Rebecca,* London, 1912.
Daniels, Jonathan, *The End of Innocence,* Philadelphia, 1954.
Dedmon, Emmett, *Fabulous Chicago,* New York, 1953.
Dressler, Marie, *My Own Story,* Boston, 1934.
Dunn, Robert, *World Alive,* New York, 1956.
Elliott, Maud Howe, *This Was My Newport,* Cambridge, 1944.
Halsey, William F., and J. Bryan III, *Admiral Halsey's Story,* New York, 1947.
Harriman, Mrs. J. Borden, *From Pinafores to Politics,* New York, 1923.
Hoyt, Edwin P., *The Vanderbilts and Their Fortunes,* New York, 1962.
James, Henry, *The American Scene,* New York, 1907.
Kavaller, Lucy, *The Astors,* New York, 1966.
Lehr, Elizabeth Drexel, *King Lehr and the Gilded Age,* Philadelphia, 1935.
Lewis, Oscar, *The Silver Kings,* New York, 1947.
Lodge, Henry Cabot, *Early Memories,* Boston, 1913.
Logan, Andy, *The Man Who Robbed the Robber Barons,* New York, 1965.
Lydig, Mrs. Philip, *Tragic Mansions,* New York, 1927.
Lynes, Russell, *The Tastemakers,* New York, 1954.
McAllister, Ward, *Society As I Have Found It,* New York, 1890.
McLean, Evalyn Walsh, *Father Struck It Rich,* Boston, 1936.
Mesta, Perle, and Robert Cahan, *My Story,* New York, 1959.
Morris, Lloyd, *Incredible New York,* New York, 1951.
Myers, Gustavus, *History of the Great American Fortunes,* New York, 1936.
O'Connor, Richard, *Courtroom Warrior,* Boston, 1963.

——, *The Scandalous Mr. Bennett*, New York, 1962.
Sirkis, Nancy, *Newport Pleasures and Palaces*, New York, 1963.
Strange, Michael, *Who Tells Me True*, New York, 1940.
Taylor, Charles C., *The Life of Admiral Mahan*, New York, 1920.
Tharp, Louise Hall, *Three Saints and a Sinner*, Boston, 1956.
Vanderbilt, Cornelius, Jr., *Queen of the Golden Age*, New York, 1956.
Wecter, Dixon, *The Saga of American Society*, New York, 1937.

PERIODICALS

American Mercury
Collier's Weekly
The Gentlewoman
Harper's Magazine
Harper's Bazaar
Theater Magazine
Town Topics
Vanity Fair
Baltimore *Sun*
Boston *Herald*
New York *Herald*
New York *Times*
New York *Tribune*
New York *Sun*
New York *World*
Newport *Daily News*
Newport *Mercury*

INDEX